CHOSEN TO CARRY THE GLORY

Carry THE FIRE OF JESUS

BECOME A CARRIER OF THE WORD OF GLORY

✨ LEARN how to host, carry and reveal the ABIDING GLORY
✨ LEARN how the Holy Spirit picks and anoints His CHOSEN ONES

🔥 Carry   🔥 Lead.   🔥 Serve

The Great Move of God

Norman Morea Trent Sabadi

Norman Morea Trent Sabadi

Chosen To Carry The Glory

Carry the Fire of Jesus

© Copyright 2023 - Norman Morea Trent Sabadi
(The Place Where He Speaks)
(Norman Sabadi Publishing)

All rights reserved. This book is protected by the copyright laws of Australia. This book may not be transmitted, copied or reprinted in any form for commercial gain or profit, without the prior written permission of the publisher or author. Permission will be granted upon request. The use of short quotations or occasional page copying for personal or group study, sermons, and social media posts, for audio and video content, is permitted and encouraged, with acknowledgements.

Unless otherwise identified, scriptural quotations are taken from the Holy Bible (The King James Version).

Cover Design by Norman Sabadi Media Productions 2023

ISBN (Paperback): 978-0-9756110-1-2
ISBN (Hardcover): 978-0-9756110-2-9
ISBN (Ebook - pdf): 978-0-9756110-0-5
ISBN (Ebook - Epub): 978-0-9756110-3-6

For Worldwide Distribution

Norman Sabadi Publishing
8 Allen Rd, Gracemere, QLD 4702, Australia
https://www.normansabadi.com/

Revival is God's answer to the one who possesses the posture of worship.

—

Worship is Divine purpose. It's your worship posture that draws and carries the Glory of God.

—

Revival—when the extravagance and magnificence of God's Power meets with the contrite heart that trembles at His Word.

Dedication

I dedicate this book to the Lord our God for Your everlasting faithfulness and grace. To You, I am forever grateful.

I also want to make a special mention to all the faithful servants of God throughout the world; past, present and future. Keep going after God with all of your heart.

I would like to salute and honour two great men of God who have had a tremendous impact on my life—my dearest father, the Late Leonard Henao Leana Bogana Sabadi and my spiritual father, the Late John Thomas. For the special part, you played not only in my life but in the lives of many others and also in the Move of God. Your efforts were not in vain but are now truly your treasures in Heaven. We remember you both, the warriors of God. For you have shined the light of Christ Jesus on us and have demonstrated to us that no matter how unworthy a believer may feel about themselves if they choose to follow Jesus with their whole heart, they will be used mightily by the Lord.

Acknowledgements

*J*esus, my Lord—I thank You so much for the grace that You have placed upon me. Thank You Holy Spirit for every anointed Word written in this book, and for the Anointing to write this book.

My beloved wife, Olivia, and our precious children, Ethan and Jazmina—thank you for the amazing love and support you pour upon me every day. You have faithfully, confidently and joyfully walked with me in the Revival Fire of God.

Miriam Lili—for your special gift in editing and for flowing with the Holy Spirit so powerfully in His River of Revelation. Your valuable inclusions have truly made a difference and prepared this special 'Revival' book for God's people.

To my dearest mum, Torea C.T Sabadi and my brothers and sisters—for your unceasing love and prayers for me.

I also want to extend my gratitude to the faithful saints of God who have stood with me—You are *God's Chosen Army*. For you also have walked in the Revival Fires and have diligently pursued God's Presence. We have, with much grace and discipline, carried the Word of Power and walked in the oneness of the Holy Spirit. It's a great privilege and honour to walk alongside each of you as we continue together to *host and reveal His Presence*.

And lastly, to the one who reads this book—thank you for listening to the Holy Spirit and believing with your heart. May the Revival Fire of God clothe you and become for you, Rivers of Living Waters.

Contents

Foreword..11
Preface..13
Ch.1 - Where it all began...21
Ch.2 - Baptised with the Holy Ghost & Fire..............................31
Ch.3 - The Baptism of Fire is your Induction Service................51
Ch.4 - Our Heritage—Endued with Power................................69
Ch.5 - The Glory Cloud & Australia..79
Ch.6 - Why Revival? (The Archangel Michael Message)..........91
Ch.7 - The Water Baptism..99
Ch.8 - The Revivalist & the Posture for Revival......................115
Ch.9 - When Desperation meets the Word.............................141
Ch.10 - The Great Induction & Anointing Service...................157
Ch.11 - My Dad receives a vision - before the Throne............189
Ch.12 - Moses Anoints me a second time before the Glory Cloud.....193
Ch.13 - The Anointing - Mantles & Impartations....................199
Ch.14 - A Second Baptism with Fire by Jesus.........................229
Ch.15 - The Emerald Revival..237
Ch.16 - Experience The Great Move of God...........................255
Ch.17 - The Revival Mentorship - Another Level....................269
Ch.18 - The Posture that Brings & Carries the Glory..............291
Ch.19 - The Place Where He Speaks.....................................311
Ch.20 - Final Thoughts...327
About the Author..333

Foreword

It is with great honour that I am presented the opportunity to give you 'The Foreword' to this book. The Truth and Message presented by Norman, will awaken and stir up your desire and hunger for God. It will give you a firsthand experience of Norman's journey with God, his life experience in the Baptism of the Holy Spirit, and more. I resonate deeply with the Power of the testimonies he has shared. This has also had a great impact on me and has changed the way I once viewed the mysterious work of God. True indeed, God certainly chooses 'the hungry believer.' They that seek God will certainly find Him.

Most Importantly, God wants to be actively involved in your walk with Him. God wants to intervene in every area of your life. He wants to be a part of your Faith Journey. But you will never be able to experience that without the Holy Spirit. As you read what Norman has written, this will unlock doors filled with answers to the questions you have about the workings of the Spirit of God and other related questions. You will be Amazed! You will be Transformed! Your perspective on every level of your faith and knowledge of the things of God will be elevated and confidently grounded in the things of the Spirit.

I am so glad for you, that you have picked up this book, "Chosen to Carry the Glory—Carry the Fire of Jesus." You are now 'Divinely Appointed' to experience the Power of the message within it. That Power is the Spirit of God given without measure to do mighty works in your life. Saints, God is no respecter of persons. He can choose you if you are *willing to listen and obey His instructions*. This is your appointed season for REVIVAL.

– James Sabadi
(Twin Brother, Comrade and fellow Warrior in God's Army)

PREFACE

I have 'One Assignment' from God, and that is to teach, mentor and impart to you 'The Knowledge of the Glory of God.' I am burning with God's Fire because His Spirit rests upon me. That power that rests is the Divine Assignment of God given to God's 'Chosen Ones.' Every assignment from Heaven has God's Royal Seal and Marking on it. That Marking is the Power of the Spirit resting upon that assignment and upon the Vessel who has been appointed to carry out that assignment. My assignment is to elevate your mind to Divine perspective on what the Revival Fire really is. Indeed, God is looking for vessels who will submit to the 'discipleship' of the Holy Spirit to 'Carry the Glory of Jesus.' They are called and marked to carry the Glory of the 'Abiding Word.'

Therefore, it would be correct for me to say, that REVIVAL is all about carrying the Glory of God. Revival is the passion and desire of our God revealed. Habakkuk 2:14 speaks about 'THE KNOWLEDGE OF THE GLORY.' That is the Revival Fire I speak of. It is not just about the Glory, but a dimension of understanding of how the Lord of Glory operates and Moves in the midst of His people. It is entering into a clear understanding of the posture and heart attitude that God requires of us to host, carry and reveal His Glory on earth. The Church in its current state, is lacking that superior Holy Spirit level of understanding. The full reason why we must study and pursue, by the enabling of the Spirit an

Preface

elevated perspective of the Knowledge of the Glory, is to become God-focused and to come into a continuous 'Living Experience' with God. Carrying the Glory of the Word is a LIVING EXPERIENCE. That, my friends, is REVIVAL. The time of God's passion and desire has come and His Holy Spirit is moving amongst us. I have heard many say, that Revival is still coming. This is far from the truth. The only way we can correct this kind of talk is to come into an understanding of what the Revival Fire of God is, from God's perspective.

If we are referring to an event like the Day of Pentecost in Acts 2, the saints of the Upper Room never used the term *Revival*. They were simply obeying what Jesus had instructed them to do. To them, they were waiting for the initial manifestation of the Promise of the Father; when the Holy Spirit would come upon them and clothe them with Power. Then it happened again in Acts 4:31-33. A great shift in their paradigm occurred when the Glory of the 'abiding Word' descended mightily upon them. That is the Revival Fire. Revival is not just an event, but a continuous 'Living Experience' of the Fire of God.

The highest desire of God for man is to dwell in our midst in the fullness of His Power and Glory. This is not properly conveyed or represented by the statement that Revival consists merely of bringing the Church back to life or restoration, including the drawing of all others to Christ for salvation. If you twist the truth, it no longer carries the true power of its meaning. We must, therefore, elevate our thinking to the desire of God for us. Or have you forgotten what Christ said (note the bolded)?

John 14:23

Jesus answered and said unto him, If a man love me, he will keep My Words: and My Father will love him, and We will come unto him, **and make our abode with him**.

What about the Heavenly song that was sung by the host of Heaven on the night of Yeshua's birth? "…Peace on earth and goodwill to man." The true meaning of that proclamation is God saying, it is His 'intent and goodwill' to come and abide in our midst. Christ is the Glory of God made flesh, the ensign of Divine Peace appointed to man. That's why Christ is called the Prince of Peace. Therefore, Revival Fire is more than what you think it is. It is the 'Word made flesh' in our midst.

Now, there is the Move of the Spirit upon an individual. Then there is a God-Movement for a group of individuals in one accord. And both are supposed to be a constant or perpetual happening in our lives. So, if you have experienced the outpouring of the Holy Spirit upon your life, that is *Revival*. The Spirit doesn't only come upon you once, He continues to do that through the rest of your life. The Revival Culture is *Kingdom Culture*. For we live and walk in the Spirit of the Word, experiencing a continuous renewal, and refreshing from the Lord.

Revival is already here. Revival is and has always been the Holy Spirit *Himself*—the Power from on High and the Word of Glory revealed.

> **"**
> Revival is and has always been the Holy Spirit—the Power from on High and the Word of Glory revealed.

Preface

This working of the Holy Spirit is appropriately addressed as the *Move of God* or the *Work of God*. Only a vessel filled with the Spirit, who also is led by the Spirit, becomes the instrument by which the Holy Spirit reveals Jesus Christ.

The purpose of God's outpouring is to manifest Christ and cause the hearts of many to turn to Him. And I submit to you a greater thought: that we are called to be 'Living Epistles' written with the ink of the Holy Ghost. But we cannot be Living Epistles if we are not 'Living Examples' of those who carry the Glory of Jesus. That is the 'Living Experience' I speak of.

The Revival is also the *Awakening Power of God*. An awakening occurs in our spirits when the Power comes upon us. When the awakening happens, we are empowered or girded with Holy Spirit Knowledge and Power to be witnesses for Christ. That Awakening Fire, then burning upon us flows from our beings to those who hear us testify. Again, when I say, "Fire," I am referring to another elevated thought. I am referring to 'The Glory of the Abiding Word.' There is a Word from God, that when received in the spirit of a man, becomes in him a burning Fire. That is the Revival Fire I speak of.

The Spirit will come to them that respond to the *Call*. And Just as Gideon blew the trumpet by the power of the Spirit resting upon him, Jesus blew a spiritual trumpet when He told the disciples to wait for the Holy Spirit in Jerusalem. A great positioning was needed for that great and mighty outpouring of the Holy Spirit. The power of God would come to those who were thirsty for God and ready to receive Him. For as many as believe in Him, to them, He gives the power to become children of the Most High (John 1:12).

Leading from this understanding of the Knowledge of the Glory of God, we can then go further to define with much clarity, what the Move of God is. Delving deeper, we gather here that

attributes of the Revival Fire can also be described in various ways, by specific insights from the Bible, and by the workings of God as:
- The Knowledge of the Glory of God revealed
- The Revival Fire of God,
- The Awakening Fire of God;
- The Outpouring of the Spirit
- The Promise of the Father
- The Wind of the Spirit
- The River of God
- The Tide of the Spirit
- The Baptism of the Holy Ghost and Fire
- The Work of God
- The Move of God
- The Spirit of Elijah
- The Kingdom of God has come
- The Former and Latter Rain
- The New Wine of God
- The Glory of God in our Midst
- The Glory of God manifested
- The manifested or tangible Presence of God
- The Word of Power in our midst (The Abiding Word of Glory)
- The Power of His Anointing

When that magnificent power of the Holy Spirit's *Revival Anointing* comes upon His people, that is when the Spirit of the Word resuscitates, reignites, rebirths, regenerates and restores the Church to her foundations established in Acts 2. That is the 'Rock' upon which Christ said He would build His Church. All of the aforementioned *Revival outputs* become the continuous experience of those who have chosen to respond to the 'call' of the Spirit and have believed in the Word of Power and are therefore aligned to a continuous encounter with the Holy Spirit.

Preface

A revived Church becomes a carrier and spreader of the outpouring of the Spirit. This is much like the spilling over of that Glory in the Upper Room of Acts 2; described above, which *awakened* Jerusalem, and spread to Judea, Samaria and the uttermost parts of the earth (Acts 1:8). That Fire has reached us, who have also become the recipients of the glorious overflow of the Gospel of Christ and of His Spirit.

When this Great Move is birthed in the midst of the Church, it reaches those who have not yet believed Christ by the Power or enabling *witness* of the Holy Ghost resting upon a Church.

So, this book starts with the example and model that the early Church left for us to follow. We must be revived and set on Fire by the Power of the Holy Spirit so that we can become effective witnesses of Christ. We must come under the influence of that abiding Glory just as they did. And we are only on Fire for God because God's Glory has set us ablaze. This is a fact. A real experience. It is more than an emotional drive. It is the inspiration and desire of God burning within our bodies, our minds and our souls.

> "
> We are only on Fire for God because we are
>
> burning
> with the Fire of God's Glory

Without the working of the Holy Spirit, there is no Power to transform lives, there is no conviction of sins, and therefore no repentance, not only for us who are believers in Christ but for those who are yet to encounter the Power of the Gospel of Jesus Christ. We need the Holy Spirit if we are to be on Fire for God. It is the Lord who knows how to reach the lost more effectively than we do. Jesus said (John 12:32), "...when I am exalted I shall draw all man unto Myself."

That is what the outpouring of Acts 2 is all about. God drew all those who could hear that new sound of the Holy Ghost at work in the hundred and twenty saints so that He could reach their hearts and transform their lives. And not only that, He wanted to make His Home in them. He wanted them to be a people of His Presence. But how can the people know His Presence, if they don't know their God? How can God be their dwelling place, if they do not know what it means to, seek after God with all their hearts? If they say that they do not need His Presence, then they're also saying they do not need His Promise.

I have been on my knees for you my brother and my sister. I have laid myself prostrate before the Lord, so that you may also know Him and come into a full understanding of what it means to carry His Glory (Ephesians 3:9-21). That is all I desire.

And just as Moses asked God in Exodus 33:13-15,

> "Now therefore, I pray thee, if I have found grace in Thy Sight, shew me now Thy Way, that I may know Thee, that I may find grace in Thy Sight: and consider that this nation is Thy people. And He said, My Presence shall go with thee, and I will give thee rest. And he (Moses) said unto Him, If Thy Presence go not with me, carry us not up hence."

I have the same request. I have been broken before the Lord God of His Great Revival Fire. I plead the same before Him, "God if Your Presence won't go with me, don't let us go after the Revival Fire without You. If Your Presence won't be with me to write Your Revival Book, don't let me write it."

Opening Prayer:

Set us on Fire with Your Power, Heavenly Father. We bow before You and repent of our sins. We ask You to forgive us for missing the mark and cause our hearts to return to the place where You had ordained for us; to be empowered by the Spirit to carry the glorious Gospel of Jesus to the world. Lord, we realise that You truly love us with an everlasting love and You want us to be a people of Your Presence. You desire that We know You.

Dear Jesus, I thank You for the grace and opportunity to be able to share the revelation of Your Glory and Power with Your people. I pray You will release the Fire of Your Move; Your Revival Fire upon Your saints in these end-times and cause our hearts and minds to come into the fullness of the knowledge of Your Glory so that we may be full and overflowing with You. Great is our God.

In Yeshua's glorious Name. Amen!

CHAPTER 1

WHERE IT ALL BEGAN

*God sees all that I am. For He has been there from the beginning.
I decrease that He may increase more (John 3:30).*

The REVIVAL FIRE is the one thing that has had the most significant influence on my life. I am able, by the grace and power of the Holy Spirit, to speak of the Glory of God in such a powerful way right now, only because that journey for me, started many years ago.

I gave my life to the LORD Jesus when I was twelve years old, in 1995. I tell my whole story of how I came to know the LORD in my first book, *'Wisdom Calls Out To You.'* But my Baptism in the Holy Spirit and Fire was four years later in 1999. It was the beginning of my high school life. As I look back to those times and reminisce, I can see what God was doing: God wanted to work mightily in my life and in the lives of my friends. At that time we didn't realise that God was looking for vessels to set ablaze and use for His glory. Revival had broken out in Papua New Guinea (PNG) and when it hit our small town of Goroka in a tremendous way, I wasn't expecting that I would be so impacted and transformed by the experience.

CHAPTER 1

Where It All Began

Col Ples (cold place) Goroka, contrary to its name, became the place burning with the Fire of God. Goroka is a little town in the Eastern Highlands Province of Papua New Guinea, often referred to as the gateway to the highlands. The highlands is a green and luscious tropical region, with an unbroken chain of rough terrain and mountains. The climate there is always cold to mild and often rainy all year around. The name Goroka is derived from the original language word, *Gouloka*, which means, 'DAWN OF A NEW DAY' or 'AT THE BREAK OF DAWN.' It couldn't be more true. The very meaning of the place carries heavenly significance. At the beginning of a particular new day in my life, it would be the place of a literal encounter with the Living God. This was not just a new beginning in Christ, but the birthing of the Move of God in my life and the lives of many others; a wave of change that we didn't expect, that came upon us at the appointed time.

I was only nine years old when we moved from Port Moresby (the capital city of PNG) to Goroka. My mum took up her posting at the Goroka Technical College as Deputy Principal in 1992; later becoming Principal in 1993. In 1994, she took up further studies for the role, which meant we had to move back to Port Moresby. She was then reappointed as Principal at the same college in Goroka in 1995 and remained in this role until the end of the year 2002. So I call Goroka my home.

So in 1997, my first year in high school, my twin, James, and I were just settling into high school life. There was so much already to take in. I had this feeling that it was going to be an exciting experience of exploring the pathway our older siblings had already travelled.

In the second term of school that year, a particular teacher, who oversaw the Scripture Union Students Fellowship, was being used by God to introduce the Move. The wave of that initial experience of God's Fire quickly caught on as stories spread about meetings that were held towards the end of the school day. These gatherings were held twice a week and many of the students attended them. Students were being transformed instantly by the Fire of God as God added to His Church daily (Acts 2:47).

At the very beginning, I was sceptical about it and only a bystander observing from afar. Going from what I was told, some students attended because another student had spoken to them about it. They were unaware of the transforming power of the Gospel of Yeshua the Messiah. These students would walk in and never be the same when they walked out. It was the preaching of the Word coupled with the tangible Presence of the Holy Spirit that reached the ears of those who were there. The messages came with a great level of conviction as the Spirit moved upon their hearts.

A few students from our class attended the meetings also. I, on the other hand, stayed away from any form of an invitation to attend. I wasn't cynical, to say the least, but I also wasn't interested.

But the next morning I witnessed first-hand what the Power of Christ can do. Three of these boys used to smoke cigarettes and drugs secretly at a certain place on the school grounds, where no one could find them. I already didn't like them. They were a gang of their own. But whatever path they thought they were on wasn't going to last long. The valiant God was at work and the Spirit reached out to them, by stepping into their conversations unannounced, just like Christ did to the two disciples on the road to Emmaus. The powerful hand of the Spirit drew these boys to that particular meeting. Praise God for whoever sowed that seed of hope for them to attend the meeting, because The Holy Spirit did convince their hearts to turn to Him, not partially but completely.

Now they were standing before us ready to preach the same message of transformation burning in their hearts. For sure, it was noticeable that the three of them were completely different individuals as they testified about the mighty work of Christ. They were saved, and not just half saved, but completely saved. This was before the teacher came in for roll call. Usually, if we were at the classroom early we had a 30-40 minute gap before roll call.

The morning was cold as usual. The boys began to preach, but not like how my United Church reverend preached. This was preaching that carried a different kind of conviction. Now I was certain that these boys had been to those afternoon Revival meetings that I had been hearing about; although, I hadn't yet attended any of those meetings.

The Fire of the Spirit's conviction burned in our hearts as they spoke with all sincerity.

"What happened to them?" I thought.

I was already saved by then but I never publicly shared my faith like these three. I was taken by their boldness and courage to preach Jesus. It was not only confronting but refreshing. It was the Holy Spirit drawing me.

I was determined to know more, so I decided to join them. Two of the three were Kenneth and Fabian (I can't recall now who the third person was). They were now part of the AOG Church in Goroka and the Fire of God's Word burned in their hearts. It was not only visible outwardly, as their countenances seemed to have gotten brighter, but there was evidence of change in their voices.

I had never heard them talk like this before. Their annoying jokes and jesting stopped, along with whatever other silly things they did; all that ceased immediately. They were completely transformed and I was captivated. I wanted in on this experience. Was there more to God than I knew?

It would be appropriate to say that up until then, I was still a Sunday-going Christian. I was strongly rooted in my religious culture and not fully given to God like these brothers in Christ. Growing up under the umbrella of the United Church (formally known as the London Missionary Society) taught me that life as a Christian was a religious practice and it seemed a world far apart from that of these new converts to the Pentecostal Movement of God. Their countenances continued to shine like lights in our midst. For they also had with their conversion something else more magnificent, and far greater than my religious nurturing.

Brother Kenneth boldly encouraged me on in my journey to find the Holy Spirit. He was the one who invited me to my first-ever meeting with the Scripture Union group. I wasn't ready for the unrestricted, unsuppressed prayer, praise and worship session that was about to begin. To make matters worse, I got myself stuck. I chose to sit furthest from the exit door, and the room was soon so full of students that there wasn't any way to easily slip through the crowd without being seen.

The meeting started with the group bursting out with loud prayers and strange tongues. I thought to myself, "What have I walked into? This is no place for a conservative, religious Christian, like me."

But I stayed. I stayed through that prayer and worship session. As unusual and unfamiliar as it was to me, I stayed. I am glad I did. I wanted to worship God like this but didn't know at all if such a thing was allowed or possible in 'devotion'—as we called it. For the first time, I saw worship that was free and it was a place free of judgement from anyone.

This kind of life in Christ was a wonderful idea, but I still wasn't yet too serious about it. Our friend Peter Nemesi was a classmate of ours in 1997. Peter became close friends with us over that year and ended up living with us (of course, with permission from our parents) to attend school with us.

James and I were blessed to have him and our parents opened their arms to receive him. It's important to mention Peter now, as he would later become a part of the biggest event of our young lives.

About three months before my Baptism with the Holy Spirit and Fire things began to build up for me. I began to hunger for God. I was reading the Bible and I found that the more I read, the hungrier I got. So James, Peter and I decided from about the month of May 1999 onward that we would fast by skipping all our breakfasts and lunches, and just only have dinners. We noticed that our prayer life and worship increased over that period. Also, Kenneth would come over and do sleepovers at our place during the weekends. Kenneth's walk with God was a great encouragement to us. Such wonderful times are had when you have the right people around you. When you have others to help stir up the hunger for God, it becomes in itself a kindled Fire that burns to lead the way. And together, we kept pursuing God.

> "Such wonderful times are had when you have the right people around you. When you have others to help stir up the hunger for God, it becomes in itself a kindled Fire that burns to lead the way.

As we grew a keen interest in the Word and Bible study, I learned about the gifts of the Spirit in 1 Corinthians 12. I learned about the Upper Room Baptism of the Holy Ghost and Fire and oh, it took my heart. I desired to experience the same too. I was so captivated by the idea of pursuing this same experience. I became intentional about the pursuit and began to cut out things that once mattered but didn't matter anymore; as they were now a distraction and a hindrance to me.

We noticed all the AOG boys were flowing with God differently. Some were already speaking in tongues and we certainly wanted this experience to be ours also.

Peter didn't want to miss out either and he told me he was going to follow my fasting program. He became steadfast and disciplined. He would check with me every day to find out if I was fasting or not. If I said I was, then he would confirm his own similar status. I smile now thinking about it. How precious our dear friend was. His willingness served him well and became for him deep insight and joy.

> **"** When your willingness for God is genuine, it will serve you well and become for you, deep insight and joy.

Although he didn't need my validation or approval, he was sincerely a keen follower. We didn't know it then, but God required it of us, for He was positioning us through our pursuit. And without Peter, me, or anyone knowing the near future, only just ahead, would bring about its yield and that promised Fire from on High would eventually come to us at the appointed time.

We kept on with our fasting through May and continued throughout June and July. Soon we were in August 1999. Revival meetings were happening everywhere in the country and quite a number of them were held almost every second week.

Heaven was aligned and soon it was our turn. Our student leaders had planned to invite an anointed man of God to come and preach at our school and the word was passed on to us to prepare the atmosphere and grounds for a mighty Move of God.

We had never heard anything like this before. Even the subject of 'prayer mapping' was new to us. But our hunger for God was getting bigger. This was shown in our commitment to fulfilling the request. We, the young men of the Scripture Union, were to hold our first all-night prayer meeting on Friday 27th August 1999.

CHAPTER 1 — *Where It All Began*

The Sunday prior to that, my brothers and I, with Peter, were leading worship at our United Church University Campus Church. It was *BouBou* Day (Thanksgiving Day) that Sunday. *Boubou* Day is celebrated annually. It is a day marked down in the Church's calendar when the members of the Church would come together on that one day and give to the Church, gifts and offerings as a token of their appreciation and thanks to God. As I remember, it was a day of singing, dancing and celebration with plenty of food to share, kind of like a 'Firstfruit Giving.'

While the singing and presenting of gifts went on, a strange thing happened. As I mentioned earlier, Goroka is a mildly cold place to live. Everyone was dressed in cold climate gear: jumpers, jackets and beanies being the common attire. But for James, Peter and me, our faces were burning hot as if we were sitting right up next to a fireplace. This strange heat started from our heads and began to course down through our bodies and just remained with us for the entire *BouBou* celebration service. But there were no visible signs of the tongues of Fire of Acts 2, and there was no speaking in tongues. And I wondered to myself. Was this it, or a sign that we were getting close to it? By this point, we had read the Upper Room encounter of Acts 2 so many times, our hunger had surely reached a point where I believe it was ripe. For certain, we were fully given to the LORD and ready to receive ours from Him.

I digress a little here, but the Azusa Street Revival and the Upper Room Fire of Acts 2, were both very much like this. The tarrying led to the endowing of the Power of God, and that resulted in the Baptism of Fire that overflowed into the streets that day and went as far as Jesus Himself had said, to the uttermost parts of the earth.

Our hearts were in one accord and we could sense that the time of our Upper Room encounter was approaching and was waiting at the doorstep. How close was this? Very close indeed.

Where It All Began **CHAPTER 1**

The doors of our hearts were wide open with anticipation that He would step through at any moment. Heaven was smiling down on us during this *Boubou celebration*. The unseen *initiative of God* was at work in us to bring us to a place of alignment and fulfilment. The Plan of Heaven wasn't going to be hindered and the appointed time was set. It so happened that this enormous heavenly surprise was waiting to be released on us the following weekend.

CHAPTER 2

BAPTISED WITH THE HOLY GHOST & FIRE

Endued with Power from on High.
The Spirit of the Lord God is upon me

𝒪h, the transforming Power of God that manifests so beautifully in the Baptism of the Holy Ghost and Fire. *The Move of God is* certainly one of the most exciting subjects of all.

If ever you notice hunger for God burning like a Fire amongst the saints, it's a sign that the Revival Fire is at 'The Break of Dawn —Gouloka'. In my own experience, that hunger continued to grow until God's appointed time, which was a particular weekend. When dawn broke, that weekend finally arrived and it was everything we expected and more. Here's how it all happened.

THE NIGHT OF THE BAPTISM OF THE HOLY GHOST & FIRE (27th AUGUST 1999)

I am keenly aware that I can't tell this story to you by myself. I was not alone in this experience and I don't want to miss the opportunity for you to hear from someone else who was there and has always been with me in this life. So, I would like to introduce my twin brother, James Sabadi and let him share his testimony of our Upper Room experience that weekend.

James also shares a special insight into that glorious night of the Baptism of the Holy Ghost and Fire that will help you to understand what God was doing from a broader perspective. So before I share my version of that blessed event, here's what James has to say:

MY ACCOUNT OF THE HOLY GHOST BAPTISM EXPERIENCE 27TH OF AUGUST, 1999.

We arrived at the school at around 5:00 p.m. The teacher in charge (TIC) had given us the keys to map out the all night prayer session for the Goroka Secondary School. I was 16 years of age at that time and doing my Grade 9. That evening, fourteen boys had turned up for the prayer night. These are their names as I remember: Onnevo Michael, Peter Nemesi (our friend who lived with us), Fabian Dominic, Kenneth Sage Ropra, Robert, Norman Sabadi (my brother), myself (James Sabadi), Pastor Peter, David, Toby, Joel, and three more, I can't recall their names now.

It was an amazing night. We started on an ordinary note. The TIC had come to see us and advised that he wasn't going to be around so he kindly asked us to take care of ourselves for the night of prayer. We assured him that we would. Then he left. At around 7:00 p.m. we began our praise and worship. Kenneth and I led our praise and worship. We had done almost three hours of praise and worship and at around 11:00 p.m., the singing became deep and we were about to have an encounter with the Holy Spirit.

We praised till we were soaking with sweat. And when we worshipped we were literally lost in His Presence. It was quite an experience. By this point, everyone was praying in their own corner. Some were standing, some still pacing the floor, and some were kneeling. As for me, I was sitting on top of a desk playing the guitar. I was positioned in the first row closest to the door. I noticed Peter Nemesi was on the second row of desks from me.

As the worship intensified, I felt in my heart to sing, "There is none like You."

As I began to sing this song, Peter fell on his knees and began to speak in tongues. He was praying but this time I could not make sense of what he was saying. He was struggling to speak. And I then looked over to the other side and saw Norman had also been baptised by the Holy Spirit. One thing for certain is that it didn't make sense at first.

When Peter was praying and pleading and speaking in his prayer, he wasn't formulating words anymore. Everybody stopped to check on him and check on Norman. That's when we realised we were in for a big night.

By that time everyone was just finishing off worship and just about going into warfare prayers when this happened. The Spirit was truly leading and we were all there completely surrendered to His leadership.

Robert...honestly, that brother really knew what was happening. And he asked the Holy Spirit to tell us what to do. We were trying our best to keep Norman on his feet, as the Power of God flowed through him. I remember by this time, most of us were a little bit afraid and that's when the Spirit of God spoke. "Do not be afraid," Robert said to us. "The Spirit of God has taken over them."

Pastor Peter quickly asked us to get together and listen to what Norman and Peter were going to do or say.

The experience was new to us. All fourteen boys did not know what was going on. But I believe the Spirit of God was there to guide as Robert and Kenneth helped Norman and Peter up to the front of the classroom. It was at that very moment that all of us knew we were having an Upper Room experience like the saints of the Upper Room in Acts 2. And in that very hour, God began to use both of them mightily for the night's events that were about to unfold.

As a side note, most of us came from a United Church of Papua New Guinea background (previously founded as the London Missionary Society of Papua New Guinea). Our Churches never really talked about the Upper Room experience nor the Baptism of the Holy Spirit. It was all religious practice to us. We only read about it. We didn't know this was real. That experience alone changed my whole life; my whole perspective of the way I thought about God.

Norman would speak in tongues and Peter would interpret what he was saying. It was a whole new experience for us. We did not waste any time. All fourteen boys marched out of the room and began to pray and warfare over the whole school area; visiting each classroom and building as we went. It was quite an experience.

To cover the whole school area, we had to break up into two teams. This was around 1:00 a.m. when we began to pray for certain segments of the school grounds. It was quite an extraordinary experience. In every classroom we went to, Robert was responsible for opening each door. The other team: Brother Toby was in charge.

At one classroom we came to, the Spirit of God moved Peter Nemesi and we felt an urgency to get into that classroom. Then a miracle happened before us. Peter simply stepped forward and pushed that door right open, before Robert could find the keys to unlock it. Brother Robert stood amazed at what just happened. A locked door just opened with the locked bars still in place. Peter hurried in and began casting out the strongholds in that classroom.

After mapping and praying through some of the darkest places in the school, we discovered so much evil presence in our walk. I felt, there was a great battle in the spirit over the young people we prayed for. The warfare itself was so real. We felt it. Even the urgency in the Spirit was something I noted also.

Once our task was completed, we then moved back to the main classroom where it all began. We were soaked by the experience. Still dazed from the prayer walk, we began to worship the LORD again. There began the laying on of hands. A lot of spiritual gifts and impartation were done during that night as Norman and Peter Nemesi began to lead in the Spirit, prophesying, giving words of knowledge and laying hands with evidence of the Power of the Spirit.

Then it was my turn to be laid hands on, and I will never forget it. But it didn't happen in the usual way. God had set it up. This peculiar event would lead to me receiving the Baptism of the Fire of the Holy Ghost.

Norman, being led by the Spirit, called Brother Kenneth forward and announced that God was going to release a mighty Anointing. I was standing right behind Kenneth as he was going to be prayed for. I was the appointed catcher, and that was the setup.

Norman began to pray and at the very moment when he was about to say, "Receive it!" Kenneth, quickly stepped or skipped slightly towards the side, to his right (because he was afraid), clearly giving way and there was I the catcher. All of a sudden I got hit by this tremendous force of wind.

I remember being thrown about two metres back before hitting the concrete floor. After that, I blacked out for a while. I was in between the natural and spirit realms. What I felt was consciousness and I looked at everything around me and noticed that the air was filled with white smoke. It was the Presence of God; the Cloud of God had settled in the room. And true as it was, my spiritual eyes of discernment were open from that moment on.

Then, as it seemed to me, Norman and Peter, who were still in this spiritual trance of the Holy Ghost, woke up from it and realised they were in the classroom, where we had first gathered.

They had so much to say, and there was so much they had seen by the enabling of the Spirit. We spent the rest of the early hours of the morning listening to their stories and recollecting all the events that took place that night until the break of dawn.

This is my account of my first Holy Ghost Baptism experience and one that is our story to tell. How wonderful that we get to share it with you. It's an experience that church-going Christians may have never had.

And if you've never received the Baptism of the Holy Ghost and Fire you will never be able to truly relate to Him (The Spirit of Christ) until you have had a personal encounter with The Spirit of the LORD Jesus like we did that night. The Baptism of the Holy Spirit is available for all those who seek Him with all their heart.

> "The Baptism of the Holy Spirit is available for all those who seek Him with all their heart.

I tried to sing some songs after that, but every time I did my lips would become heavy. I would mumble something different from what was going through my mind and my body would become so heavy and weak on occasions when I began to worship during the night. The weightiness of the Presence of God was still upon me. I then realised that I had received my Baptism in the Holy Ghost and Fire also, and was already speaking in tongues. I remember how the Presence of the Lord would fill the room as I worshipped Him. It was so wonderful.

Every one of those fourteen boys…we were changed forever. My twin brother Norman, who is now Senior Pastor of *The Place Where He Speaks* was a totally different person after that night. And since then he has never been the same person I knew before that experience. He has never looked back after that experience.

Since then I have seen God in a very different way compared to what others think of Him. And my message to the world is that if you think that there is no God, or that God is a myth, then think again. God is real and Heaven and Hell are real and Jesus is calling us to repentance, for His return is very near. That experience changed my perspective of who God is, and since then my prayer life and daily conversation with God have never been the same. Sure, the journey wasn't easy after that. There were many trials and temptations along the way. Even through the hardest of seasons, God has seen me through them all.

Even when I have gone astray so many times, the Lord in His goodness and grace has continued to lead me back to His loving arms. Oh, the wonderful mercies of God. Amidst all the shortcomings that one may encounter, the call of God remains faithful. I considered then it was time to truly follow Jesus.

I decided to recommit my life to Jesus in 2008 and I have, once again, enjoyed fellowshipping with Him every day since.

James S. Sabadi

As told by James Sabadi

What a privilege and blessing to read my brother's account of the event. Talking about the Holy Spirit brings me great joy. I desire to make God the focus and emphasis as I reach out to your heart to believe with me and to recognise and receive the Move of God. The Great Wind of the Spirit is right now fresh and ready to touch, transform and disciple many who will turn their hearts to the King of Glory. God wants to pour out His Spirit upon you also. God is looking for willing vessels who will say yes to that glorious call and yield to Him until His Power rests upon them.

Prayer:

Oh, God of Heaven. We love you. We surrender ourselves completely to You. We are ready Lord. We are ready. Come and use us for Your Glory...Amen

ENDUED WITH POWER FROM ON HIGH

Now it's my turn to tell you my testimony of the story. There was a coffee expo at our school that Friday 27th August 1999. We were informed by our Patron that there was only going to be school time in the morning and then the expo would take up the rest of the day.

Because of the expo, the principal decided a special lunch would be served for all students. What a treat, right? Well, if this was the absolute test of our commitment to fast. I mean, who turns away delicious food, especially when you don't usually get a special lunch like that at school? But we were fasting that day, so it was either we break the fast or push the plate away.

We lined up for lunch and our plates were served full of many varieties of yummy food. At that same time, our student leader was arranging (with the Scripture Union TIC and the Deputy Principal) for the keys to the classrooms we were going to be praying over that same night.

The weekend was set apart for the all night prayer in anticipation of a great week of ministry ahead. There we sat—all fourteen Scripture Union boys, including myself—in one of the Grade 12 classrooms that faced the main assembly area of the school. We said a prayer for the meal and as the others got right into enjoying their plates of food, I paused. I couldn't do it. I couldn't break my fast. My tummy grumbled but I was so hungry for God. I hungered for Him more than for anything on that plate of delicious food in my hands. I passed it to the others in the room.

Peter had already eaten a quarter of the food on his plate when he noticed what I had done. He quickly passed his plate on to another brother saying to him, "I'm all right. You can have the rest of my food." It is important for you to understand that I didn't seek his commitment. Nor did I try to communicate my thoughts to him to influence his decision. I was being driven by my own hunger. It was his own decision to make. It was clear that same hunger had gripped him too, and now we were certainly both seeking the deep things of God. I remember our young pastor, who was there too, declared to everyone in the room, "God is going to use the Sabadi brothers, and Peter tonight"

My eyes were wide as I looked at him. Was it really going to happen? I thought, "God knows. He must have seen our hearts."

And, of course, I was a new Christian, and these types of questions are expected, especially when you are new to the things of the Spirit and new to the Gospel of Jesus Christ. Internally, I felt that I was ready. But I wondered if it was enough for God to move in and through my life. If that feeling ever gets to you, just know it's an indicator that you're on the right path. Without a doubt, *desperation for God* is certainly part of the traits of the pursuit of God. Hunger after the Spirit is in itself: a mentor with no voice yet it speaks and stirs the heart to yield until God comes and transforms the heart with Power.

> **"** Hunger after the Spirit is in itself: a mentor with no voice yet it speaks and stirs the heart to yield until God comes and transforms the heart with power.

The evening came quickly. We had gone home briefly to get ourselves ready and were soon back at the school grounds. The night was cold but we were fired up and ready to worship God. Toby and Joel; our leaders, briefed us on the night's events. The prayer map was made and we were going to be praying for the school area. That's all we knew.

We knew the school campus was quite a big place to cover but our hearts were ready for the prayer assignment. After the quick prayer map briefing, we started with praise and worship. Oh, how wonderful it is to worship God freely. Kenneth and James played the guitars and led the songs. Every one of us joined in and we sang our hearts out. This seemed to build us together into a place of overflowing adoration for God. I could already feel my heart so overwhelmed by the grace and goodness of the Lord.

The worship progressed and got deeper and at this point, I found myself in tears on the floor crying out to the Lord, "Touch me, Lord. Here I am God, so hungry for You. Here I am Lord, use me for Your glory. I want to be completely Yours."

The prayers intensified all across the room, and our hearts were in one accord (Acts 2:1-4), and then suddenly, a tangible Wind began to fill the atmosphere. Across from me, two rows of desks away, Peter Nemesi burst out in tongues and was completely taken by the Holy Ghost. Like rivers, the tongues of God gushed out of his mouth and from the depths of his being. The living waters of God's Spirit began to flow (John 7:37-39).

I remember raising my head briefly to glance at Peter and thought to myself, "Peter got it. Lord, he followed me in my hunger and pursuit of Your Presence, but You gave it to him first?"

As funny as it sounds, I was stirred even more and my heart reached for Heaven as I began to groan before the Lord. "Don't forget me, God. Touch me too. Please, Lord. What about me? Here I am Lord. I surrender….r…r…r…"

And before I could say any more, the Baptism of the Holy Ghost and Fire came down like a wind upon me and it was real; that glorious Power from on High.

My mouth and tongue became heavy under the influence of the Power of the Spirit. He rushed into my being like a mighty wind. It was so intense that it threw me to the floor. I tried to get up but wave after wave of that Power kept rushing into my being. I simply wasn't able to remain standing. Once again, I fell to the floor overtaken by the Glory of God. Oh, how glorious is the Power of the Living God.

Then the heavenly tongues gushed forth and with them, tears of joy. My heart swelled with joy and praise for the one true God.

God was pleased with our offering. That offering was a broken heart and contrite spirit. Immediately, King David's words flashed before me.

Psalms 51:16-17

> "For Thou desirest not sacrifice; else would I give it: Thou delightest not in burnt offering. The sacrifices of God are a broken spirit: a broken and a contrite heart, O God, Thou wilt not despise."

I was completely consumed by Divine Power. I felt whole and I knew that I was cleansed; I was washed by His glorious Presence, Hallelujah!

That same night the Spirit led me and His VOICE was so clear. I had never heard it before, but at that moment I knew Him and He knew me.

And an Anointing for warfare rested mightily upon me, I knew it was for the prayer assignment we were about to embark upon together. The brothers helped me to my feet and held me up. I then said to them, "Let's go! The Spirit wants to clean the school up."

I knew God was with us and that we were going to win a mighty spiritual battle. As I recall, demons began to flee before us, and angels descended upon the school grounds to help drive out the demons and evil spirits. One vision after another flashed before me as the Lord led us. And with every praying moment came an instruction on what to do in that moment. Darkness had no grip and was powerless before us because the Holy Spirit was at work and the mighty Presence of God had been poured upon the school grounds. I realise now as I look back in hindsight, that our dependency was fully upon the Holy Spirit to show us what to do, and at the same time the Spirit enabled us to do it correctly.

There were times when we had to pause and wait as the dialogue from Heaven (through tongues) was received. It was like a transmission waiting to reach the receiver. This was a real battle indeed, and the gift of heavenly tongues was like encrypted messages going to and fro, from the Throne of God to us. In that exchange of information, the Holy Spirit would reveal to us what was happening and what to do at those exact moments. I understood straight away that the gift of tongues is critical for spiritual warfare.

I remember also a particular girl who was shown to me in a vision. When I mean, a vision of her, I mean it was like I was literally standing with her. I was in a trance, guided by the Spirit. It seemed to me that I was in two worlds at the same time. The natural realm and the spiritual realm. The spiritual realm wasn't just in my thoughts. It was as real as the natural realm and both realms were before me. The girl was covered by thick darkness and all around her, including her entire being, was consumed with evil. She had been overtaken by the horrendous grip of wickedness.

Immediately the Holy Spirit spoke to me and said she was bound by a chief evil spirit: a stronghold. The Bible mentions them as principalities and rulers. I then directed the team of boys to pray for her as I described the vision to them. I said to them that the girl was a student who had her lessons in the classroom we had just entered, and it seemed this evil force had held her bound for a very long time. So they all began to pray and bind the evil spirit and call out the functions that it operated in, but none of these strategies seemed to deter or dislodge the stronghold.

This was no small demon. We learned another important lesson here. We learned that the other demons fled without looking back. They were minor demons; subordinates ruled by other demons that were much stronger than them. So it was easy for us to remove these hordes of minor demons in one mighty blow, led by the Spirit. When we declared them bound, and then rebuked and drove them out, they would leave immediately.

But this one didn't react at all; it had possessed and controlled her for a long time and wasn't going to budge.

I then called out to everyone to begin praying in tongues. I had a knowing that God was going to give us victory over this principality. And, sure enough, the Holy Spirit spoke clearly into my spirit the actual creative name of the stronghold. Just as my name is Norman, the demons all have their names given to them too. The Spirit then told me to call it by its name and that this would expose and defeat the stronghold. I stood before the demon in the vision, and the boldness and might of the Spirit became intensified in my spirit. I shouted with a strong and firm voice calling the demon by its name. "—— Leave her now!"

Immediately, the light of God beamed on it, and the ugliness of the creature was exposed. The evil spirit didn't even wait for us to say the Name of Jesus. It was gone instantly and abandoned any attempts to defend its position. It fled from before us and was gone. The brightness of God increased in the room and the girl was now free. Hallelujah! We had seen firsthand how the Lord leads us to victory by His Spirit.

Zechariah 4:6

> Then he answered and spake unto me, saying, This is the Word of the LORD unto Zerubbabel, saying, Not by might, nor by Power, but by My Spirit, saith the LORD of hosts.

As we were about to complete our warfare prayer, we were led to this dilapidated boys' dormitory that was at the northwest end of the school and there the Spirit led us right into this poorly lit place. As we walked down the dark corridor, my eyes were shut tight but I could see the path and I could see the rooms lit up before me. But then I noticed one room wasn't shining bright. The Holy Spirit led us to that room. I walked up to it and looked in and, there sitting by the window were two boys who were smoking marijuana. This was their secret hideout and they would come to that room to smoke it. I saw them bound with heavy chains as they each took turns puffing their marijuana, and I knew these were chains of addiction and chains of demonic influence. The enemy had them trapped and they couldn't break loose from the bondage of this evil influence. It seemed also that they were unaware of the chains.

This should speak to your heart if you are right now bound with an addiction and you can't seem to break free from it. It is important for you to know that any form of addiction from demons is a spiritual chain that binds the soul. God wants to set you free from those chains by the Power of the Name of Jesus and the Authority of the Spirit of God.

Prayer:

> Lord, Holy Spirit, I pray for that brother and sister who is bound in those chains right now. I declare by the Power of the Name of Jesus those chains that are binding you be loosed from you in Jesus' Name and I declare you be free in the Glorious Name of Jesus. Holy Ghost I ask you to fill that person with Your freedom and Rivers of life, in Jesus' Name. Amen...

By the Spirit, I directed the team to pray for the two boys whom I had identified. I described what was happening to them spiritually. This gave the team specific heavenly insight into what they needed to pray for so that these boys could be set free.

In my vision, the chains came loose and I saw them free. I do remember sometime afterwards when the vision was told to the individuals concerned, they admitted to feeding their addiction to marijuana right there at that very location. Their sins were exposed and the fear of God gripped their hearts.

After this, I could see in a vision that the atmosphere was changing. The warfare was complete. In the middle of total darkness in the corridor of this run-down dormitory, gifts from the Holy Spirit began to fall from above. I saw glowing boxes with ribbons on them that had begun to descend upon all of us boys in that old place.

We can decorate a room and have the perfect lighting to suit and still have no Holy Spirit manifestation. That's because the true encounter is not determined by our mood, but by our hearts.

The Spirit of God fell again in that old building upon us. Only one person carried a torch, but we could hardly see each other's faces. One would think otherwise to control the Spirit but that would be a direct misalignment to God's will and what He was doing right there in that poorly lit, old corridor. This manifestation taught me that the Holy Ghost's program is not restricted to what we as believers might consider, to be an appropriate place and time. He chooses the place and time. He works purposefully and powerfully according to what He decides must be done in that place.

There was abundant grace as we were all learning to move with the Holy Ghost. The Spirit was also leading Joel and Toby, our team leaders, and they realised what was happening and quickly mentioned that we should all head back to the classroom (our Upper Room) where we had started. The Spirit was patient with us as they led Peter and me back to the main classroom. The Power of God was with us, and our hearts were ready for whatever the Lord required of us. We returned to that classroom, and sure enough, the Holy Spirit continued to speak to us there. God was moving fast and in order to stay in the flow of His plan and purpose we had to respond quickly to His leading.

There I understood, by the counsel of the Holy Spirit, that the Anointing for warfare had played its part and was complete, and now a different type of Anointing had entered the room. These were the Anointings and operations for ministry and included everything mentioned in 1 Corinthians 12.

This is an important insight also into the operations of the Spirit. It is important to understand that there must be spiritual preparation and cleansing of the atmosphere before the Anointing that we receive for ministry, can function freely in that place. We must first win the unseen battle in the spirit, a battle that the Holy Ghost reveals and fights for us. When we overcome the enemy in the spirit realm, our victory becomes manifested in the natural realm. When we win the battle for the atmosphere over that place, it becomes an open heaven for the Holy Spirit to work, without any hindrance from the enemy. Having this understanding grants us the confidence to be bold in ministry and to know what to do when we are confronted with a spiritual enemy.

2 Corinthians 10:3-6

"For though we walk in the flesh, we do not war after the flesh: (For the weapons of our warfare are not carnal, but mighty through God to the pulling down of strong holds;) Casting down imaginations, and every high thing that exalteth itself against the knowledge of God, and bringing into captivity every thought to the obedience of Christ; And having in a readiness to revenge all disobedience, when your obedience is fulfilled."

BE HUNGRY FOR GOD

Matthew 5:6

> Blessed are they which do hunger and thirst after righteousness: for they shall be filled.

A key lesson to learn from my testimony here is that there is a *trigger* that causes you to go down the path to search for answers. That trigger can come out of any circumstance and it is HUNGER FOR GOD.

Spiritual hunger is a prerequisite for the infilling and overflowing of the Holy Spirit. Every one of us can access His Presence just by being hungry for Him. A genuine hunger after God aligns your heart, mind and soul to the purposes and promises of God. Hunger after the Spirit prepares you to receive the Power from on High. As Jesus puts it, "This kind can only be driven out by prayer and fasting."

Jesus was not only referring to the type of spirit being dealt with (a chief unclean spirit; a stronghold in this case), nor just the method or Heavenly weaponry alone that deals with it. Jesus was alluding to something ingrained and foundational: *the hunger of a saint whose bones have been consumed by the Fire of the Holy Ghost*, the Fire of His Divine Word of Power because that believer in Christ has chosen to surrender their life completely to the Lord.

It is holy desperation that causes you to separate yourself from the world and draw near to the Spirit's desire for you. That hunger and thirst for God becomes in the hungry the cup that eventually must overflow. It is also described as our need to be covered by the clothing of the Power from on High. This clothing is far more glorious than any garment we could produce from what we can gather with our own resources. It is being clothed with

Christ, the Messiah, the one who died so that we could be reconciled to God. It is a glorious truth, that has always been true. God wants us to seek and find Him.

Isaiah 55:6

Seek ye the LORD while He may be found, call ye upon Him while He is near:

Jeremiah 29:12-14

Then shall ye call upon Me, and ye shall go and pray unto Me, and I will hearken unto you. And ye shall seek Me, and find Me when ye shall search for Me with all your heart. **And I will be found of you...**

CHAPTER 3

THE BAPTISM OF FIRE IS YOUR INDUCTION SERVICE

In the volume of the book it is written of me (Psalms 40:7)

Jeremiah 1:4-5

Then the Word of the Lord came unto me, saying, Before I formed thee in the belly **I knew thee**; and before thou camest forth out of the womb **I sanctified thee**, and **I ordained thee** a prophet unto the nations.

It is with prayerfulness and sincerity that I seek your willingness to respond to what I will share now on the subject of ordination. My intent here is not to divide the Body on doctrinal matters. The reason why I am raising this point is that it has everything to do with understanding God's Move, and God's Awakening. When we come into an understanding of the Anointing and our ordination from God, the Church will function correctly out of revelation knowledge, and pursue God in the correct way. This will also help the Church to identify and acknowledge God's anointed vessels in our midst. By this, I mean God doesn't want us to miss the mark. The Holy Spirit is with us. God wants the Church to walk and live in the Power of the Spirit and not void of Him.

I talk about *the Anointing* in more detail in Chapter 13, but at this point, I want to focus on *Ordination*. The ordination of God upon our lives is His mark of favour and ownership. We belong to Him. That ordination of Power that rests upon your holy calling comes from God.

The early Church started this journey in the Upper Room of Jerusalem. They were obedient to the command that Christ gave to them. They were to wait for the Power from on High before they could become effective witnesses for Christ. The Power that would come upon them would enable them to give powerful testimonies about salvation, reconciliation and eternal life through Jesus the Messiah. When that promised power finally came upon them, their Mantles (or their Anointings for ministry) rested upon them on that day and they were ready to go forth and be mighty vessels used for God's will.

Our callings are all prepared in Heaven's wonderful plan and we need not try to figure out the calling. The Spirit of God will help us with that. The Baptism of the Holy Spirit and Fire that clothes us will assign the *Call* and make it known to us. As the Apostle James wrote (in James 4:8), it is important for us to understand that to *draw near to God* means to become hungry for God and seek His Face just as it was with the early Church.

When God began to Move in my life, I noted these same traits of the workings of God right from the beginning. My own observations are evidence of this one truth: the only part I played leading up to these Glory encounters was HUNGER FOR GOD. I was continuously hungry for God and I also pursued a personal relationship with Him. I wanted to abide under the shadow of His

Wings and dwell in *His Secret Place*. I wanted His Presence. I was completely given to His abiding grace and Power upon my life.

I drew a deeper understanding with every God-encounter, and I gained wonderful insights about different A*nointings* and their *ordinations* each time the Holy Spirit ministered to me. The Lord made it clear to me that the starting point of ministry is to seek after God with all your heart. My encouragement to you, brothers and sisters in the Lord, is to first have your Upper Room encounter appointed by God. It's God who calls, empowers and sends forth. I became aware that effective ministry was when the Holy Spirit ministered through me and this was how He operated. I would rather it be God and none of me. I learned through many God-encounters that when the Glory of God's Word rests on me and also upon the room, He moves mightily in our midst.

The God of Glory wants to abide with us. God wants to be in our midst continuously by inhabiting our worship and praise. I have also observed that the Holy Spirit can clothe a vessel more than once, in their lifetime here on earth. When we read the Old Testament books about the Judges and Prophets of ancient times, we note them saying consistently, "Then the Spirit of God came upon him." The Spirit didn't just do it once, He repeatedly came upon chosen vessels that were marked to fulfil a God-purpose presented in those crucial moments when God's people needed Heavenly intervention. And through those individuals, God demonstrated His power and decisive response to give them a favourable outcome. On every occasion mentioned in scripture when the Spirit clothed these individuals, it was God who had the upper hand. Establishing this truth, we can then with confidence state that the Holy Spirit's Baptism experience works in our favour and aids or empowers us to bring the desired outcome. Also, we are assured that it is a repeated experience of the clothing of the Power of God whenever the Lord wants to Move and all He needs is a vessel to work with. This has happened to me more than twelve times and I am confident that there is more to come. But this is not something that should be unique to my experience. God desires to fill us all with the treasures of His Glory.

2 Corinthians 4:5-7

> For we preach not ourselves, but Christ Jesus the Lord; and ourselves your servants for Jesus' sake. For God, who commanded the light to shine out of darkness, hath shined in our hearts, to give the light of the knowledge of the Glory of God in the Face of Jesus Christ. **But we have this treasure in earthen vessels**, that the Excellency of the Power may be of God, and not of us.

So now, this is the point I want to make. The initial Baptism of the Holy Ghost and Fire is your *'induction'* into office for Kingdom service. It is your Heavenly Inauguration. You are empowered from that point on to be an effective witness for Christ.

> " The Baptism of the Holy Spirit and Fire is your ordination service. It is your Heavenly Inauguration.

After the initial Baptism, there are continuous encounters with the Holy Spirit's power clothing a vessel. Acts 4:21-33, being a separate event from Acts 2, is an example of this. The saints had already received the Power from on High in Acts 2, yet after they prayed in oneness again in Acts 4, the place was shaken by the Power of God and the disciples were again filled with the Holy Ghost. Verse 33 goes on to say,

Acts 4:33

with great Power, the apostles gave witness and testified of the resurrection of the Lord Jesus Christ.

This pattern is not exclusive only to the New Testament Saints of Acts 2. The Spirit has been poured out on many Christians since then. The work of the Spirit is very rich and has been manifested openly to the world in the Church's *Revival History.*

One that is certainly worth mentioning here is *The Azusa Street Revival,* in Los Angeles, USA (1906-1909). Then there was that same experience of *A Mighty Wind and Fire* upon a Protestant Church, in Soe Village, Timor Island, Indonesia (1965). Evangelist Mel Tari's book reveals in detail that encounter.[1] Similar to the Upper Room account of Acts 2, and that of the *Fire on Azusa Street,* the 200 people gathered there were praying and they heard and felt the wind that blew into that building. And all of sudden the Spirit began to move in their midst baptising all of them with the Holy Fire from Heaven. Soon the fire bell rang from the police station nearby and it was to alert the villagers that the Church building had caught on fire and was engulfed in the flames. The villagers with their buckets of water hurried towards the burning building and when they reached the Church building they could see the flames but the building wasn't on fire. This wasn't a natural fire but it was the Fire of God that had come upon those praying in the building. That same night, the water bucket carriers became 'Heavenly Fire Carriers;' they also were converted and received Jesus Christ as their Lord and Saviour. They were even baptised with the mighty Fire from Heaven that rested upon the place. Hallelujah!

God also worked in the same manner of empowering His servants in the Old Testament. You will read that when the Spirit of

God came upon a particular individual, that person rose and acted upon a specific direction with the might of the Spirit resting upon him, and moving him. They would, by the moving of the Spirit, either do something, speak something or both.

Here are some examples in Scripture:
- The 70 elders - Numbers 11:25-26
- Balaam, a heathen who was told to bless God's people - Numbers 24:1-9
- Othniel, Caleb's younger brother - Judges 3:9-10
- Gideon - Judges 6:34
- Samson - Judges 14:6, Judges 14:19, Judges 15:14, Judges 16:28
- King Saul - 1 Samuel 10:10, 1 Samuel 19: 21-24,
- King David - 1 Samuel 16:13
- John the Baptist - Luke 1:15
- Mary, the mother of Jesus - Luke 1:35-38
- The Prophet Isaiah moved by the Spirit prophesied about *the Power: that holy Anointing of the Holy Ghost that rests upon a prepared vessel.*

Isaiah 61:1-4

'The Spirit of the Lord GOD is upon me; because the LORD hath anointed me...'

- Jeremiah could not fight it, and he said it was because the Power of the Word burned in his heart like Fire shut up in his bones (Jeremiah 20:9).
- That same Power came and rested upon the disciples in the Upper Room.
- Elisha received it as it fell upon him and clothed him as Elijah was taken from him. Elisha received the double portion

from Elijah when the Mantle fell and he picked it up. He was at that exact moment, endued with the Power of the Most High. Later, his bones still carried the *Fire of the Word—That Holy Anointing* that raised a dead man (2 Kings 13:20-21). Just think about it, a man who no longer lives, whose body now rest in his tomb, but yet his bones still carried power to raise a dead man to life. It was the *Power of the Word that was still resting upon Elisha's bones* that spoke resurrection life into that dead man and brought him back to life.

• John the Baptist, who himself was a Revivalist, was sent with the Anointing to call the people to repentance and to prepare their hearts for the Messiah. This is what John declared as recorded in Matthew's Gospel (note the bolded words):

Matthew 3:11

'I indeed baptize you with water unto repentance: but He that cometh after me is mightier than I, Whose shoes I am not worthy to bear: **He shall baptize (IMMERSE/ CLOTHE) you with the Holy Ghost, and Fire**:'

The Lord Jesus is The Chief Revivalist. When He came to John to be baptised, John would rather have the Messiah baptise him. But Jesus said to John, "Let it be, for we are fulfilling all righteousness."

In other words, "We are obeying what the Father wants."

Jesus, being the Word of God made flesh, knew very well that John had to play his part in the Heavenly plan because it was in line with Heavenly protocol and God's ordination—God's plan for the mission that was upon Christ's shoulders. Then, when Jesus was baptised and came up out of the water, this was what John saw and heard (again, note the bolded words):

CHAPTER 3 *The Baptism Of Fire Is Your Induction Service*

Matthew 3:16-17

'he (John) saw **the Spirit of God descending like a dove and lighting upon Him**: And lo a Voice from Heaven, saying, This is My beloved Son, in Whom I am well pleased.'

Here, we see that Jesus the Messiah (The Anointed One) was now being Anointed or Baptised by the Power from on High—the Spirit of God. Jesus was being inaugurated into His office. He received His calling, and His Mantle to be the Messiah and Saviour of the World.

Christ's Immersion into water does not mean He was a sinner repenting of His sins and needing to be cleansed by water. Christ was dedicating Himself to *His Commission as God's Messiah and Saviour*. He was simply committing Himself to the call of His Father, in obedience and surrender.

And just as the Prophet Isaiah declared (Isaiah 61), the Spirit of the Lord God came and rested upon *The Anointed One*. So Christ was also *endued (baptised or clothed)* with the Holy Spirit.

It is important to note here that Jesus Christ was already the Christ before the foundations of the world were laid. The Jordan River Baptism was His ordination appointment (meaning this was what He was called and purposed to do). We understand then that His *ministry* as Christ didn't start officially until the Jordan River Baptism. So what really was happening right before John's eyes here was that when the Spirit of God came and rested upon Jesus, in that very moment, He was being *inducted* into His Office as *The Anointed One*. And *the cloak of His Mantle that clothed Him as the Christ came upon Him like a Dove*. That Mantle was in effect from that point on.

We can see a striking similarity with a previous account when Elijah's physical Mantle fell upon the ground. It was the evidence of the Holy Spirit Mantle that fell upon Elisha. The Prophet Elisha only started operating in the double portion of his mentor's Anointing as soon as he saw Elijah go and responded by picking up the Mantle from the place where it fell.

Likewise, John had to obey God and baptise Jesus in water (Matthew 3:16). This act of obedience was the physical evidence that would initiate the release of the spiritual Mantle that would fall upon Christ. It should be noted that you read nothing about Jesus ministering with healing, miracles, signs and wonders before the Jordan River Baptism. The only stories of Christ's early years that the Gospels have documented are His nativity story and a snippet of His time as a twelve-year-old in the Temple.

So from this, we can see how God appoints His chosen vessels: the Spirit must rest and abide upon them. Let's look at yet another example in the Old Testament.

David was the youngest of eight sons of Jesse. His father gave him the job of tending the sheep and David gladly served with diligence. David loved worshipping God, and he was able to concurrently watch the flock and spend time worshipping God.

It was to Jesse's family that the Prophet Samuel was sent by God to go to Bethlehem to anoint David as the chosen king of Israel. God was going to reveal to Samuel the selection for Israel's next king. God had found His man; *a man after His Own Heart*. Samuel didn't know who it was but Heaven had marked the young David out. Jesse and Samuel thought alike. They both assumed that God would pick the firstborn or one of the others after him. But it was not so. God's selection was *based on the heart*. As soon as David stepped into that room, God said to Samuel, "Arise, anoint him: for this is he." David received his call and

Mantle to be king of Israel as soon as the Spirit of the Lord rested on him (1 Samuel 16:12-13).

Samuel didn't know who the chosen vessel was until God revealed that person to him. Samuel, by the instruction and command of the Lord, took the horn of oil and poured it on David to officiate the appointment.

1 Samuel 16:13

Then Samuel took the horn of oil, and anointed him in the midst of his brethren: **and the Spirit of the LORD came upon David from that day forward**

This was David's commissioning and induction service done by the Holy Ghost and not man. Samuel's experience was similar to that of John the Baptist, who didn't know who the Christ was until the Lord Jesus stepped into that water and God opened John's eyes to see who it was. And in like manner, as John was sent to mark out the Christ by the sign of Baptism; the Prophet Samuel was sent to mark God's chosen king with the Anointing oil.

I know I am repeating this point, but you really must get it. An induction into office happens when the Spirit of the Lord rests upon a chosen vessel. You are only called and anointed because an Anointing came upon you. You are only marked as anointed when the Spirit rests upon you. That's when the Purpose, Call and Commission of your ordination begins.

> " You are only marked as anointed when the Spirit rests upon you.

The *Mantle (coat) of the Spirit* that rested upon David was the official commissioning and induction into his calling as God's chosen king. Notice also that the Spirit of God was with David, and his Anointing as king started from that day onward.

I did mention Elijah and Elisha earlier but let's look a little deeper into their experience. Elisha was already chosen by God to be the one to take over from Elijah. Elijah had thrown his physical Mantle over Elisha's shoulders earlier in their initial meeting, but at that point, the Mantle did not remain with Elisha. Elisha returned the Mantle to Elijah and Elisha became his disciple right up to Elijah's departure. Therefore the double portion that Elisha was to carry wasn't given to him until he saw Elijah caught up by chariots of Fire. Elijah specifically told Elisha that if he saw him being taken away, he would get the double portion of Elijah's spirit that he had asked for. The Instruction was simple, "If you see me when I am taken from you, it shall be so for you."

2 Kings 2:9-10

> And it came to pass, when they were gone over, that Elijah said unto Elisha, Ask what I shall do for thee, before I be taken away from thee. And Elisha said, I pray thee, let a double portion of thy spirit be upon me. And he said, Thou hast asked a hard thing: nevertheless, **if thou see me when I am taken from thee, it shall be so unto thee**; but if not, it shall not be so.

Elisha did see when Elijah was taken and also saw that Elijah had dropped his physical Mantle. Elisha picked it up and from that day onward Elisha carried the double portion of the *Anointing of Elijah* (2 Kings 2:13-14).

God's calling and timing are perfect. Don't rush into ministry. Wait upon the Power from on High.

CHAPTER 3   *The Baptism Of Fire Is Your Induction Service*

> " God's calling and timing are perfect. Don't rush into ministry. Wait upon the Power from on High.

Now let's look at a New Testament example. I don't think you'll be surprised that I'm referring to the Baptism of the Holy Ghost and Fire that fell upon the saints who were obediently waiting in the Upper Room in Jerusalem. They were all endued with Power from on High to be witnesses for Jesus. Oh, how glorious and wonderful is the Power of God, that not only saturates us but also sanctifies and appoints us with a holy Anointing.

The disciples' ministry to Jerusalem, Judea, Samaria and the uttermost parts of the earth, could not happen until the Power of the Spirit rested on them in the Upper Room. They needed to be clothed by the Spirit of God; or, in other words, *inducted into their calling* and a specific Anointing was given to each of them for the part they would each play to fulfil the Great Commission of our Lord Jesus.

Note here that they were instructed by the Lord Jesus to *wait* in Jerusalem for the forthcoming *evidence of God* to descend and clothe them with Power. Hallelujah! It would be a day like no other in their simple lives. Jesus, the Chosen One of God, the One sent from the Father, was now sending the Spirit to all those who would *yield to the call* to wait in Jerusalem (As you read the verse below take careful note of the bolded words).

Luke 24:49

And, behold, I send the promise of My Father upon you: but tarry ye in the city of Jerusalem, until **ye be endued with Power from on High.**

Acts 1:4-8

And, being assembled together with them, commanded them that they should not depart from Jerusalem, but **wait for the Promise of the Father**, which, saith he, ye have heard of Me. For John truly baptized with water; **but ye shall be baptized with the Holy Ghost not many days hence.** When they therefore were come together, they asked of Him, saying, Lord, wilt thou at this time restore again the kingdom to Israel? And He said unto them, It is not for you to know the times or the seasons, which the Father hath put in His own Power. **But ye shall receive Power, after that the Holy Ghost is come upon You; and ye shall be witnesses** unto Me both in Jerusalem, and in all Judaea, and in Samaria, and unto the uttermost part of the earth.

If you are a believer in Christ, I encourage you to be hungry for *the Fire from Above*. I urge you to follow the pattern that God has laid out for us and be prepared to wait upon the Spirit till He comes.

And I plead with you, my fellow labourers in the work of God. It is time for us to adopt the correct doctrine on the subject of ordination and service to God. Let us return to the precedent that was set in the Upper Room. Let us no longer choose to ordain people, whose fruits don't match their callings. The authorisation and work of our ordination belong to God and it should remain that way. It is no wonder that there are segments of the Body of Christ that are struggling. We have dead Churches and no Revival because we have chosen and ordained individuals by earthly perception and not by the Anointing that rests upon them to mark them out. Furthermore, there will certainly be no Revival if the people who are ordained by God and who carry God's Mantle are not permitted to minister. We can see from scripture that the people God chooses and anoints are often those that would not naturally be chosen by the people around them.

So, let our consultation and conversation be toward Heaven and let us submit to the leadership of the Spirit of God. For God is waiting for us to be hungry and call out to Him. He is waiting for us to align with His plan and purposes. When we align with God we come into oneness with God and there a harmonious flow from Heaven begins to cascade into our lives. That's when miracles, signs and wonders will happen as heaven's appointments, purposed to be fulfilled on earth through earthen vessels. So come, let us return to that Upper Room Fire; that Glory and Power that becomes like the dew that settles upon those that are anointed of God.

That being said, we do have believers amongst us who have already received the blessed Fire from Heaven. So let us make it our priority to identify these certain individuals who have been graced and anointed by the Spirit of God. For they have received the Baptism of the Fire of the Lord Jesus Christ and of His Holy Spirit. Let us yield to the Lord to allow these selected men and women of God to take up the purpose of their ordination in the midst of the congregation. And if there are none among us, we must encourage those who are hungry to continue to wait. Or become hungry for this experience ourselves.

With that said, I need to clarify that I am referring to men and women marked by humility and sincerity, who will decrease so that Christ can increase. It's not about exalting a man or a woman. The Glory doesn't belong to man. It did not come from man, so why should man get the glory for what belongs to God? The glory must go to Jesus—He is the One we exalt. All who are chosen and anointed must be vessels that desire to behold His Glory and to give their lives over to Him. They must desire to reveal Jesus and His Presence.

Ordination is of God and our part is to recognise His choice by the Holy Spirit, as Samuel and John did, and make room for the will of God to be manifested and fulfilled in those upon whom He has chosen to pour out His Fire. It's time we allow those who are anointed of God to arise and obey the calling they have received from the Spirit of the Word. Let us repent of our dead works and return to the place of hunger, expectation, and submission to His work of ordination. His Spirit will be poured abundantly on all who are continuously drawn *to the brightness of His rising* (Malachi 4:2, Isaiah 60:1-3).

MAN DOES NOT GIVE ORDINATION. GOD DOES.

Jeremiah 1:4-5

'Then the Word of the LORD came unto me, saying, Before I formed thee in the belly, I knew thee; and before thou camest forth out of the womb I sanctified thee, and I ordained thee a prophet unto the nations.'

ORDINATION is not supposed to be a human institution. It is not authored by flesh, nor given by flesh. If human knowledge, skill or wisdom was the source of the Baptism of the Holy Ghost and Fire, then we could argue the point that man has the authority to ordain a minister. But the Power is from on High. It is God's gift. It has always been from on High and will remain that way forever. You can ordain all the ministers you want, and give them permission to function in a particular place but that doesn't mean that they carry a particular Mantle to function in the Body of Christ. We can only know our place of appointment when the Holy

Spirit comes upon our whole beings and reveals to us that holy calling.

People who want to serve God often look for ways in which they can equip and prepare themselves to do the work of the ministry. They look for places where they can learn knowledge and skills and gain credentials that recognise their achievements. If you desire to go to theology school, by all means, go get your diploma, and get your degree if you have to. But don't use that as the primary reason or evidence for your being called into ministry. Be certain that the Lord has called you and seek his revelation of what your ministry will involve. The knowledge you gain from Bible college or seminary will be relevant for ministry but don't settle with knowledge, rules and traditions of religion. Seek the heart of God and know what God wants from you. If you think your salvation or your calling is based on a piece of paper, well then you've got it all wrong. The Anointing marks your heavenly graduation day and goes with you throughout the rest of your life to accomplish every purpose that Anointing was assigned to do. You must understand that the work of God is more important than any preparation that you can do. *The Calling and Selection of God* are far greater than a piece of paper. The Move of God never started with a 'degree paper from completing theological studies,' but the one hundred twenty disciples waited on the Holy Ghost. God is the one who sends, and therefore God is the one who will empower you and assign you to the work you must do.

Our Lord Jesus was confronted with similar issues by people who challenged His credentials and the source of His authority to minister during His time on earth. The chief priests and the elders questioned Jesus' approach to ministry and whether it was valid or permissible. But they couldn't answer Him when He answered their question with a question (note the bolded words):

Matthew 21:23-25

And when He was come into the temple, the chief priests and the elders of the people came unto Him as he was teaching, and said, By what authority doest Thou these things? and who gave Thee this authority? And Jesus answered and said unto them, I also will ask you one thing, which if ye tell me, I in like wise will tell you by what authority I do these things. The baptism of John, whence was it? **from heaven, or of men?**

Ordination is Divine Appointment. It is, therefore, from Heaven and authored by God. You can see this in God's first recorded conversation with Jeremiah that you read at the very start of this Chapter. The Lord God said to Jeremiah that he was ordained as a prophet even before he was formed in the womb (Jeremiah 1:1-4), which means that *God knew him and His purposes for him.*

Does God know you? Is your heart turned toward Him? The Prophet Jeremiah was not called by a man. He didn't have his ministry because someone laid hands upon him and commissioned him to be a prophet. Before he was even formed in his mother's womb, God knew him and had already ordained him to be a prophet unto the nations.

The choice of God is the choice of God, whether you agree with it or not. Let ordination be of God, and let surrender be our posture.

Endnote:
1. (Tari, Mel, "A Mighty Wind." *Like A Mighty Wind,* New Leaf Press, 1971, 1978, pp. 24-25)

CHAPTER 4

OUR HERITAGE—ENDUED WITH POWER

The Power that rests upon us reveals Yeshua the Messiah

The Prophet Isaiah was able to see the future by the Spirit. I believe he made reference to the Power of God when he spoke of *'the Heritage of the Servants of the Lord and their Righteousness being of Him.'*

Isaiah 54:17

'No weapon that is formed against thee shall prosper; and every tongue that shall rise against thee in judgment thou shalt condemn. This is THE HERITAGE of the servants of the LORD, and their righteousness is of Me, saith the LORD.'

I am particularly interested in the word, *heritage* that Isaiah used in Isaiah 54. Taking from what we read above, let's look a little deeper into what the word *heritage* means: Heritage has to do with (including the spiritual context applicable to us):
- Allotted portion (Our allotted portion)

CHAPTER 4 — *Our Heritage—Endued With Power*

- A special possession (Our special possession)
- Inheritance (Our Inheritance)
- Birthright (Our birthright)
- A provision (Our provision)
- A benefaction to the benefactor (Our benefaction)
- An endowment (**Our Endowment**)

Now let's unpack what is meant by the last word 'endowment.' An endowment is something that is received. Another word for endow is 'endue' or 'invest' with a gift or special quality. The same in Greek is 'Enduo' which means to sink into a garment, (an immersion) to clothe or to put on. The Latin word sounds similar also: 'Induere' which means to put on clothes. The word: *endue*, is what Jesus used to describe the Power of God that would come upon the disciples at the appointed time Acts 1:4-8.

We can then derive this revelational insight from our short word study, that the Power that rests upon us is our inheritance from God. We are equipped, clothed or supplied *with Power from on High.*

Isaiah declared, seven Chapters later in Isaiah 61, "The Spirit of the Lord is upon Me." So now when you look again at what happened to the one hundred twenty disciples in the Upper Room in Acts 2, you can understand that they were literally clothed with or immersed with Power. As John the Baptist said, they were "Baptised with the Holy Ghost and Fire."

Jesus also anticipated this moment as He instructed His disciples to wait for the promised gift of Power:

CHAPTER 4

Luke 24:49

'And, behold, I send the Promise of My Father upon you: but tarry ye in the city of Jerusalem, **until ye be endued with Power from on High.**'

The promise was that a gift would be given, and they had to wait for it. Notice, also that the *true witnessing* came after the Power from on High rested upon them. For certain none of them were ever the same again.

The Baptism of The Holy Spirit and Fire is:
- the promise of the Father,
- God *clothing* a believer with His Spirit and Fire (Power from on High) at a God-appointed place and a God-appointed time,
- the Induction and ordination of a believer into their call to be God's witness in the way that God has purposed for them.
- the Anointing and call poured upon an earthen vessel ready for the Lord's use.

The Upper Room, therefore, was a place of obedience and complete surrender to God. We don't decide the time and place—God does. We don't determine when and where the Power falls—God does. Our part to play is to become hungry for God and wait upon Him with all our heart, mind and soul. A surrendered vessel is the most effective vessel in God's hands.

> " A surrendered vessel is the most effective vessel in God's hands

JESUS—LED BY THE SPIRIT

Luke 4:1,14

> And Jesus being full of the Holy Ghost returned from Jordan, and was **led** by the Spirit into the wilderness...And Jesus returned in the Power of the Spirit into Galilee: and there went out a fame of Him through all the region round about.

L-E-D by the Spirit of God. Led. It's a three-letter word so short and exact that its meaning should be clear and yet it seems that it's misunderstood by many who seek God. Maybe it seems too simple and too literal. Satan and his demons have worked hard to deceive us and one strategy has been to make that simple word complicated so that we end up replacing it with religious practices, ceremonies, methods and systems. Or it could be also that these alternatives offer us more control. If we follow the Spirit we must expect to do things differently when the Spirit of the Lord is leading and we know that doing so would not fit into the religious and culturally ingrained practices of the day. But we are to not conform to the standards of the world but elevate to where the Spirit is. We are supposed to be world changers. We are supposed to bring and walk the *God-culture* on earth. We shouldn't pray, "Thy Kingdom come, Thy Will be done" and then just work on building our own kingdoms where we do what we want or think is best. We must own these words, and in our surrender become the vessels that the Lord empowers in order to establish His Kingdom. If we want God's dominion, then let us choose to be LED by the Spirit.

Our Lord Jesus Christ left us the model of the Spirit-led life, with His own example of what happens when we keep in step with the Spirit and do the Father's will. Why then do we deviate and stray from it? We must go back to the foundations of the doctrine of our empowerment—*we must be empowered and led by the Spirit*. That is God's way. We can either be led by the Holy Ghost or driven by our desire to uphold a form of godliness that lacks the Power that marks the people who, by waiting on and keeping in step with the Spirit, respond to *God's Call*.

It is clear that in all of Jesus' ministry, Jesus was led by the Spirit. The Spirit also led Him in all of His preparation for ministry.

In the reported event of the water baptism of Christ in the Jordan River, the Spirit descended like a dove and rested upon Jesus. But the initial phase of Christ's preparation for ministry didn't stop there. The Spirit then led Jesus to take the journey into the wilderness for a time of fasting. It was the Holy Spirit who led Christ into the wilderness as it was the Father's will and when Satan was done tempting Jesus, then our Lord Jesus returned *in the Power of the Spirit*.

This goes back to the keyword that I want to point your attention to in bold in the verse above, but it is so important that I will state it again:

> Jesus was **LED** by the Spirit

I would like to point out some observations here concerning John's words, "The Christ shall baptise you with the Holy Ghost and Fire." Jesus was already filled and empowered by the Spirit at the Jordan River Baptism. The Lord knew that He had received His Anointing at the Jordan River, and John was witness to it. Jesus later affirmed this when He read the Isaiah 61 passage in the synagogue in Nazareth (note the bolded words):

CHAPTER 4 *Our Heritage—Endued With Power*

Luke 4:18-19

The Spirit of the Lord is upon Me, because He hath anointed Me to preach the Gospel to the poor; He hath sent Me to heal the brokenhearted, to preach deliverance to the captives, and recovering of sight to the blind, to set at liberty them that are bruised, To preach the acceptable year of the Lord.

After reading this passage, He then declared before everyone there, "This day is this scripture fulfilled in your ears (Isaiah 61:21)."

Jesus, by the leading and power of the Holy Ghost resting upon Him, took ownership of that scripture and the prophetic Mandate that was resting upon His life by Divine ordination.

The Apostle Peter was also directed by the Spirit of God to go to somewhere he didn't expect: Cornelius's house. Cornelius was a Roman centurion who had been seeking God with his fasting, prayer, and generosity. He had sent his servants to find Peter and bring him to his home. This was in obedience to a message that he received from an angel in a vision. Before the servants arrived, Peter had also seen a vision that challenged his thinking. Peter was prepared by the Spirit to be led to the house of this Roman centurion. The Spirit also led Peter in what to say to the large gathering of Gentiles who were waiting for him at the house. He not only referred to Jesus' encounter at the Jordan River but went on further to establish the foundation of sound doctrine that is based on that experience that Christ left as an example for us to follow.

I think there is a reason why the Biblical text says "Then Peter opened his mouth and said (Acts 10:34)…" In this instance, he was receiving the revelation that he then spoke. This expression is also used for Jesus in Matthew 5 when He spoke the revelation of the

Beatitudes, and Philip in Acts 8 when he spoke revelation truth about Jesus from Isaiah (Isaiah 53) to the Ethiopian eunuch. Peter said (note the bolded words):

Acts 10:34-38

....Of a truth I perceive that **God is no respecter of persons:** But in every nation he that feareth Him, and worketh righteousness, is accepted with Him. **The Word which God sent unto the children of Israel, preaching peace by Jesus Christ: (He is Lord of all:)** That word, I say, ye know, which was published throughout all Judaea, and began from Galilee, after the Baptism which John preached; **How God anointed Jesus of Nazareth with the Holy Ghost and with Power:** who went about doing good, and healing all that were oppressed of the devil; for God was with Him.

God was with Him. The Holy Spirit rested upon Him. He was *anointed with the Holy Ghost and Power.* That is what you must seek and what your ministry in God should be marked by. You must be led and empowered by Him.

Why should you settle for anything less? Why should you be satisfied with taking on and adopting systems, ideas and practices that may support the work to a certain degree but are not a replacement for the Power of the Spirit of God?

Peter let the Spirit lead him into unfamiliar territory and declared the words that the Spirit gave him. And then...oh, I just love the next part of the story that describes what happened next to Cornelius and his household. While Peter was still preaching these words, Peter and all the other believers that came with him then witnessed and experienced a mighty and astonishing Move of God's Spirit.

Acts 10:44-45

"the Holy Ghost fell on all them which heard the Word... that **on the Gentiles also was poured out the Gift of the Holy Ghost.**"

God truly demonstrated that He is no respecter of persons in that wonderful meeting where the Gentiles also came into that glorious encounter of the Holy Ghost and Power.

Note that Peter used the word 'Power' to describe the Anointing of Jesus. He was using the word that he had heard Jesus use to denote the sign of the promise and, of course, this is the fire that had been declared by John the Baptist.

Jesus had told His disciples to go to Jerusalem and wait for the promise of the Father (Acts 1:4). Jesus had first said they would be "Baptised with the Holy Ghost (Acts 1:5)"

Jesus then expounded a little further saying, "**Ye shall receive Power, after that the Holy Ghost is come upon you**: and ye shall be witnesses unto me (Acts 1:8)"

It is clear then that when the Spirit comes upon a person to baptise them, He empowers them to be His witnesses. A witness testifies to what they have seen, heard and known. Jesus wanted His followers to be empowered by the Holy Spirit so that they could see, hear and know the ministry and might of the Spirit's work upon them. And by that Holy endowment, they would witness to many the powerful Testimony of Jesus Christ, who came to set us free from the power of sin and death and give eternal life to as many as would believe (Acts 2:38-39).

We are commanded to live and walk in the Spirit (Galatians 5:25) and to walk in the law of the Spirit of life in Christ Jesus which sets us free from the law of sin and death. As we walk in the

Spirit, we grow deeper in our revelation of God. Our walking in the Spirit leads us to walk *in the Power of the Spirit of God.*

> When you are LED by the Spirit, then you are EMPOWERED by the same Spirit of God.

There are two things I would like for you to keep in mind as you are led by the Holy Spirit. Firstly, it's a journey. There is a place in God that carries a greater weight of His Glory than is assumed possible in the ordinary.

> There is a place in God that carries a greater weight of His Glory than is assumed possible in the ordinary.

Secondly, there will always be differences in explaining the great experience of the Power of God that is manifested. We give God the Glory for the marvellous work He continues to do in each of our lives. Regardless of how each of us may view and describe the Presence and Glory of God, the fundamental truth is that God's Power is real and God can change a person, a society, a city, and a nation when He comes upon vessels that are made ready through surrender to be used for His Glory.

Are you one of those chosen by God? If you answered yes, I praise God for you. I encourage you to keep seeking to be led by the Holy Spirit by pursuing the will of God. And if you have not yet come into your own Baptism experience with God, I also encourage you to stay hungry, wait on God and seek that glorious encounter of the endowing Power of God. Seek His face with an open heart. Yield with expectancy, with this thought, that God is looking at your heart. And He is waiting for you to align your heart with His. That alignment I speak of is when you desire after Him. You are drawn to Him because you have become obedient to the Spirit. Obedience and Surrender is alignment with God. God will only pour out His Power upon the heart that has become fixated and completely given to what the Holy Spirit wants.

Wait eagerly and earnestly till the Fire falls on you, Hallelujah!

> " Wait eagerly and earnestly till the Fire falls on you, Hallelujah!

God's heart is always towards us. God has a notable, splendid and inspiring plan to pour out His Spirit upon all flesh (Joel 2:28, Acts 2:17); He has a good and perfect plan for you and me. It is by the empowering of the Spirit that He will turn the hearts of many to Him. Oh, Hallelujah! And He shall do this magnificently by His Spirit in those who have yielded completely to Him.

CHAPTER 5

THE GLORY CLOUD & AUSTRALIA

*Go I send you—Go I send you—Go I send you—
Go I send you—Go I send you—Go I send you—Go I send you!*

𝓑ack in 2002, I occasionally visited the Thomas family, who lived in a double-storey house. My dear friend Emmanuel would invite me over and I had many wonderful and precious moments of fellowship with his family. We were both in Grade 12 at Goroka Secondary School. I was nineteen years old and full of vision and drive for my future in the ministry of God. Often when I visited 'Manu' (as we called him), I would be joined by Jason (whom we called Isaiah) and Emmanuel's younger brother, James. Initially, they were short visits, which then turned into sleepovers and eventually, I stayed with them for about 2 months.

My relationship with the Thomas family is special and close to my heart. In those early days, their love for the Lord was a beacon that lit the path for many young people. Mr John Thomas and his

CHAPTER 5 — *The Glory Cloud & Australia*

dear wife Veronica were so welcoming and I have no doubt that they were a true Holy Ghost-led couple. They had grace for every person they met and the individuals they spoke with, were inspired, motivated, nurtured, prayed for, guided and encouraged with many words of wisdom and insight from the Lord. I quickly understood that this was standard procedure for them. They were constantly hosting God's Presence and I loved flowing with the Holy Spirit whenever I was with them. Though I eventually went on my way and parted from them to pursue the path that God had for me, I remain eternally grateful for their input in my life.

The short time I spent with them has a part to play in the story I am about to tell you. This is my story of the 'Glory Cloud of God' encounter.

It was in the early hours of the morning at the beginning of September 2002. At about 3:40 a.m., I lay prostrated with my face down on the floor. I prayed quietly as I lay before the Lord. I said to God, "I am not worthy to lay down here before Your Presence. I want to be lower than the floor that I am lying on. Lord, I surrender to You. I give myself to You. I worship You. For I am not worthy before Your holy Presence." I lay there for about an hour completely surrendered to God. I then got up from the floor and sat on my bed.

I thanked God for the time of worship and was about to lay my head on the pillow when all of sudden, while fully awake and conscious, I saw a thick white Cloud appear before me. I couldn't see anything except the Glory Cloud. I had a knowing that the Glory Cloud of God had entered the room and I became afraid of the Presence of the Lord God. Yet, at the same time, I felt a great peace flood my soul. Then the Lord God spoke. His voice was a deep bass voice that echoed and filled the whole atmosphere as He spoke. Immediately a vision like a floating TV screen appeared before me. It had no edges but I was able to see everything that was happening on screen. In it, Mr John Thomas stood before me. He was wearing his grey suit and facing me. The map of Australia appeared also before me. A large hand came out from the Cloud and pointed at a place on the map of Australia. The Lord Most High then spoke to me saying, "Tell him (referring to Mr Thomas who stood beside the map), GO I SEND YOU! GO I SEND YOU! GO I SEND YOU! GO I SEND YOU! GO I SEND YOU! GO I SEND YOU! GO I SEND YOU!"

Seven times did the Lord say, "GO I SEND YOU!" And seven times it echoed all around me.

The vision then faded before me, and the Glory Cloud of God rested another few more seconds. Then suddenly the Cloud was gone and I was back in the room again. It is important to note here that I was not asleep. I was fully awake when this happened.

I then thanked the Lord for the Word and knew in my heart that I needed to deliver this Word straight away. So I quickly got off the bed to go upstairs and see Mr Thomas, who was praying and worshipping in the living room by this time. Papa John was always up as early as 4:00 a.m. and could sometimes be found worshipping the Lord till 6:30 a.m. He would play a particular song (which was one of his favourites) and begin to walk in a circle, dancing at times, all while praying in tongues. This was the posture I found him in when I stood at the top of the stairway looking straight at him. He sensed something was different about me and asked, "Man of God. How are you this morning?"

I smiled and said to him exactly what the Lord God said, "Mr John Thomas. The Most High God came to me this morning and His Glory Cloud filled the room. He said to me as I sat awake. Tell him (referring to you) GO I SEND YOU! GO I SEND YOU! GO I SEND YOU! GO I SEND YOU! GO I SEND YOU! GO I SEND YOU! GO I SEND YOU! Seven times did the Lord say this to me for you. Mr Thomas, you are commanded by the Most High this morning to pack up your bags and get ready to fly to Australia. God wants you to go."

What I didn't know at that time was that John was in the middle of sorting his travel visa to Australia and there was some kind of delay.

That same morning, John and Veronica called up the Australian High Commission to follow up on that visa and got an immediate response that his visa would be issued. The visa department of the Australian High Commission later called back and said he was good to go, much to his amazement as the delay had seemed to be going on forever and now all of sudden in one day it was done. His visa to Australia was approved and he flew to Wagga Wagga, a regional city in New South Wales, Australia. Wagga Wagga lies by the banks of the Murrumbidgee River.

John knew in his heart that this trip wasn't for the thesis he was trying to complete for his course but it was for something far greater than he could perceive. It was truly a notable work of God. The Lord had it on His Heavenly Calendar and He had appointed a particular task to John.

I also couldn't shake the thought that God really wanted John to do something special; something marked on God's Calendar. And Papa John was the man for that assignment.

How divine and how splendid are the ways of the Most High. Our pathways, mission statements, and destinies are all marked on God's Calendar and we were ordained before the foundations of the world were ever laid.

I often think about this mission statement given to John. God could have made it simple. Why didn't God just pick one of His servants locally based in Wagga Wagga, or even in Australia and send them to that exact spot to do what the Lord desired to be done? The answer, I am sure, is an important truth that is confidently evident from the part I had to play in this story. God had sent John to Australia and John had obeyed *the Call.*

Can you see that to be led by God is to be chosen and sent by God? Even though you may consider yourself an unworthy vessel in your own eyes, you have been marked to do something Holy for the Living God. And in partaking of the Holy Command, you are made clean by His Words (John 15:3).

I've come to learn that God works in very specific ways because He knows the end from the beginning. The reason why a specific person has to do a specific task has everything to do with their ordained purpose on earth.

God looks from Heaven and sees amongst many. He knew you while you were yet formed in your mother's womb. God knows your flaws, and yet He chose you because He loves you and wants you to be a part of Him—His people, His family, and His Body—in every way possible. He has always had a good plan for your life.

Even the Prophet Elijah's catching away was in a very specific place and at a very specific time. We see this also with the Upper Room of Jerusalem, and the Azusa Street Revival, which began at that humble home on 216 Bonnie Brae Street. Don't despise your humble beginnings. Make room for God and let Him come and rest upon that humble place and cause an overflow of Heaven upon you. The DNA of a world changer from God's perspective lies in the Fire that proceeds from the Holy Spirit. The Baptism of the Holy Spirit is given to empower you for your mission. For you are called by God.

Therefore, we can establish the thought that *times* and *places* and *the specific person whom* God will call and use as His *vessel in a specific situation and for a specific task,* are all important to God. I will share more about that when I discuss God's Altar that Elijah rebuilt on Carmel.

CHAPTER 5   *The Glory Cloud & Australia*

I have also thought about how God could have just given the Word to me in a prophetic way through another man of God, or an angelic encounter like those described in the Bible. But I have come to realise that this message was too important. The timing was also very important. He needed no middleman, and so the Most High decided it was appropriate to deliver it Himself in His Glory Cloud, and I had the privilege and blessing of receiving it directly from Him for Mr Thomas, who was in the living room above me, praising and worshipping God at that very moment. Consider how the prophets of old prophesied about the coming Messiah. Their messages contained specific details: that at some time in the distant future, the Messiah would come and be born in a specific town called *Bethlehem* (meaning house of bread), in the nation called *Israel* (meaning a prince that prevails with God and man). God is very much into the details and far more than we tend to think. It's all in His plan.

God needed a *John* (meaning, God is gracious) to pave the way by travelling from Goroka, PNG to Wagga Wagga, Australia. God knew about the visa issue that would cause a delay and His message that He would deliver to me at the appointed time so that I could give to John Thomas. God did it this way because He was going to give John the 'prophetic declaration' for *Revival* that would connect later in the years ahead and *the Revival Mandate* and *Ministry* would align to that Holy Message concerning Australia. There is more that God wants to give to His people; There is more.

So what did God get John to do? Well, while John was there in Wagga Wagga, on a particular day, the Spirit of the Lord God came upon him and as God led him, he obeyed and reached down to the ground beneath his feet, picked up a handful of soil and raised it to the Most High God, and he declared the following proclamation in a loud voice, "I claim the land of Australia and its people for You. Let the Wave of Revival rise up out of this land and reach to the ends of the earth. I declare Australia is the Great South Land of the Holy Ghost. I declare in Jesus' Name that Australia is Chosen and prepared by the Lord as the platform for the greatest Move of God the world has ever seen. To You, Lord, be all Glory forever. May Your will be done."

When he had finished saying this, the Lord spoke again to him telling him that this was the reason why God sent him to Australia.

A task like this, which is so simple in man's eyes is not viewed the same way in God's eyes. Such a task carries the weight of Divine authority and there is a Holy Commission behind it because it is the outworking of God's own intent.

Hence, for this reason, we should never judge a God-ordained task with our natural perception. For what no eye has seen, no ear has heard, and what has not yet entered the heart of man, is what God has intended for those who love Him (1 Corinthians 2:9-10). Your obedience to the Word that you receive from God carries and fulfils God's Intent.

> " Your obedience to the Word that you receive from God carries and fulfils God's Intent.

On the same day that John had made the proclamation, but back in Goroka, God spoke to me in a vision. An Australian 20-dollar note appeared before me, but I noticed something different about it. On it was written $26. I asked the LORD what He meant by $26 and He gave me another Instruction for John. This vision was on the 22nd of September 2002.

John was not to return to Goroka no earlier or later than the 26th of September 2002. And I thought to myself, "Well, this is an official trip for Heaven, so it is only fitting that as John was sent by Divine Commission, he also must return by Divine Order. The Almighty God has spoken. Let His Will be done."

CHAPTER 5   *The Glory Cloud & Australia*

After arriving back in Port Moresby, John had no sense that his travel plans were about to change. He had already pre-booked his return ticket before he went to Australia. He was scheduled to fly to Goroka on the 24th of September, 2002. When he called home from Port Moresby, I said to him, "Man of God, Papa John, You are not to come back to us till the 26th of September because that's what the LORD told me. I am only His messenger but that's up to you."

He was somewhat confused, but he believed me. That in itself is amazing. What did I know about the fact that spending money on changing flight times and rebooking tickets was an expensive ordeal, especially when you are aware of ongoing bills to pay? But in John's mind, the issue wasn't the finances that would need to be used for the travel that God purposed. The issue had everything to do with what God wanted. I spoke only what the LORD had told me to say and nothing more and John received what I said, and left it in God's hands. Interestingly, he didn't rush to change his ticket even though he believed me. He had pre-booked his return ticket at the time when God had sent him to Australia. So he trusted God to do whatever He wanted to do for his return. Well, can you guess what happened?

When John went to the airport on the 24th to catch the plane for his pre-booked flight, he found out that his flight was cancelled due to some technical issues with the aircraft and that the next available flight was not until the 26th of September, 2002. He just stood there smiling with amazement, as he remembered the Word that the LORD had spoken.

Why would the return date be so specific and why would God be so concerned with it? Believe me, I asked the same questions too and the Holy Spirit made it clear to me in this way. It was to prove to John and all of us that this had been no ordinary trip. This was official business for Heaven. *God's protocol needed to be adhered to for a God-ordained mission.*

> " God's protocol needs to be adhered to for a God-ordained mission.

This kind of protocol can be seen in the Bible when Jesus told John the Baptist to follow through with God's calling on his life, to baptise all who came to him. Jesus asked John to baptise Him too, even though Jesus had no need for repentance, Jesus told him that it was necessary to fulfil all righteousness (Matthew 3:15). The Father verbally testified of Jesus' righteousness, and the Holy Spirit descended and rested on Him, demonstrating God's intent. John the Baptist couldn't see the point of what he was about to do, but in God's sight, it was very important. In our case, it was that if any one of us still did doubt, even for a moment, the Glory Cloud encounter, the LORD made sure we understood that He was at work, and He would have His way and get the Glory.

It would be years later after I had permanently migrated to Australia, in October 2008, that I began to realise the importance of this event and how it was connected to my future and the call of God upon my life: to blow the trumpet for Revival.

At that time, I heard about a long-standing prophecy uttered by Smith Wigglesworth. In it, Smith declared by the Spirit that the last great Move of the Spirit will start in Australia and spread throughout the world. It would start at the end of the twentieth century and move into the twenty-first century. This Move would usher in the Second Coming of the Lord Jesus Christ.

Then I had a dream on the 5th of August 2012. In the dream, the Spirit of the Lord came upon me and I began to prophesy, "Before it happens I declare it. It is going to happen soon! I prophesy that we will see the greatest outpouring that the world has ever known! I prophesy that the River of God will never stop flowing and it will never run dry. I prophesy that this outpouring will begin with us: the Church!"

The Glory Cloud encounter will remain in my life as one of the most significant events I have ever experienced.

The writing of this book was done in January and February 2023. I am thirty-nine years old, heading towards my fortieth birthday in June 2023. It's been just over twenty years, since that encounter. I long to be in God's Glory Cloud again; soaking in His Presence. I long for His Glory to abide continuously. I long for Him. Do you also have this longing? I am careful to note that what God wants is very specific. At the same time, God has not restricted Himself to one place. The experience of God's Glory is for every person everywhere who will turn their hearts to the Lord and bring an acceptable offering upon His Altar.

The Spirit is moving in different parts of the world right now. He is moving in big and small ways, in large gatherings and small gatherings alike. It is one and the same Spirit who works in all and through all who hunger for God and are willing to be led.

As I write, I am very aware of the Move of God that is progressing strongly throughout the world. That said, I can't deny, ignore, or be disobedient to the directive God has laid down for the Church. I must declare, and share with you here what the saints in Australia must do to align themselves with the purpose of Heaven.

There was a prophecy for Australia received in December 2021, by Prophet Barry Wunsch from Canada. Barry was told by the Lord, "Keep your eyes on Australia. For I am about to light it up. I am about to release My Fire across the land and I shall blow upon **the burning ones** who are standing in My ways. They shall ignite cities, towns and regions. Australia, for you, have been forced down under and yes, from that place I am going to BIRTH A MOVEMENT; A REVIVAL..."[2]

It means God wants us to pay attention to what He is saying to the Church in Australia. God's promised Revival, the one that will reach everyone else, is already at work and will increase in a greater measure as hearts yield and come into alignment with the Moving of the Holy Ghost.

Let us be ready and prepare our hearts and minds to receive the Power of God and the will of God, so that the *Word of Glory* may dwell in our midst.

Are you willing to pay the price for Revival? Are willing to pay the price of *obedience, submission and surrender to His Voice?* To wait in His Presence until the Baptism of Fire rests? Will you say yes to the Move of God? God is looking for carriers of the Glory. He is looking for Fire starters.

Prayer:

"Yes Jesus, here am I. Use me for Your Glory."

Endnote:
2. Wunsch. B. 2021, *Prophecy for Australia.* https://www.facebook.com/TheCanadianHammer/

CHAPTER 6

WHY REVIVAL?
THE ARCHANGEL MICHAEL
BRINGS ME A MESSAGE

'NËR`VIL`LË

Isaiah 60:7

...they shall come up with acceptance upon Mine Altar, and I will Glorify the House of My Glory.

*J*ust before the break of dawn, on Sunday 9th February 2003, the Lord God sent His angel to deliver an important Word to me for the Church.

At about 1:00 a.m., in the boys' bedroom (At that time I shared the room with three of my brothers). I had adopted long praying sessions as my usual routine and had become

CHAPTER 6   *Why Revival? The Archangel Michael Brings Me A Message*

aware that visions from God often appeared to me without fail, so I had an eager expectation every time I engaged in unceasing prayer that I might see something that He wanted to reveal to me in response to my prayers. These were my deep communion times with God.

At about 4:30 a.m., I sat facing the window praying in tongues, and focusing my attention on worshipping God. I felt tired. I often feel tired by this point of a long praying session and not long after, I would begin to fall into a deep sleep. That's usually when the visions happen before I fall into that deep sleep. Usually, when I get to that place of communion with God, I have a knowing in my spirit that I am about to see and hear something from the Lord.

In my experience, I found that visions and trances from the Holy Spirit, and travelling in the spirit (like Ezekiel did), came to me in a very specific manner.

But it is important to note here that we don't decide what we want to see or how we want to see it. Visions from God are God-initiated and revealed by God in whatever way He chooses. It is the Lord God who decides these encounters. The Bible records that the prophets of old, right up to the apostles, all had different visions of Heaven, including seeing God Himself in the Throne Room and encounters with angels. They never told God what they should see and hear. It was God who revealed these Heavenly truths and mysteries to them. For me, as I went into a vision, I would willingly surrender to the Holy Spirit to lead the way.

In this particular vision, a bright blue light hit the floor in front of me and quickly began to grow bigger and bigger. I looked up immediately to see where it was coming from. This all happened in seconds.

When I looked up, I saw the Glory Cloud begin to flow with great intensity, grace and Power before me. As it continued to flow,

I became aware that the window I had been looking through wasn't there anymore. I suppose I was lifted out of the room to see the vision.

Suddenly there in front of me standing with great might and Power and moving towards me, was this gigantic and fierce-looking being, carrying great authority. As he drew closer to me, knowledge from the Holy Spirit entered me and I knew who it was. The one who stood in the beaming pillar of Light, shining like the midday sun, was the great Archangel Michael. He is the Prince who stands for God's people and the Mighty Commander of the Lord's Army.

He had blonde curly hair that went down to his shoulders. His eyes looked like they were burning with flames of Fire, and his whole body was covered with the brightness of the Glory of the Lord God. And in his right hand, he had a beaming sword that glowed with Fire.

At that very moment, I was terrified and afraid in my spirit because of the Glory of the Lord God and the countenance of His angel. It truly was magnificent to behold and yet so frightening at the same time. The Commander of the Host of Heaven stood with a strong warrior-like posture looking at me with fiery eyes.

CHAPTER 6   *Why Revival? The Archangel Michael Brings Me A Message*

A picture I drew to closely resemble the Archangel Michael

The Archangel Michael then spoke with a deep strong voice from the Light and the Glory Cloud of God and said "NËR`VIL`LË! This is an acceptable saying of the Lord God! NËR`VIL`LË! NËR—the Temple of The Lord is His Dwelling Place. It is His Holy Altar! VIL`LË—the Lord God will glorify the House of God, His Temple. It is Holy and the Lord shall sanctify it for Himself!"

Then he paused and pointed at me, and looking intently at me with those piercing fiery eyes, he then said to me, "You are the Temple of the Lord. Amen!"

I felt those words flowing through my being, and the Power of the Lord God came rushing through me. It hit me with force, and from there I came out of the vision.

Before I thought to look up scriptures relating to the vision, I paused to worship and thank the Lord for the vision. I knew in my heart that one day I would have to preach the contents of this vision to the people of God.

Straight after this wonderful encounter, the Lord led me to look at certain scriptures relating to this word. I came upon a few passages which are a direct reference to what the Archangel Michael said to me. There are two key points in the words that the Archangel Michael said to me in the vision. The first is that "We are the Temple and the Altar of the Holy Spirit. Holy and sanctified for the Lord. And God shall glorify the House of His Glory and We are that House." The few scriptures I noted were Isaiah 60:7, Haggai 2:6-9, 1 Corinthians 3:16-17, 2 Corinthians 4:6-7, Colossians 1:25-29, Habakkuk 2:14, 2 Thessalonians 1:10-12, 1 John 3:2-3 and 1 Corinthians 15:42-57.

God really wants His people to know His heart and to understand what His great plan is for us. It has everything to do with why Jesus came and what God is going to do through a mighty Revival to prepare the Church, which is the Bride of Christ, for the Second Coming of our Lord Jesus.

It was only right for me to not just observe the holy visitation of God, but to also consider the Words of our great God. I knew the Holy Spirit had led me to find these scriptures to confirm this message from the Archangel Michael. I often remember and think about that encounter and marvel to myself about how the Sovereign God has planned all these things, and that in His timing they will all become true. We, as the Temple of the Holy Spirit, respond to God. Our hearts are washed with His Presence and we are made ready by His Holy Spirit. We are called to bring the offering of our yielded hearts and place it upon the Altar of our God. And while there in His Holy Presence, we become one with Him through the working of His Glory and Power.

CHAPTER 6 *Why Revival? The Archangel Michael Brings Me A Message*

Isaiah 60:7

All the flocks of Kedar shall be gathered together unto thee, the rams of Nebaioth shall minister unto thee: they shall come up with acceptance on Mine Altar, and I will Glorify the House of My Glory

When we consider the current state the Church is in, there's no doubt that we must be revived, replenished and cleansed, and the Altars of our yielded hearts prepared for the Coming of Christ. We must, by the leadership of the Spirit, grow in our knowledge of God from Glory to Glory until we reach the fullness of our preparation.

For God shall glorify the Church with a mighty Baptism of the *Spirit* and *Fire*. The Upper Room of Jerusalem in Acts 2, helps us to understand what a prepared Church looks like.

1 Corinthians 3:16-17

Know ye not that ye are the Temple of God, and that the Spirit of God dwelleth in you? If any man defile the Temple of God, him shall God destroy; for the Temple of God is holy, which Temple ye are.

And with this, I again exhort you to turn your eyes upon Jesus. Look fully into His wonderful Face. Seek after Him with all your heart and make room for Him to come and be Lord in your midst.

For this is an acceptable saying of the Lord,
Nër' Villë Saints of God,
Nër' Villë Burning Ones and Carriers of the Glory,
Nër' Villë Remnant of His First Love,
Nër' Villë Priesthood of His Holy Calling,

Nër' Villë to the generation that will go up to the Holy Hill with clean hands and pure hearts, and be made ready for the Lord *to Glorify the House of His Glory.*

> Nër' Villë

Prayer:

Ëlilë Pitëkā. Māran thā.—Vision of God come forth in Word and Power. Oh Lord Come. Mighty God, we acknowledge that Your Temple is Your Dwelling Place. It is Your Holy Altar and You will glorify Your House according to Your Word—You will glorify Your Temple because we belong to You. We acknowledge that we have been made Holy unto You through Yeshua our Lord and that You have sanctified us for Yourself. We surrender our lives completely to You and we ask You to have Your way in us. In Yeshua's Holy Name, Amen.

CHAPTER 7

THE WATER BAPTISM

Truly we have died with Jesus in baptism so that we may live for Him by the Power of His Spirit upon us.

We had moved from the beautiful cold mountains of Goroka to the seaside, to Gabagaba Village (my father's home country), in the latter part of 2003. Our new home was going to be Kapalagere Homestead. On the first day, when we arrived on site, we saw that it was covered with thick bushy grass, some of which had grown to my height. We all took to clearing out the place on Dad's portion of the land at Kapala. There was much work to be done.

Although I had missed out on a university placement, I was happy to be a 'village boy' for a season if that was what the Lord wanted.

We started with the basics: living in a house that was partially built as a tent, with heavy tarpaulins as walls and corrugated iron roofing. A timber platform about waist height was used as our floor. The same floor was our sitting area and sleeping platform. At least it was a start and we had a roof over our heads and food to eat. This was our home for quite a long while as the family worked towards building a permanent home structure near the tent site.

I remember the many nights when all I did was pray while looking up to the star-littered sky dreaming about what God had in mind for me. I guess it was a quiet place but we could certainly hear the noise of God's creation. Apart from the noise of the buzzing mozzies, were the laughing kookaburras, the whistling of the birds, and the choruses of the crickets by the river.

The holiday season passed and it was time to go back to school. All my brothers left to embark on their next journey of studies. Seeing as I would be there for a time, I put my hands to the plough. My daily routine was filled with helping Dad. I would fetch water from the dug-out water holes at the river nearby and collect firewood for the morning and evening meals. I also helped Dad with planting some coconut trees, and banana trees. This would be my lifestyle for most of the year, and this continued right up to early September 2004.

During that time, my dad's sister Aunty TK (as we all knew her by) and her dear husband had invited a minister from Port Moresby to come out to the village and begin teaching the Word of God in their home. This was a journey of about one hour drive for the minister.

Would my aunt and uncle do anything for such a time of fellowship? Yes indeed. They must have known what they were getting themselves into and that this was going to be met with persecution and criticism from the village Church elders. The old Church was established by the early missionaries to our people back in the 1870s under the London Missionary Society (LMS)—now the United Churches of Papua New Guinea.

Come to think of it, just like in those early days for the village the new visiting minister would bring with him the same changing spiritual wind and would also see some changes on the spiritual front. At the time, no other Christian denomination was ever allowed to come to the village.

Bringing an "outsider doctrine," as it was perceived, was considered heresy, and those who attempted such a thing were immediately reprimanded and excommunicated. There was no doubt the actions of my uncle and aunt were going to stir up trouble, but they had been touched by the Lord through this visiting pastor's ministry and they wanted us to come along to their beach home (that stood over the waters) and join them in a teaching session with the visiting pastor. Aunty TK was adamant that the visit was a good idea and a God-idea. She convinced my dad and mum. She said, "I am confident God is going to do something wonderful. You must come and meet this man and hear him speak."

The minister's name was Pastor Peter Dege; a wonderful man of God. This man was a walking, talking Bible. Before we had Bible audio apps, there was Pastor Peter! He could recite whole chapters in one go and string them all together into a well-presented study of scripture. He was also knowledgeable in the Greek and Hebrew root meanings of many words. I was mesmerised by his ability to flow with scripture and recite—letter by letter, line by line—the whole passage.

I felt God was up to something. This was going to be our first-ever meeting with Pastor Peter Dege and I was excited. But on the whole, I gave little thought to the unsuspecting miracle awaiting us. God was up to something and it would be a whole new experience for my dad and mum and me.

When we attended the meeting the next evening, we found that Aunty TK had also invited a few other people. I can't remember how many were actually there, but I'd say about thirteen of us sat for the Bible study as Pastor Peter introduced

CHAPTER 7 — *The Water Baptism*

himself and began the teaching. His subject that evening was *the Water Baptism.*

I quickly looked around the room. I figured that since I was the youngest in the group it was my chance to sit back and let the elders engage with the pastor. But this was not going to be a normal Bible study session. How was I to know that the subject to be discussed was going to cause a heated debate with the strong-headed United Church doctrine followers and Pastor Peter's teaching on water baptism was already venturing into a no-go zone?

My late dad, bless his heart, and the elders stood their ground and guarded the fort of their beloved teachings that had been passed down faithfully by the missionaries.

Whooooiiii! It was like watching a movie scene play out before me. Yet, the end was so much more than that. I was about to witness a miracle that would leave the whole room in great conviction and tears.

You see, up to that point, no one had ever challenged the indoctrinated belief about the sprinkling of water baptism before. And now a man full of the Word of God stood before us to dismantle and dissolve everything we and our fathers thought was correct about water baptism. Pastor Peter was truly full of the Spirit of Grace. He ever so gently led and guided the debate to every key scripture. Pastor Peter's point: Baptism is not by sprinkling but by *immersion according to scripture.*

As you know, from what I shared in an earlier part of this book, I was already baptised in the Holy Ghost and Fire. I had received this back in August of 1999. But I was never taught about the water baptism; at least not in the way I had heard it taught from Pastor Peter's mouth that evening. And I myself was not water baptised either. In all of my endeavours in the Word, it never occurred to me to study the subject of water baptism, but here I was now witnessing the Word in action.

The more scriptures that Pastor Peter expounded on, the less fiery words were hurled at him. The debaters began to lose their argument. Their doctrine wasn't founded on scripture but on the traditions of man passed down from the early missionaries to our people. Pastor Peter, with the grace of God, was leading them to a glorious pathway and one that, as I look back now, opened the doors spiritually over Gabagaba Village and broke through the thick cloud of religious disparity.

It was certainly funny to me that I have to write that my champion dad led the protest and he seemed to have more fire to throw than the others. He didn't like Pastor Peter stepping on forbidden holy ground. He was easily the leader of the pack, and he shot back with question after question. Was he to let an outsider destroy the long-beloved religious traditions of the London Missionary Society? But now, God was showing, by the Spirit, the transforming Power of the Word.

At first, the attendees were all stirred up with anger. But as the teaching went deeper, they became stunned into silence. This was going to be a night to remember. I watched in wonder as scripture after scripture peeled the layers off of each of us until we were left undone before the Lord.

The room went from hot anger to calm and acceptance in less than an hour. The gathering of verbally hostile protestors soon became convicted under the might of the Spirit of the Word. They were captivated by the pure Word of God. No one could rebut the scriptures spoken by Pastor Peter. His words were from the superior authority, the original book from and by which all true doctrines are formed. For the listeners, the Word became for them truth and light. They were pricked to the heart deeply, as were the three thousand on the day of Pentecost in Acts 2.

CHAPTER 7   *The Water Baptism*

God had done His job thoroughly through Pastor Peter. Dad slouched back into his chair briefly, and then sat back up again without a pause, right on the edge of his seat. He was profoundly convinced. He stood up and declared to the preacher, in almost the exact way the Ethiopian Eunuch spoke to Philip in Acts 8:36. "Listen Pastor. There is water under this house. The tide is about right. Why don't you lead us down there right now and baptise us? What is holding us from doing this right now?"

Talk about *Revival-Revival-Revival!* I had never seen my dad this way before.

The Pastor smiled. A sense of the moving of God was felt. He knew we had finally understood it. I too was convinced just as they were. I knew that all of us seated in that room were ready to get baptism right according to the true doctrine of the Word. We were ready to humbly but boldly correct the mistakes the missionaries made. The conviction of the Spirit was burning in each of our hearts as each man and woman stood and declared the same logic to the Pastor.

Tears of joy are rolling down my face as I write this. God was changing the literal DNA of our way of worship. The voice and identity of our people were being released into a new way as we obediently responded to the Word and we received a new mark.

This group would be the pioneers of the new way signifying our submission to God.

Now Pastor Peter was glad that we understood the story of the Ethiopian Eunuch but he had a suggestion that was prompted by the Holy Ghost. "I know you want to be baptised right now, as you have learned tonight, according to the scriptures. But I am stirred in my heart that we must make this a public declaration for all the villagers to see. God also wants to reach their hearts. In light of this suggestion, I ask if you can meet me at the river mouth tomorrow morning to do the baptism so all other villagers can see the new thing the Lord is doing in their midst. Would that be okay with you all?"

Everyone agreed. If this change was to impact the village, we were going to be the examples of the new way established by God. We were going to be the first ever, in the history of our little village, to be immersed in water according to the scriptures. And this would happen right at the 'Sirovai' River mouth, which flowed at the footstool of the old 'Hisiubada' Church building. Not only were we going to be in view of the Church, but also in view of the villagers whose homes were over the water. They would watch this unfamiliar event right in their backyard. We were aware of the rebuttal that was likely to follow, knowing that this action would be considered apostasy and heresy in the eyes of the Gabagaba reverends, deacons, and Church elders of the 'Hisiubada' United Church.

We all knew persecution would follow but the persuasion to serve Christ was stronger than any consideration of the persecution.

That night as we got back to our tent-home, God's peace was with us. The newness and awareness of God were in the air. The joy of taking a new step filled our minds. What made it even more special was that I was going to be water baptised along with my parents.

Wednesday, the 12th of May 2004, was the day marked for the Baptism. The same small group gathered now at the river mouth. One of the brothers played a worship song on the acoustic guitar as Pastor Peter and another man walked out into the water and dedicated it unto the Lord. Then came the time for all of us to be immersed. My dad and mum, along with all those same men and women, were baptised in water in the Name above all names, the Name of the Father, Son, and Holy Ghost—the Name, Jesus Christ.

CHAPTER 7 — *The Water Baptism*

When it was my turn to be baptised, I walked out to Pastor Peter and I felt the weightiness of the awesome Power of God. His Presence was now resting so mightily upon the waters that I soon found that I couldn't stand anymore. I fell into the water, and the brother who had led me there helped me up.

Pastor Peter chuckled as they held me up, "It looks like God has already immersed you into the water. But let us do the formalities..."

The Power of God that was upon me was so intense that I had to be carried out of the water and back onto the beach. Mum and Dad stood by me waiting and praising God with joyful tears. For the joy of God had filled our hearts and we had a definite knowing inwardly that we belonged completely to Him.

We understood that the baptism was our declaration of our love and thankfulness toward the Lord Jesus Christ, and the God of Salvation. We were dead to the world by our proclamation, and alive in Christ by the Power of the Spirit! We had the joy of knowing God on the inside and it was overflowing to the outside. What a precious moment for us.

As I lay there on the beach, Pastor Peter who had now finished baptising everybody walked up to me. Pastor Peter sat me up and a Word from the Lord came to him. He spoke it over me, "You are the instrument in God's hands. You are God's mighty instrument which He shall use for His Glory. And you shall bring great Glory to His Name. And with you, the Lord God shall gather a mighty harvest unto Himself. For the Lord shall use you as His Holy Vessel, His Instrument in His hands to draw the hearts of many unto Him. And God shall truly be glorified in your life."

Even if we weren't fully knowledgeable concerning the subject. What happened was, that its core message reached our hearts. That message was this: Jesus gave His life for us on the Cross so that we through believing in Him may receive His

Salvation. Our proclamation of faith in Him was demonstrated in love and surrender to Him in the water of our baptism.

Not only did we learn the true pattern of water baptism, but we also learned the reason for the water made available for the baptism.

THE WATER BAPTISM—THE CELEBRATION

Luke 23:42-43

> And he said unto Jesus, Lord, remember me when Thou comest into Thy kingdom. And Jesus said unto him, Verily I say unto thee, Today shalt thou be with Me in paradise.

The water baptism is a declaration of our love for God and our surrender to His love. We are proclaiming before the host of heaven and a cloud of witnesses that we desire to come into oneness and wholeness with Jesus. It is a handing over of our lives to the One who is the Keeper of our body, soul and spirit and the Captain of our salvation. It is the day of our Joy. When we are immersed in that water, we are simultaneously immersed in the love that came to reach our hearts. That love is Jesus Christ. So in that way, we declare that we are in Christ.

When we said yes to Christ we were immersed into the power of His Word; which is the true and spiritual water of our baptism. The earthly water is a demonstration and public declaration of that true baptism. When we are immersed in that water, we are also declaring that we will walk after the Spirit.

Water baptism is a declaration of new life. Our confession has been sealed by the Spirit in our hearts and in our water baptism, our hearts have been made new by His Spirit. We declare God's work, just as we declare the Lord's death until He comes to unite us together again with Him in Holy Communion. It is when we believe and accept Jesus as the Messiah and Saviour, that we become a new creature in God. The water baptism then is the outward act and symbol of our confession and commitment to Him. It is the event we share before God, to mark the occasion that our hearts have become His.

Now I understand that you may be asking, "Well, what about the man on the cross, whom Jesus accepted into Paradise? He didn't get water baptised and he was saved." The man on the cross did exactly the same thing as we did, minus his physical immersion into water. While he hung on his cross next to Jesus, he gave his life completely over to the Messiah and he believed on Him. He was baptised into the death of Christ by His confession of Christ and entered the new and eternal life with Christ in Paradise. Although he was not able to celebrate by physical water baptism, the declaration of his commitment to Jesus, and his belief in Jesus, was counted also as his spiritual immersion into Christ. Therefore, we can establish here that the true doctrine of our baptism is the one we have made with all our heart before the Lord. So, the outward act of our water baptism is only a declaration of our true baptism; the change that happens within when we say yes to Jesus.

> "The outward act of our water baptism is only a declaration of our true baptism; the change that happens within when we say yes to Jesus.

This, therefore, is our article of faith: in our true baptism, our heart, mind and soul are immersed into the cleansing and rejuvenating work of His Salvation by the Spirit: we are immersed into the Power of His Word. This is the Father's good purpose.

The Water Baptism   **CHAPTER 7**

In the case of our Lord Jesus's water baptism, He didn't need cleansing or rejuvenating. But He was the example of what it truly means to hand your life over to the Father and to trust and obey Him. Jesus laid the foundation for those who would accept Him as their Lord and Saviour and by the declaration of their immersion, they too would also be immersed into the Commission of God's great work. These are they who have been born of the Spirit and the Word and not of the will of man.

Now if Jesus, who is the Lord of our Salvation, accepted that man on the cross, because of his confession and the condition of his heart, who are we to say otherwise? That man on the cross was immersed into Christ's love and Christ's sacrifice, just like we were. He understood that Jesus was giving Himself to save us. We deserved that punishment, but Christ didn't. When the man on the cross asked Jesus to remember him in Paradise, this was him actually trusting in Christ and giving his life over to Jesus fully.

Jesus declared to the man, "Today you shall be with Me in Paradise." Hallelujah! For the Son of man truly has the power to forgive sins.

This touches my heart so deeply because that man, in the eyes of everyone, was still a criminal right up to the moment of his death. He hung as a criminal before many and, to them, he died as a criminal. How easy it is for us to judge others and never know the condition of their hearts.

The onlookers knew why he was crucified on the cross. The lawbreaker deserved the punishment for his crimes. But they lacked spiritual eyes to see and understand the truth before them. When the man confessed to Jesus, by His confession he had given his life to the Lord. Jesus became for that man, The Way, The Truth and The Life. The convicted criminal in that moment of his confession became a transformed man. He, by the Blood of the Lamb of God, was no longer a criminal hanging on the cross beside

Jesus; he was a new creature in Christ. He was now hanging there as one justified and accepted in the eyes of God, our Father. And he died as one whose sins were pardoned and washed away with the precious Blood of the Lamb. For Yeshua, the King of Salvation had washed away all his record of wrongs and had received him into the baptism of his redemption. For sure that man was going home with Jesus.

Are you in need of the saving grace of Jesus Christ today? If you haven't yet made that choice, today is the day of your justification and acceptance. Now is the day of your salvation. Jesus is waiting for you. You can accept Him also by believing in Him. All you have to do is confess with your mouth the Lord Jesus and believe in Him with your heart that God raised Christ from the dead.

Romans 10:10-11

> For with the heart, man believeth unto righteousness; and with the mouth confession is made unto salvation. For the scripture saith, Whosoever believeth on him shall not be ashamed.

And because our true baptism is a spiritual baptism by the Word of the Spirit, should we then neglect or disregard the public proclamation of our faith through water baptism? Not at all. That grand and open statement is our testimony to the world and to the spiritual forces working to stop us from reaching the salvation decision. It is right to proclaim on the mountain tops and to proclaim it confidently, that we were once bound but Christ has set us free. We were once lost but now we are found. We like sheep had gone astray, but the Shepherd of our souls didn't give up on us. He led us back to the Father. All of Heaven rejoices with us, as they witness this declaration of the new birth experience in Christ.

CHAPTER 7
The Water Baptism

The water baptism is a special event for our hearts. It is our baptism unto repentance and publicly declares our surrender and commitment to Jesus. The earthly water is of no effect if the true baptism of hearts hadn't happened. We have been washed by the Holy Word of God, which is Christ our Lord and the Spirit of God now abides in us.

You can see why John rebuked the pharisees and the sadducees who came to be baptised (Matthew 3:7-8). He told them to, "Bring forth therefore fruits meet for repentance." The real issue was the lack of repentance in their hearts. These teachers of the law were just putting on a show. John knew their hearts hadn't truly repented. They had no inner baptism so the outer baptism would mean nothing.

When we celebrate a birthday, it is not to make that person another year older. Rather, we celebrate the birthday to acknowledge the fact that they have turned another year older. And even if we didn't celebrate it, that person will still be another year older. Yet, there is something about celebrating birthdays that causes us to rejoice in our hearts and often encourages the one whose birthday is being celebrated (the birthday celebrant) to cherish the moment, reflect on the foregone years, and look forward to the year ahead.

This is very much the same with our water baptism. It is a celebration of the true baptism; the inner baptism that happened in the heart, mind and soul of the person that turned their eyes on Jesus and made Him Lord of their life. That person was completely born again at that moment (1 Peter 3:21). The water baptism, therefore, becomes the celebration event acknowledging that person's new life in Christ. The old has departed and the new has come.

And like the 'birthday celebrant,' the 'born-again celebrant—the person celebrating their baptism' (born not of earthly water, but of the Heavenly water of the Spirit and Life), cherishes the moment, lets go of the past, and looks forward to their new life in Christ Jesus.

Recently, in Texas, USA, satanists attempted to hold an 'Unbaptism' service, at their pagan fest, to 'unbaptise' attendees. A certain group of Christians gathered to pray against the event, determined to stop it from happening. The event still went ahead though.

This is not really surprising. The real truth was that those who attended that ceremony had already backslidden in their hearts before they even attended that fest. In fact, they might have never actually known Jesus or given their lives in surrender to him. Any baptism they had received may have meant nothing anyway. They were already 'unbaptised' in their heart, mind and soul. Their claimed baptism was already of no effect and non-existent before the Lord. They didn't need a satanic ritual to confirm the fact that they were already on the wide path of apostasy, leading to hell. Their attempt to undo the baptism, was already a waste of effort because the truth is they were already reprobate in God's sight. What the satanists were celebrating was the lost soul. They were publicly declaring their rejection of Jesus. Their reprobate minds had already walked away from the Lord and much like what Judas Iscariot had done, they too had chosen to betray and deny the Lord Jesus. Although Christ had washed Judas's feet along with all the other disciples, Judas's heart was what needed cleansing. That's why Jesus said, "I have washed your feet, but not all of you are clean," referring to Judas (John 13:10-11). For Judas, the washing of his feet had no effect, because his heart was already hardened against the Lord.

Again, I emphasise here that our true water baptism is the spiritual one, made in our hearts. The celebration of our true baptism is a public declaration of our testimony in Christ. We do it, but not to be saved (that, should have already happened inwardly). We do it to proclaim our new life in Christ—the celebration marks the occasion publicly in the presence of our rejoicing spiritual family, before the host of Heaven and before the Lord our God who sits on the Throne of Glory.

Baptism is for the person who believes in Jesus. Their confession and conversion is what bring about their transformation and is preached through their proclamation in water baptism. This is the tenet of our faith—rend your hearts and not your garments (Joel 2:13-14). We are to give our hearts to God in true surrender. That is our true baptism. We can't fake it like an outward garment because the outward baptism will mean nothing if the inward baptism of our hearts has not been done. Will you, therefore, surrender to God with all your heart? Let God make you a new creature in Him. He can if you will give yourselves completely to Him.

I exhort you to boldly declare your faith in Christ. Be immersed in the Living Water of the Spirit.

Let the old die in the Living Water of your true Baptism and let the new become yours in Christ. What a joy it is to come into a life-changing experience with God. When we believe in Christ, we experience the same life-changing power of Christ, like that pardoned man on the cross; and former criminal in the eyes of God. We, like him, have made that same request: "Yeshua, will You remember us in Your Kingdom? We give ourselves completely to You, to be baptised into Your love and the commission of Your Call. We believe in You, Lord."

And because of our sincere declaration, made in and from our hearts, we affirm that we no longer belong to this world. For our true allegiance is now with the Lamb of God.

For God so loved the world (that is you and I) that He gave us His Only Begotten Son, and whosoever believes in Him, will not die but have Everlasting Life (John 3:16).

2 Corinthians 5:17

Therefore if any man be in Christ, he is a new creature: old things are passed away; behold, all things are become new.

CHAPTER 8

THE REVIVALIST & THE POSTURE FOR REVIVAL

*Holy Spirit Revival has one fundamental and powerful trait:
God abides in the midst of His people*

Joy fills my heart because I am about to talk to you on the subject that is God's heartbeat: a vessel like no other —*The Revivalist,* and *the posture for Revival.*

Let's first talk about the Office of the Revivalist.

GOD'S REVIVALIST

Other names we can call the Revivalist by:
- Fire Starters
- Glory Carriers
- Fire Carriers
- Carriers of the abiding Word (or Word of Power)
- Ministers of obedience to God

- The messenger, sent to Preach and demonstrate the Revival of God.
- Servants of the Cleft of the Rock
- The Burning Ones
- The Anointeds of God
- The Messengers of Discipline
- The Chosen of the Lord, marked with the Spirit of Power

Everything I share here, I share out of experience, encounter, revelation by logos (principle) and by rhema (utterance of the Spirit), observation, discipline, and how the Lord Holy Spirit has specifically trained me. I have seen much and I have been thoroughly prepared to *preach to you the Gospel of Peace and Power of Christ by the Holy Ghost*. Now is the time.

In delving deeper into who the Revivalist really is and the correct posture for Revival, my intention is not to create exclusivity amongst the ministers of God, leaving it only for a few, but to highlight the markings of a true Revivalist, chosen by God and to draw your attention to the stirring, direction and leadership of the Spirit of God for the Church.

The Lord wants you to take up this fiery call to be a *Burning One*. For you to grasp this without any filters, I must be direct because I desire to see the Church step into this role correctly.

God wants you to carry the *Revivalist's Mantle* but are you willing to go where God goes? Will you lay down your crown willingly to serve at His feet? Will you be a *carrier of the Glory of God?*

> "
> God wants you to carry the Revivalist's Mantle but are you willing to go where God goes?

First and foremost, a Revivalist is called by God. Their calling will often contain a testimony of a fiery encounter or Baptism with God.

The Revivalist is God's message, not just the messenger because they carry the message wherever they go. I'm not talking about a notebook full of sermons—that's not enough. We must go beyond that and soak in the message of the Spirit. I'm talking about sermons burning in the heart of the carrier. They are *carriers of the Abiding Word of Power.* They preach only the sermon pressed upon them by the Holy Spirit. The message ordained of the Spirit rests on them like dew from Heaven (Psalms 133). That message lives in them and is alive in them. The Prophet Jeremiah also described this weighty and potent experience. Because he was unable to keep it in. And the *burning ones* are exactly like that. The Power and Glory of the Word burns in them intensely as Fire, shut up in their bones, so much that they are often unable to contain it, nor hold it back, that they overflow with the Word (Jeremiah 20:9).

The Revivalist answers directly to God, their Supreme Commander-In-Chief. Their ordination is a specific kind and their Anointing is peculiar. The Revivalist is *God's Sign* to the people and the carrier of God's firstfruit because the Word they carry bears the traits of Jesus Christ—the Firstfruit of God (James 1:17-18). Wheresoever they release the Power of God, a blessing flows in that place that entertains the Word on their mouth. The Revivalist is called to carry out the desire of God. You will often see them broken before the Lord; humble and surrendered to the Spirit. When the Spirit moves them, they respond without hesitation because these *servants of the Cleft of the Rock* have given themselves completely to the Holy Ghost. This kind of individuals are marked by a special Anointing of the Lord. Their call and Anointing is a *Revivalist's Mantle.* The Revivalist Mantle is not given to everyone. But one can carry and all others can partake of it by helping carry that *Rod of God* in the hands of the chosen vessel. Like Aaron and Hur, holding up Moses's arms so Moses could keep the Rod raised before the people: Moses being the Revivalist in this example (Exodus 17: 8-15).

To the Revivalist, the *Prayer-Closet-life is Revival-life*. It is the 'Psalms 1:1-4' life and the 'Psalms 91:1-2' life. It is a life of abiding in God to live by the Spirit to adhere to the will of the Lord Jesus.

And because I am already into the subject, it would be fitting for me to describe further in detail the particular difference the Revivalist carries. To do this, we must first observe the outlined ministerial calls the Lord gave to the Church.

In Ephesians 4:7,8,11-13, Paul talks to us about the five-fold ministry:
- the apostles,
- prophets,
- evangelists,
- pastors and
- teachers.

God gave the Church these specific Mantles by the *Grace* resting upon each of these offices in the Lord according to the measure of the 'Gift of Christ' ministered only through the Holy Ghost.

The reason for these offices was for,
- the perfecting of the saints,
- for the work of the ministry,
- and for the edifying of the Body of Christ.

To what ultimate outcome was God looking at for the five *rooms of calling* to pursue after? The five offices' commission was to work till the Church came into *the unity of faith, and knowledge of the Son of God—then the Church would be a perfect man reaching the measure of the stature of the fullness of Christ.*

In other words, the Church must go from Glory to Glory till we reach that level in which have become fully overtaken by the fullness of Christ in us.

These five Mantles are very much in function and alive in the Church today.

Now there are diversities of gifts, administrations and operations under these five *ministries* and all are given by the same Holy Spirit. Their functions find their full strength to operate only by the leading of the Spirit of God and without the Holy Spirit, no man is able to carry out these ordained duties correctly. Thus, all five offices have their purposes and foundations deeply rooted in the governance and guidance of the Holy Spirit, who is the *Giver and Operator*. It is the Spirit of Christ, at work in these vessels to fulfil the *Commission of the Kingdom*.

With that said, where does the Revivalist come into the picture concerning the offices and operations?

Looking at what we already covered, we can establish that an apostle can carry the Revivalist Mantle; a good example is, Peter. Likewise, a prophet; example—Elijah and Moses. An evangelist; example—Philip. A pastor; example—The apostles themselves were perfect examples of pastors and teachers also. Last, but not the least; the teacher, *can* also be the Revivalist.

Contrariwise here is where I must now point out the difference. This particular error has come about because the Church has forgotten that the Holy Spirit is the one who calls this role into existence. If we attempt to put all ministers under this one covering and mark them all as Revivalists, we'd be making a very big mistake because we won't find God working this way anywhere, not in the old times, nor in the current day Church, even if we wanted it to be. We'd be lying to ourselves if we let a pastor believe that he carries the Revivalist's Anointing; claiming a Mantle but demonstrating no traits and signs, nor the mindset and

Power of the *Revival* Mantle—being distinct markings of the Revivalist that sets them apart from the rest. Concerning the five ministries of God, the *platforms* under these offices and that of the Revivalist, aren't the same. This is how we must see it; there are the five Mantles of ministry and then there is the Mantle of the Revivalist. This *General of the Move of God* walks with God at a level governed by the Lord Himself.

Why is this the case? The answer remains steadfast in what God wants and not how we want it. The Revivalist is different because they possess a deeper seriousness with God, and that profundity is predominantly influenced by God. It is God, who has caused their life to be marked by the demonstration of the Holy Spirit and Power. (1 Corinthians 2:1-4).

The Revivalist knows God and God knows them. They came into that call, not of their own will, nor did they force their way into it. Only the *Call of the Most High is the determining authority that sets them apart*. Their call is not to build organisations but to build the Kingdom. This is the Commission of *the burning ones; They are sent to preach and demonstrate the Revival—which is Christ's Gospel of Peace and Power.*

They are not enthusiasts or fanatics. Nor are they motivational speakers, stirring man with outward charisma, and with their gifted oratorical speeches. Their desire is not to entertain the people with well-crafted sermons. That is not the way they work. Rather, Their ambition, commission and aspirations come from the Holy Spirit. The *Revivalist message* burns within them. It consumes and overtakes them. They are broken and, at the same time, captivated by that message and yearn for nothing more but to grab with both spiritual hands the fullness of that Heavenly Word poured like hot water into their hearts.

The compassion of God pours out of them to reach out to the people because of the Word burning in them. They are not emotionally driven, they are Holy Spirit led.

Because the Revivalist is a *carrier of the Word*; the authority of their Mantle is established to reveal the Glory and Presence of God on earth—They are called to reveal Christ.

Hence, that peculiar Anointing of the Revivalist, like other Anointings, is its own offices with a platform, position and influence to act as God's *Sent One*. A Revivalist doesn't look for platforms. But the Anointing that rests upon the Revivalist is their platform.

This in no way disregards the five offices, which are also appointed by the Spirit. Rather, it becomes the elevated privilege presented to the five offices. This happens when your hunger turns God's attention to you, and draws the invitation from God, to grant you access by the Holy Spirit.

The Revivalist is also *the Minister of Discipline*. Although he is separated from the five ministries, He is authorised to function in all five offices and he will usually carry a dominant office out of the five. That is also to say, any of the five offices can be elevated to step into the office of the *Burning Ones*, again, only by the invitation of God and not by the forceful eagerness of man. They can be an apostle and a *Glory Carrier* at the same time. They can be a pastor and also be called *to preach and demonstrate the Revival*. The same applies to the evangelists, prophets and teachers.

I emphasise again; that we must note with high regard, that the *Revivalist Calling*, like that of the five offices, can only be appointed by God. God picks the vessels that are ready to host His Presence and Carry His Fire. He knows their hearts. He knows they are ready for Him because they have been yielding unceasingly to Him. They are the ones that have already started to feel out of place, but they can't settle. The Mandate upon their lives won't let them stop pursuing. God has marked them out for great things. These have been forged through the Holy Spirit Fire and when they do rise, they will know their place in God, because the Spirit will reveal it to them.

AN ANGEL DELIVERS A MESSAGE

—

THE MESSENGER OF DISCIPLINE

I had this dream on the 21st of April 2021. In the dream, we had travelled out from Rockhampton to attend a conference where I was going to be speaking. When we got there, the scene changed and I was walking down a corridor at a 5-star hotel. I entered a hall looking for the meeting place. When I entered a certain conference room, there was a handful of Christians sitting on the table tops and I thought, this must be it. However, upon speaking with them, I was bemused by their unfriendly and jesting response toward me. They were criticising me and mocking me for something I wasn't aware of.

Wanting to avoid a discussion with them, I left the room and walked down the corridor and finally found the reception desk to get some directions to the meeting place.

As I entered into the reception's large foyer, it led out to a vast beautiful outdoor garden. I greeted the receptionist and proceeded to ask for her help. There also was another man waiting patiently at the counter about a few metres away from me. I noticed as I took a brief look at him, that something was different about him. He observed me for a while before he broke the silence with an unusual statement that immediately got my attention, "Did you know God has given you a Ministry of Discipline? Did you know you are God's Messenger of Discipline?"

I turned fully and looked at him in a daze and I sensed something familiar; it was Heavenly. Although, I didn't quite understand his rhetorical question. A knowing from Heaven was evident on his countenance. And now that he had my full attention, he proceeded to say to me, "God will use a Messenger of Discipline to start His Revival. Revival requires Discipline to carry it. It requires a Messenger of Discipline to carry, lead, and serve it. Revival also requires that Messenger, who is obedient to the Voice of God. This messenger will release the fire of Revival wherever he is sent. God will not use any messenger who is not disciplined. God is going to use His Messenger of Discipline to Release Revival in this meeting. And there is one that God has already picked. You are that man. You are His Messenger of Discipline."

I stood there wide-eyed and awestruck by what he had just said to me. His countenance glowed brighter as he spoke to me. I realised immediately that I was standing before an angel of God. I had no sooner come to the knowledge of this in my mind when he disappeared before me in a flash.

END OF DREAM.

> "God will only use His Messenger of Discipline to Release Revival.

You may have already worked it out at this point of the book that every time I encounter something new from God, there is always a lesson in it. And that's exactly what I've been led by the Spirit to do here—to talk to you about God's *Messenger of Discipline.*

God teaches us more about Himself and more about His Work through these holy visions and dreams. In these spiritual encounters, we learn about God's heart and desire. We also learn more about ourselves in Him.

With that said, what can we learn about God's preferred vessel—the Messenger of Discipline?

To do that, we first have to study what God meant by Discipline. I have learned through many of these heavenly experiences that God sees things differently from us. And when He uses a specific Word, He sees things at a heightened level of understanding compared to our earthly definition of the same word. There's more than meets the eye when it comes to Holy Spirit revelation. When we lean into the Spirit we are then able to receive God-perspective and insight concerning His Will for us.

1 Corinthians 2:9-10

> But as it is written, Eye hath not seen, nor ear heard, neither have entered into the heart of man, the things which God hath prepared for them that love Him. But God hath revealed them unto us by His Spirit: for the Spirit searcheth all things, yea, the deep things of God.

DISCIPLINE has several meanings. Let's look at them:

1. The practice or system of enforcing control or training to enforce obedience to rules, conduct and patterns of behaviour.

2. Punishment for breaking rules or stepping out of line.

3. A field of study or branch of knowledge.

4. To train or develop by instruction and repeated exercise in order to acquire through guided focus and self-control.

The etymology of 'discipline' is from the Latin word, *discipulus*—pupil, which became *disciplina*—*instruction and knowledge*. This provides the source for the word *Disciple*—*a follower of Jesus Christ*.

Discipline for Revival is *Obedience to the Voice of the Spirit*, and nothing more than that.

God's main thrust in Revival is to draw a group of people who will come under the submission and weightiness of the Baptism of Fire. They are willing to grow in an unusual and almost unrecognisable way. Unusual, only because the Church has forgotten her unique birthplace; that holy and magnificent event of the Day of Pentecost when the Spirit of God descended and rested upon the saints (Acts 2). The Church has also forgotten her discipleship and discipline to walk in total submission to the Holy Spirit and His abiding Word.

The Discipline I speak of requires humility, honour and love for another. The governing aspect of that Discipline is to hear what the Lord says and only proclaim what He speaks.

That messenger of Discipline will wait. There will be many things happening around him, but he will wait until the Lord speaks.

The first trait of this *Heavenly Discipline* is the ability to recognise the Voice of the Holy Spirit. And when the Messenger of Discipline knows his Master's Voice, He becomes the vessel by which the Blessing and Fullness of Revival descend upon a meeting place, where that Messenger is sent to speak. His main focus is not even on the crowds. He is completely fixated on the Voice of the One He follows—That is Discipline.

Our programs can distract us; even we can distract ourselves. That is something we are very good at. But when you want Revival, you must stop entertaining the noise, and focus on *the Voice of the Spirit*.

The Messenger of Discipline: his main intent and passion, is the Revival Fire of God. Revival is God's heartbeat and that same heartbeat becomes the Messenger's too, as he yields to God's leadership. Therefore, he is willing to go through the process of moulding to be a carrier of the Move. He is trained to deliver the Heavenly assignment. He loves what God loves—he loves God's people and he loves God.

This type of Discipline is not only restrictive in nature as we may think it to be, but more than that. It is Power with God, and the Power to Walk with God—That is the Heavenly Discipline I speak of (Acts 10:38).

The Messenger of Discipline did not choose Revival, Revival chose him (John 15:16).

This *Minister of Discipline* will be the one that turns the hearts of the children to their fathers and the hearts of the fathers to their children (Malachi 4:5-6). The 'Messenger desires to behold *the beauty of the Word*. He has been caught up in the Presence (Psalms 27:4).

And when he beholds his Lord, the desire to be more like God overwhelms the Messenger. The servant of the Move has become one completely overtaken by the goodness of the Presence (Psalms 84:1 -2). The messenger is a vessel of humility before the Lord. His desire is to be broken before his God (Isaiah 66:1-2)—This is, that Discipline.

> " It is a worthy and wondrous experience to be broken before the Lord

Revival is always on his mind. This holy vessel knows that his *Discipline* is to pursue the Presence and obey the Voice of the Living God. He is led to walk with the great and mighty God of the Revival Fires. He was born from the Fires of Revival and he lives, immersed in the intensity of that Heavenly Fire. He is willing to lay down his life for the Fires of the Great Awakening of God (John 15:13). Nothing is more wonderful to His soul than to see God have His way in the midst of His people. He has the attitude and intent to decrease, so that Christ may increase. This Messenger of Discipline wants no glory from man. He knows he is not perfect but is willing to go where the Lord leads.

This same *Vessel of Discipline* prefers to be the least in the Kingdom, to be the servant that serves tables of other ministers, the usher willing to catch for the ministering team, the one willing to serve wherever he is required. He seeks no recognition. He seeks no fame. He would prefer others to be above him. But when it comes to hearing God's Voice, He will not buckle nor refuse the Voice of the Saviour—That is the Discipline I speak of.

Although he may live a very normal life, and even have a nine-to-five job, yet when God speaks, he responds with due diligence because the Fire of His Commission burns bright in God and He understands the significance of the Holy Mandate that rests upon Him. The *Minister of Discipline* knows that Revival cannot come from the efforts of man. No way under God's Heaven. Revival is ordained and initiated by God, who is the author and accomplisher of His Work. God will look for His *Vessel of Discipline* to do His bidding. He will search the hearts and find one willing to become the *igniter-initiator* of the Fire. God is looking for one who will not compromise or suppress the purpose of Revival (1 Samuel 13:14). That person is called 'The Messenger of Discipline' and he carries the Word of his God upon his lips. He is the appointed Revivalist known by God (Isaiah 43:10).

Measure yourselves against these above descriptions and ask yourself on every ground—Do you qualify or do you want to be that person?

EVALUATION TIME–

Are you committed to REVIVAL?
Are you willing to go where God is going?
Are you willing to obey God when He leads you?
Do you have the desire to behold His Face?

CHAPTER 8   *The Revivalist & The Posture For Revival*

When God said,
"Seek My Face,"
My heart said to Him,
"Your Face, Lord, will I seek (Psalm 27:8)"

Isaiah 6:8

Also, I heard the Voice of the Lord, saying, Whom shall I send, and who will go for us? Then said I, Here am I; send me.

DISCIPLESHIP FOR REVIVAL

" We can walk where He walks when we have fully become dependent on where He walks

The Holy Spirit spoke a revelation to me that for the Revival to be received, it must be taught to the Church. The Church must be willing to submit to discipleship or mentorship for Revival. Part of that mentorship is to correct our understanding of Revival, or as is correctly defined by the Bible, 'The knowledge of the Glory of the Lord' (Habakkuk 2:14). For the Church to accommodate the Glory, the Church must first be taught the knowledge on how to host the Glory.

You have read in Revelation 19:10 that the Testimony of Jesus is the Spirit of Prophecy. What this means is that everything God reveals to us, He does with the intention of revealing Jesus. All that God does for us prophetically reveals Christ. Jesus Himself said the Holy Spirit would take from Him and reveal it to us.

John 16:13-15

> Howbeit when He, the Spirit of truth, is come, He will guide you into all truth: for He shall not speak of Himself; but whatsoever He shall hear, that shall He speak: and He will shew you things to come. He shall glorify Me: for He shall receive of Mine, and shall shew it unto you. All things that the Father hath are Mine: therefore said I, that He shall take of Mine, and shall shew it unto you.

This is where I am going to be direct with you. Only the Holy Spirit who reveals Christ, is the one who is able to mentor us and disciple us into that greater place of overflow in Christ. What we call apostolic, has one strong characteristic—REVIVAL. And how do we experience Revival? We *follow* the leading and leadership of the Holy Spirit. Following the Holy Spirit is at the heart of Revival and is where the fivefold ministries are founded. This is the principle and foundation of ministry in God.

The 'following' part is what we know as:
- the 'yielding',
- the 'obedience',
- the 'surrendering', and
- the 'turning away from sins.'

Show me a man who claims to follow the Holy Spirit, and I'll show you a Revivalist who has a Word from Heaven burning in them. For they know His Voice and they follow where He leads.

There is no grey area when it comes to the Move of God. We must never let our actions leave the Holy Spirit outside of the place where He is supposed to work effectively, and rightfully be the Leader over us. Apostolic mentoring comes from the leadership of the Spirit.

CHAPTER 8 *The Revivalist & The Posture For Revival*

> Apostolic mentoring comes from the leadership of the Spirit.

I'm pointing the error out, that's if you can already see it. The mistake lies in this next statement. Study it well. I pray that in understanding it, you will be launched into deeper levels of the Holy Ghost to wade into the deep Waters of the Spirit and be filled with the fullness of God. Here's the statement:

> The Revivalist doesn't work **for** God? Rather, it is God who works **through them** to carry out what the Lord wants to do for His people.

What does that look like on a practical level? It means we do nothing but yield our hearts in worship till the Word of Glory enters the room. We don't follow our programs, we follow His Presence, His Anointing and His Voice. We don't preach or prophecy unless His Word of Power has fallen upon us to speak. We don't go ahead of Him, we wait for Him—that is the *Discipline* the Revivalist lives by.

You become one receptive to the Revival Fire of God when you worship in such a way that you are not controlled by programs but by your desire to be at His Feet and to hear His Voice. Because true worship is a heart-to-heart matter. It is the posture that draws the Glory of Heaven into the room where you have laid yourself before His holiness and have become one desiring His Presence. The Holy Spirit nourishes our fellowship with His Presence when we keep Him as the centre of our discussion. The nurturing comes when our prayers go beyond the ordinary and become *a Fire of fellowship*. Anyone who lives in this realm is totally consumed by God's thoughts for Revival and Awakening.

POSTURED FOR REVIVAL

Our submission to God is Power before Him. Our surrender to the Spirit is Power demonstrated to the world.

> " Our submission to God is Power before Him. Our surrender to the Spirit is Power demonstrated to the world.

Let us remove the veil of restriction and constraint that covers our hearts and minds. For in Christ, it has already been taken away (2 Corinthians 3:15-16). With every encounter with God, the Spirit is changing us from Glory to Glory in Him. Hallelujah!

2 Corinthians 3:17-18

Now the Lord is that Spirit: and where the Spirit of the Lord is, there is liberty. But we all, with open face beholding as in a glass the Glory of the Lord, are changed into the same Image from Glory to Glory, even as by the Spirit of the Lord.

I don't want you to just receive a touch from God. I desire for you to go beyond that. The veil has already been removed through Christ and now the Holy Spirit wants to lead you to the Throne of God, where He sits in His Glory and Majesty. I want you to catch the Fire of God and let the Glory of the Most High, which through the Holy Spirit, shall abide in you to do mighty exploits for God.

Let it burn so powerfully in you until a whole city is taken for God, and until a whole region comes under the Baptism of that Fire, and a whole nation bows before to the Sovereign God to make Him their Lord. Hallelujah!

It's time for you to come boldly into the Throne of His Grace. Do you want to be numbered amongst those who carry the Mantle of the *Glory carriers*? Then be hungry for God. And I say it again; be hungry for God—be hungry for God—be hungry for God.

Divine purpose carried in these *broken vessels* transforms lives. They are broken to experience *the God-nature*. Not only have they tasted the goodness of God, but also the boldness of God. It is *the Holy Baptism* of the Holy Ghost that overshadows them and rests mightily upon them. You might be wondering how you can carry, contain or even touch God's Glory. You might be thinking that your life is not worthy. That you are too broken and messed up. You are not alone in this. We are in this together. All of humanity is broken and messed up. But the Divine purpose is that God's Glory is carried in broken vessels and transforms the lives of both the carriers and those to whom it is carried. Glory carriers are broken people, and yet they experience the God-nature because they yield to a deep hunger for God. Their desire to worship God draws the Glory of Heaven to them. Thus, a yielding posture is the appropriate posture for all those who desire to carry the Glory.

Only a deep hunger for God meets this kind of boldness. This certain type of boldness comes upon you when you carry the Move of God. It is the audacity and boldness of the Glory of God pressed upon the soulish, fleshly mind of man to burn it up, and sear it clean out of the way so God can have His way in earthen vessels; made ready for Heaven's purpose. And Heaven's purpose is for the Glory of God to abide with us, through the mighty Baptism of His Holy Spirit that rests powerfully upon us.

Jesus described another metaphor about God's filling of our lives. Christ's work of salvation and renewal is like water pouring out and overflowing for each of us. Will you join Him there? You can come to Him and receive His Living Waters and drink of the abundance of Christ pouring out and overflowing for us today. Anyone who pursues God will find Him; they will meet the Power and Glory of the King. Jesus has never changed His posture. He is still seated in Heavenly Places with the Might of God resting upon Him. His posture before the Father is that of *the Warrior-King*; the Lion of Judah. He is postured to seek and to save the lost with a mighty Anointing, which He gave to the Church. That is the Anointing of Revival I speak of.

We are that generation that has chosen to drink of the Cup of God's Glory. Many generations before us have drank of that same Living Water and they too have been filled with the Glory of the Father and of His Son Jesus. We have chosen to walk with the God of great encounters and manifestations and He is still working mightily in those who have chosen to come before the feet of Christ and experience the blessing of His Glory. Because we know too well that to be at the feet of the Messiah, is life and liberty. We not only sense the nearness of God, but we also walk in the paths where the Spirit walks and are led by the Glory Cloud of God's Abiding Presence in us.

We are the Burning Ones - the Fire Carriers chosen by the Living God. May we together, discern the Moving of the Spirit and delight in Him (Psalms 37:4). May we seek God's Face until we find Him (Jeremiah 29:12-13). That's the posture of the saints who desire to carry the Glory by adopting a *yielding posture*. This is the main attribute and attitude of our ministry to God and one we must learn thoroughly so we can Move mightily in the directives of the Holy Spirit.

Because, the Revivalist who carries a true Mandate from God, will not be able to conform to earthly constraints. They are not built and trained that way. These *Ministers of Obedience* are a different breed of individuals who have been baptised into the holy Fire of their God and know what that feels like.

When you have been there as they have, you will never settle for anything less than that. Their training is of the Holy Ghost and they function from that place where God abides. The Revivalist will only speak from 'THE PLACE WHERE HE (GOD) SPEAKS.'

For *the Place Where He Speaks* is but the uncut stone of God's Altar, where He has recorded His Name and His Blessing (Exodus 20:24-26). This *Holy Mandate* belongs to God. The same *uncut* stone is what Jacob used as a pillow, for the comfort of his head to lie upon, and that pillow became a *pillar because the LORD SPOKE THERE.* It was anointed with oil to mark God's representation, sanctification and selection.

Even Jacob said, "The Lord was surely in that place because it was The Place Where God Talked With Him (Genesis 28:11-22, Genesis 35:13-15)."

(More on the subject, in Chapter 19 of the book).

That's the place where the Revivalist functions from. They are called to carry the Glory and release that Glory by the directives of God. They will not hesitate to proclaim it when the Spirit of God comes upon them.

Watch a Revivalist when the worship time is on. They are God-focused and their awareness is tuned towards God. To them, worshipping God is not a program; it's *purpose.* When you follow and enter into God's purpose, you enter into God's program (I talk more about this in a later Chapter).

The Holy Spirit has a program too. It may not fit the coherencies or synchronised practices of our religious gatherings and it never will. But He is God and He owns His Church. And He knows how to lead His people. He will lead His people to the fountains of the Living Waters, to a glorious City, not made with the fading glory of the first Adam, but of the latter, which is the Spirit of Christ who abides with us.

For when we thirst and call upon Him, He will give us an overflowing, and gushing River of life. Indeed, *there is a River, the Streams thereof shall make glad the City of God, the Holy Place of the Tabernacles of the Most High (Psalms 46:4-5).*

We are the Tabernacles of the Most High. We are *The Place Where He Shall Abide.*

You may still be inclined to take the *Ark of God's Glory* upon a new cart (Your form of worship—your programs), but that is a dangerous mission. Let the breach of Uzzah be enough warning for us to resist thinking we can host the Glory with our programs.

But will you be the David that hears the Voice of the Spirit, to return to that place of heart-to-heart worship toward the God of Heaven and Earth? Will you be the one that resists the temptation of the old way; reject the former and become the *new wineskin to carry the New Wine of God?*

This is where the Revivalist is. They are going to follow the Spirit, but will you follow with them, and be led by the Spirit?

You can't expect to grow in the Holy Ghost with ideas and concepts that are void of the Spirit's counsel. You can't grow in the Holy Spirit if there's no place for dependency on the Holy Spirit. You see, our dependency on the Spirit of Christ is also Power with Him.

We do that by letting the Holy Spirit come into the room of our hearts. And this is a pleasant thought: cherished worship before the Lord becomes a holy moment when the God of Heaven looks upon the room of our surrendered hearts and says, "That is where I will come and rest, abide, and dwell."

That place is what I call *the God-selection*; that place where God's heart leans into. This is the true heart that God wants His people to carry. It is also the heart of God's Revivalist.

> "The God-selection; the Revivalist—will only abide where God is. They will only align with God's program.

Will you ascend to the Holy Hill of the Lord with them? Will you join them at the *Cleft of the Rock?* These do not seek glory from man. They only want God and all of Him. For they have one Master and Lord. They also know where the King's table is. These are those who have washed their robes white with the *Blood of the Lamb of God. For they are before the Throne of God and serve Him day and night in His Holy Place (Revelations 7:9-15).*

May the Spirit of God lean into our worship. For the Lord delights in them that seek His face earnestly. He will not disappoint the one who reaches out to touch Him. He will reveal His Word to them without hesitation.

THE MANTLE HAS ALREADY FALLEN

This is a callout to the Revivalists. The trumpet of the Spirit has already been blown. A separation is before you and the appointed Gideon must pick out *the burning ones.* For many are called, but *few are chosen (Matthew 22:14).*

The Word and Spirit say, "Come." You are the spiritual *Elishas* who must respond to the Call. The Mantle has already fallen *'Elisha.'* The Voice of the Spirit has already spoken and said, "When you see me go."

And for us, it is *when we have heard His Call*. The Spirit is calling out to you to realise that the Mantle for Revival has already fallen to the ground waiting to be picked up (2 Kings 2:1-18). Hear the Call and come to the Living Waters (Isaiah 55:1-3). Elishas it's time to pick up the Mantle appointed by God. Where are the Elishas who will grab a hold of the Mantle of Revival and go forth to preach and minister with the double portion of the Spirit of Christ?

For the Lord Himself said (John 14:12), "Verily, verily, I say unto you, He that believeth on Me, the works that I do shall he do also; **and greater works than these shall he do**; because I go unto My Father."

The Mantle is for you, the appointed Fire carriers. You've been following after Revival for a long time now. Like Elisha following after Elijah. You've been following God faithfully. Your devotion has got you to a place where you are no longer satisfied with just Sunday Service. You are the one I am speaking to. Your hunger for God has taken you down paths sanctified for God; some of which are so isolated from everyone else, but you have sought after the Fire from Heaven. And down that blessed pathway of the Holy Spirit that you have followed, there have been many powerful God-encounters. But now is the time to respond to the Voice of the Spirit and take up the cup of your calling to follow after His Mandate for Revival. Now is the appointed time.

Your pursuit of the Mantle will cause you to reach out to the Holy Spirit to pick up the Mantle He has appointed to you. And the only way to do that is to adopt your worship posture as Moses did before the Lord at the Cleft of the Rock. There is no secret code to receiving what the Spirit has called you to pick up. The only thing the Spirit wants you to do is to *Surrender*.

God is looking for vessels that are willing to go up to the Holy Hill of the Lord and come before the place of His appointment to

CHAPTER 8   *The Revivalist & The Posture For Revival*

receive a Divine Word to give to the people. Are you willing to forsake all to follow the Call of the Lord? That 'Call' is the 'Cross' you must carry for Jesus. The Mantle of Revival has already fallen and the Mantle is before you, Church of God. Will you pick it up?

Elijah was a special prophet. He wasn't like the other prophets. He carried a unique Anointing for Revival only because he learned to walk in obedience to the Lord. But the question is which group are you with? Are you with 'the school of the prophets or are you following Elijah?' The school of the prophets are those who serve in the ministry and are happy with just where they are. Or, are you *the Elisha,* whose desire won't let up till he receives the double portion of the Anointing of *the Christ*?

The 'school of the prophets' love their meeting places. They know Elisha has gone with Elijah but they prefer to observe from afar. They can hear the sound of Revival but they keep saying, "I am comfortable with where I am at."

I am speaking to you minister of God. When *Revival* comes into your city or town, will you look from afar and say, "Good for them. God bless them. Hope they have a good time?" But you care nothing about the *beckoning of the Spirit* to attend that Revival meeting.

Yet, it will be the *hungry one* that crosses the Jordan with Elijah. Are you a 'hungry one?' This disciple will follow after the Mantle to serve the Will of God. They will go to that place and not let up till they have picked up the Mantle that has fallen—That same Mantle that is appointed to them.

Elisha was not hindered by earthly distractions when he followed steadfastly after Elijah. It was *obedience coupled with hunger* that became his pursuit.

But if you still choose to be with 'the school of the prophets,' you have become the bystanders and passive spectators of the very Move you were supposed to enter into and carry. You have become the sightseer and onlooker, but not a *Seer of the Move*. If you are like this and stiff-necked to the Call of the Spirit, you will forever be waiting and never jumping into the River of the Spirit.

Come away from the old way. Leave the sons of the prophets now, and follow the *Elijah* of your calling. Follow! In the Name of Jesus!

CHAPTER 9

WHEN DESPERATION MEETS THE WORD

As soon as she obeyed, the change began. Make room for God.

God will pour His Spirit where we have made room for Him. And when He enters the room, He makes that room bigger. Will you make room for Him? When I think of the words, *"Make room for God,"* I think of the widow of Zarephath (1 Kings 17:8-16) who had nothing else left but the last bit of oil in a cruse and the last bit of flour in a barrel to make a small piece of bread for herself and her son. But when Elijah asked for water, she responded kindly. But her faith was surely stretched when the prophet Elijah spoke again and asked her for bread. She had flour and oil and not even enough to sustain her own life, or her son's life. In her mind, that meal would be their last meal together. And although she knew it was her last meal, She had a glimmer of hope and made sure to provide Elijah with what he asked from her. Maybe it was faith at work or that the COMMAND OF HEAVEN was playing its course in her heart, leading up to what was to be her breakthrough moment.

For as soon as she heard the man of God speak, a response she hadn't had before came to her and she made room for the *Word on the mouth of the Prophet.* She yielded to her breakthrough and accepted the invitation of her provision by taking heed to the Word and obeying it. She allowed God to have room to move in her situation.

In fact, it was as soon as she obeyed that the change began. God starts when you start. He was already present to work through His spoken Word delivered through Elijah the *Revivalist-prophet.* When the woman yielded to the Word, that's when the cruse of oil yielded and the flour yielded too and came under the authority of the *Word of Revival* resting upon the mouth of the man of God.

Here is another important lesson to learn. When it comes to receiving the blessing of His Presence: we must make room to recognise the Fire of the Word upon the Fire Carriers who have been sent to us. So many times we turn away God's prophets who are God's Revivalists, and are we not afraid that they might receive the command to dust their feet? Are we not afraid of the Living God?

But your heart must reach the point of desperation. Desperation makes room for God like nothing else. The widow became desperate for an answer, and she had run out of options until the man of God showed up with a Word from Heaven. Those Words carried the Power to make the oil flow and keep flour in the barrel. Sustenance by the Word: that is a glorious outcome.

You can see more of this miracle-working Power of the Word in the miraculous feeding of the five thousand men. When Jesus spoke the Word over the two fish and five loaves, the food yielded to His Words and multiplied (Matthew 14:16-21/ Mark 6:38-43). Interestingly we note that it was only men that were counted. If we were to include the women and children in that total, it would be well over twelve thousand people that were fed in one sitting. All that happened because two fish and five loaves were surrendered to the hands of Christ. It may be that the one who gave them recognised the possibility and the power of the Word resting upon Christ. And what about the story of blind Bartimaeus or the woman with the issue of blood; who were healed when they pursued Christ with great desperation? They got their answer because they were desperate enough to yield. Their yielding made room for the Spirit of the Word to work. A holy Anointing touched their need.

I am filled with amazement at the powerful encounter that changed the Zarephath woman's life; when that Word from Heaven became her breakthrough as soon as she obeyed it. The Word turned her desperation into deliverance; her unfavourable circumstance into a sign, a wonder and a miracle. Desperation for God commands a type of yielding that even the devil can't fight against.

> " But desperation for God commands a type of yielding that even the devil can't fight against.

When the Zarephath woman obeyed, that's when her miracle began. If you will make room for God, God will make room for you. He will pour out abundantly on you and multiply the oil, fish and bread that is in your hands. I invite you to yield to the Word of Fire; the spoken Word of Heaven.

It is important to note that it was Elijah who received the Word to go to Zarephath. The interesting part about this Word was how the Lord God said it to Elijah, "Arise and go to Zarephath, which belongs Zidon, and dwell there: behold, I have COMMANDED a widow woman there to sustain you. (1 Kings 17:18-19)." But the widow didn't know that a *Command from Heaven* was released for her. She hadn't known it until she met and listened to the Word that Elijah carried to her door. Just think of it.

That Word could have been assigned to a rich person in Zarephath. But then, there wouldn't be a need for a miracle.

Rather, God used this circumstance to demonstrate to us the importance of the Revivalist who carries the Word, and the importance of the one who receives the appointed Word with an open heart.

Very much like when a local Church is crying out for Revival but doesn't yet know that a Word from Heaven has been assigned to them because *the Lord heard their cries and desperate plea for help.* But in order for that local Church to receive that Revival Fire, a vessel like Elijah must receive that Heavenly Word to deliver to that Church. Therefore, Revival is appointed by God and will require a carrier of the Word in order for it to be released.

The Prophet Elijah, who carried the Word, carried the influence of the Word til it was released, it became a miracle of provision for the woman. The yielding began with Elijah. He was led by the Lord to go to Zarephath. If he didn't carry that Word as God's Revivalist, the widow wouldn't have seen her miracle. *Obedience is yielding.* Obedience makes room for God to work. The Anointing upon your life will demand obedience from you. And as soon as you obey, the *Desire of Heaven* is released through your obedience.

> "The Anointing upon your life will demand obedience from you.

Elijah's ministry is quite extraordinary. His walk with God bears the marks of *a Word carrier; a Revivalist.* He was truly *a burning one.* He knew how to carry the Word because he knew how to be desperate for God and to be obedient to the Word when it showed up. He was totally committed to receiving, carrying and delivering the Word when it came upon him. Elijah understood that yielding to God released Heaven on earth and that he could be the fire starter and the vessel by which God was able to demonstrate the Power of His Anointing and Word. Elijah is our example of a *Prophet of Obedience* and one who waited patiently for the Word until it came. He waited where he was, even until the brook that supplied his water dried up. He learned how to be still before the Lord. He learned how to be aware of, recognise and know the form and weightiness of the Word when it came upon Him. He lived by the Word and walked after *the Desire of God*. And God's desire was fulfilled through Elijah's hunger and thirst for God and his obedience to the Word of the Spirit of God.

Matthew 5:6

> Blessed are they which do hunger and thirst after righteousness: for they shall be filled.

In the same manner, the Revivalist will come to you with a Word from Heaven, and God will have positioned you to receive it, but it is your yielding to the Word that will bear fruit in your life. The Zarephath woman obeyed the Word. Grace had found her out and mercy had stretched out His Hand. The hour of her obedience became for her, the banner of her Joy. She understood that in obeying this Holy Ghost *utterance* from Elijah's mouth, would mean that she would have to share her last meal, which wasn't much at all. Therefore, in the natural, this truly presented a challenge for her. She was willing to show hospitality, but she saw her lack. But she made room for God to move and, true to the Word of God upon the prophet, her obedience released the change in her situation.

The sad reality is, that so many people of God in our generation, including leaders and ministers lack the patience to wait for the Spirit. They have become like King Saul (1 Samuel 13:8-14), seeking the desire of the crowd rather than waiting on the Spirit. Many have taken their eyes away from God and have become overwhelmed by the pressure of earthly things. They are more worried about how the congregation feels and how the congregation behaves. They design their programs pragmatically but not prophetically by the unction of the Holy Ghost. They would rather leave God's *waiting posture* outside of their gatherings, because it may seem to them inconvenient, unpredictable and impractical, by their own standards. Instead, they bring in their own ideas of how ministry and Christian fellowship appear to work and then expect God to bless their plans and efforts and do His work under their carefully controlled environment. Then they ask the Lord Holy Spirit to fit into their schedule and show up when they call for Him. What they forget is that it is the Lord who calls us into that Holy Place of Worship. God calls us to that place where the intent of His heart is heard prophetically in our midst. What they don't realise is, that waiting posture is the Heavenly requirement for encounter with God and effective ministry.

I am greatly saddened when I see the ministers are so busy working for God, and in God's name, that they can't find time to wait on Him in their own time and in their gatherings with their congregations. They are ultimately conducting ministry without God's involvement. It's either a lack of knowledge or just plain discourtesy on their part. They make God look like He is weak and unable to do His own work properly by His Holy Spirit. And then they make excuses to explain it away. This mindset is close to ignorance and disobedience and it grieves the Holy Spirit. This is the error, that one can serve *the Works of God* without ever serving *the God that Works in our midst.* Instead of *the encounter* that changes lives, the ministers are caught in the busyness of service and not ministry toward God. They have replaced encounter with entertainment and exciting events. Instead of unbroken prayer, worship and word, they attempt, without hesitation, to fill every gap of time in the Church's program with activities. They don't realise that the nearness of God is in their inward posture of submission and adoration towards God. This watered-down state of mind, that they practice, has caused them to think that the outward expression or noise is enough. Enough for sure to be a clanging symbol but has no depth. May my words find grace in your hearts to make that necessary and significant adjustment to accommodate the working of the Spirit in your midst.

I am writing this, mainly to you Pastors because I care for you. My frankness is because God cares for you. I and many like me, have been burdened with this for so long. May God plead His cause before you. I am just pointing out the error to help us all. Again, please forgive me if this offends you, but know that if in this you find God rebuking you, know that it is because He loves you.

I grieve within, every time I visit a Church that wants Revival but is actually doing everything opposite to what the Holy Spirit requires of them. The people sing and raise their hands, but the worship leader is focused on the song list, their performance, and ensuring that people are actively enjoying the music. They are not receptive when the Spirit suggests a different song or a time of stillness. They start and stop according to their schedule. The 'announcement' segments often follow straight away in their Church services and have more priority over worship time. This is an unnecessary interruption of a conversation taking place between God and those seeking to worship God in a heart-to-heart attitude before Him. These practices lack the wisdom and way of *the Cleft of the Rock.* It is the way that Moses learned as he positioned himself and humbly bowed down to worship God at the Cleft of the Rock. (I share more on that in Chapter 19).

Similarly, I observe when Churches call for a prayer meeting and they announce that it's going to be only for an hour. But when you get there to pray, they fill that hour with coffee and discussions of world news. They end up with little or no time to pray and wait on God. Why do we quote 2 Chronicles 7:14 in our prayers? This verse is not just a declaration. It is an invitation from the Father's heart to ours, to enter into a season of worship, fasting and hungering for God. God wants to heal the land, but He needs His vessels to be postured and aligned with the right heart attitude for God to come and be in their midst. They must be willing to work from God's appointed time and not theirs. God doesn't take His Work lightly. Would God grant you access to His Glory when you can't pay attention to His leading?

In our individual lives, and in our gatherings in Jesus' Name, the priority should be given to getting our hearts right, getting clean before God and waiting on the Spirit of the Lord to lead us into His program, rather than us dictating what we think is fitting. The Revival Fire of God will demand our attention and surrender. The great blessing of His Presence never comes until we adopt the *waiting, and yielding posture* in our worship. There He commands a blessing because we are ONE with Him (Psalms 133).

Often I see the worship leader is 'song list and people' conscious and not 'Spirit conscious.' The worship leader should sense where the Spirit is moving and lean into the Holy Ghost's leading. Any person filled with the desire for God, who wants to see the outpouring of His Presence, will struggle with being time-conscious. The wind will blow where it will, so it is with those who are led by the Spirit. They are willing to move where the Spirit is moving and adjust to what the Spirit wants. A thirty-minute limit can be for them like a taskmaster watching closely your every move making sure you aren't failing to observe the Church's protocols and way of flowing. But what about God's way of flowing? What about following the Glory Cloud—the Spirit of the Word, where and when He leads?

Some ministers keep looking at their watches while they preach instead of looking at the Holy Spirit for leadership on what to do in a meeting. And when they make the altar call, my heart aches for them, because they seem to try to activate or stir up eagerness in themselves and the people to see the Spirit Move, while not giving the Holy Spirit a chance to move or minister at all. They try to work the Power, instead of letting God flow through them as He wills. And because they had failed to discern the Moving of the Holy Spirit, the Word of Glory refrained Himself from manifesting His wondrous works because they were too busy being ministry-focused and not God-focused.

The irony of it all stirs me to deep intercessions and inward earnestness and compassion. I once saw an anointed man of God, walk to the front of the Church to ask for prayer. He wanted to receive prayer from the minister. But in fact, it was the minister who actually needed the prayer. I too have been in that same dilemma, being full of the Spirit and yet unable to minister and deliver God's Word to ministers and the sheep under their care, only because the ministers were unable to discern with their hearts, the Spirit of God in their midst. But I still was subservient and humble before those whom I knew truly needed the Word and prayer. In my heart, I asked God, "Oh Lord you have shown me what you want to give to them but how do I help them? For they are unable to perceive the Glory of Your Word in their midst. There is just no room for this Word at all!" I grieve over this needless suffering, which is caused by a lack of knowledge and ignorance. But our awareness should be to the Presence of God, and our allegiance to God's Call. For we have chosen to be aware of His Presence.

I speak plainly here. I have seen the Lord turn a whole room around in a moment, as soon as ministers recognise where the Anointing was in the room. I have learned to look to see who God is speaking to when the Word enters the room, and to see who is carrying the Word from God. Then I posture myself to lean in that direction with great interest in what God is doing. For I have learned to *know His Voice and trust His leading*. The *Spirit's initiative and leadership* take precedence and ascendency over ours. We cannot dictate how God comes to us and how He should work in our midst. But we can submit, and we should submit, if we want to see the work of His Spirit poured upon us. The healing, wholeness and breakthrough begin when the Spirit pours out His Glory.

There is a River whose streams make glad the City of God; the Holy Place of the Tabernacles of the Most High. God is in the midst of her and she shall not be moved (Psalms 46:3-5). If we desire to jump into the River of the Holy Spirit then we must discard our rigidness and restrictions, and get caught up in the current as the River of God flows. Or have we, the spiritual *Jeshuruns (upright ones)*, made ourselves fat on entertainment and excitement, and have forgotten the *Intent* of the Spirit of God, and have lightly esteemed the Rock of our Salvation (Deuteronomy 32:15)?

Humanly *structured* worship is backwardness and leads to dryness instead of a flourishing life in the Holy Spirit. That dryness is the cause of the current state of the Church's powerlessness and ineffectiveness amongst the people. It is the result of negligence and disobedience. But the way of the Spirit is boundless and abundant. And the more we behold Him in free, full and unrestricted worship, the more we become like Him. If you are a pastor and you can relate to what I have described about humanly structured worship service, or you recognise that this describes your own Church, I caution you by the Holy Ghost to take heed to this correction. If you want Revival, make room for God. If you have planned in your Church's calendar to invite a Revivalist to speak at your Church, don't do any of those restricting practices. But let the Spirit be free in your midst. You have nothing of real significance to lose, but so much to gain. Let God *lead, rest and abide* with His people, in His way and time. We can walk where He walks when we have fully become dependent on knowing where He walks.

The Waves of God are flowing with Heavenly aspiration to break upon you. God is after your heart. Do not miss your opportunity to obey that Command from God when it is made available to you. And like Elijah said to the woman, "Do not be afraid." Sure, Revival will stir up things both good and bad, but we should not be afraid to face the ugliness of the cleanup when the Spirit is at work, nor should we fear the persecutions that dare to oppose the Mighty Wave of the Spirit. We must become unhinged and valiant before our God, moving freely with Him in great boldness.

You see when you yield to deception; to entertain the enemy, you entertain the gates of hell, and they will inflict hell upon you. Israel's leaders had done this in Elijah's day, and the people, including the woman and her son, were suffering. But when you yield to the Word of the Spirit of Christ, you entertain the gates of Heaven, and you, by the power of the Spirit, overcome the enemy and destroy the yoke of darkness. When you adopt your yielding posture before the Lord, He will put the enemy to flight when His Spirit moves mightily in your midst. For greater is He (The Holy Spirit) that is in us, than he that is in the world.

GOD'S MOVE - GOD'S WAY - GOD'S OPEN DOOR

Only a Holy-Ghost-initiated Move becomes a Wave of healing, sanctification and transformation. God is not building organisations, He is building His Kingdom.

But we must connect and align with God for us to receive a great outpouring of the Spirit. Where there is that holy connection and exchange with God, there will also be the movement and momentum of God.

> " Where there is that holy connection and exchange with God, there will also be the movement and momentum of God.

The Revivalist who is sent to you is God's *open door* for God Himself to enter through that door (His Fire Carrier) to reach you.

I reach out to you ministers, who are currently shepherds overseeing the flock; be attentive to the leading of the Holy Spirit. Be responsive to the *Anointing* and *the Word of Glory* that enters the room. And if you already noticed a certain individual who carries the marks of Revival in your Church, make room for them. Know that you are making room for God. Be obedient to God when He tells you to do something.

Pastors, I encourage you to start training the flock to not be seat warmers, but *Fire carriers*. The people of God need to make that seat their place to kneel before God and remain until a Word from the Lord rests upon them. For we are all called to go forth and shine the light not only as believers but as witnesses for Christ.

Furthermore, you must possess an attitude of waiting. Anyone who desires to be a carrier of the Fire of God must learn how to wait till the Word comes and lingers upon them. You cannot be a

Revivalist if you don't have the patience to wait for the Word. The one hundred and twenty saints in the Upper Room of Jerusalem are a perfect example of this timeless truth.

That's why I continuously preach this truth that *Holy Spirit Revival* carries this visible sign: God abides in the midst of His people, who have yielded to make room for God. You already possess that ability to yield, but don't ignore the Anointing, as you might quench the Holy Spirit, the Giver of that Anointing. If you flow with the Holy Spirit, He'll flow with you. If you will make room for Him, He will make room for you. When we make room for God, we are saying, it's what God wants and not what we want: He is looking for our hearts and not our outer works; He is looking for our broken hearts and not our garments.

Joel 2:13

> And rend your heart, and not your garments, and turn unto the LORD your God: for He is gracious and merciful, slow to anger, and of great kindness, and repenteth him of the evil.

If you say yes to His Will and go where He sends you, He will be there *when* you go and *where* you go. Go with His song, His message, His noise, His, heart, and His movement.

When you spend moments of devoted fellowship with Him, God will eventually come to you, for He loves a yielded heart. He will be drawn to your yearning and longing to worship Him (James 4:8).

For God knows how to multiply the fish and the bread in your hands. The *Rod of His Word* is in your hands also and He will lead you with it if you will trust Him. The promises of God are steadfast. And when God speaks, He speaks direction, healing, transformation, provision, promotion, comfort and encouragement. The Holy One will demonstrate His mighty works where He is made Lord. God pours generously upon those who will wait on Him. He pours upon them His gifts and callings and empowers the saints to go forth and do mighty exploits for Him. For He is the abundant God who wants to Move your heart to respond to the breakthrough that is at hand. For the Word of faith is near to you, even in your mouth and in your heart. That is the Word we preach (Romans 10:8).

Prayer:

Lord, may we obey and surrender when Your Word comes to us. Oh, Move our hearts Holy Ghost with Your holy calling so that we will not settle with what is a form of godliness and miss out on the essence and fullness of Heaven for us. We are here Lord. Have Your way in us, Jesus. Amen

HE MUST INCREASE, BUT I MUST DECREASE

Isaiah 40:31

But they that wait upon the LORD shall renew their strength; they shall mount up with wings as eagles; they shall run, and not be weary; and they shall walk, and not faint.

I love what John the Baptist said to his disciples when they asked him about the Christ,

"...He must increase, but I must decrease (John 3:27-30)."

The waiting posture is very much that. For anyone who desires to be used by the Lord, to decrease means to submit all control and leadership to the Spirit of Christ. When God leads, we experience Revival. When we lead, all we see is the Church struggling to have an encounter with God. We must decrease so the Glory of Christ can be made manifest in our midst. That is our place before the Lord. Our worship is not only an outward expression but it is the bowing down and prostrating of our hearts before the Living God. As we lie prostrate before the Lord, we decrease to the point that there is none of us and only all of Him. For we must decrease that He, our Lord Jesus, may Increase. It's *our decrease* that draws the *increase of God*. If you want the increase, then you must decrease. If you want the increase, yield before the One true God until He comes into the room.

I encourage you to draw near to God and surrender to Him. When you pour out your worship to Him, He will lead you. In fact, He will take you into the deep things of the Spirit where you have not been before. He will take you there if you will set your eyes on Him and choose to walk toward Him with all of your heart, without restriction, fear or hesitation. The *deep of God* calls unto the deep in you. That is a realm of its own. That same realm is tapped into by our surrender. It is from that *place,* that the boldness of the Spirit rises. You see, when you walk in deep places, you speak like deep places. Every Word God puts in your mouth, He puts it to bear fruit.

> " When you walk in deep places, you speak like deep places.

God is looking for a people that are willing to abide. These are they that live in *the Sound of His Presence*. They are the Psalm 91:1 person that will *abide* in His Word. They abide in the Power of the One who draws them closer to the Throne of the Living God. For they want nothing but to know Him and His Presence. They want nothing but Him. For they have understood that the great God can do marvellously in their midst only when they rid themselves of their own self, decrease before God and let all their attention be only upon Christ.

They have understood that *the abiding posture* is what God is looking for. The attitude to decrease before God is that worship posture. There is something so beautiful about that abiding posture. God works behind the scenes while you abide in Him. God goes ahead of you to make the way straight, while you abide. For the Lord knows you will respond when He Calls. And When God calls you, His Spirit will stir you to run; you have to run, you have to go, you have to respond.

Hebrews 12:1-2

Wherefore seeing we also are compassed about with so great a cloud of witnesses, let us lay aside every weight, and the sin which doth so easily beset us, and LET US RUN with patience the race that is set before us, Looking unto Jesus the author and finisher of our faith; who for the joy that was set before him endured the cross, despising the shame, and is set down at the right hand of the throne of God.

CHAPTER 10

THE GREAT INDUCTION & ANOINTING SERVICE

For this cause came I unto this hour, to preach to you the Knowledge of His Glory in Christ Jesus

John 3:27-30

"...A man can receive nothing except it be given Him from Heaven. Ye yourselves bear with me witness, that I said, I am not the Christ, that I am sent before Him...He must increase, but I must decrease."

It has taken me many years of longsuffering, strife, pain, fasting and prayerfulness to get to this point where I am now able to share this glorious event with you by the grace of the Lord Jesus. That *Release* to openly share it finally came on Sunday 29th January 2023, when God used our dear brother in the Lord, Pastor Sekove. After I had presented the document to him, he read it and then spoke from the sincerity of his heart, "Pastor Norman, I know how much this means to you.

CHAPTER 10 — *The Great Induction & Anointing Service*

But no one will ever know about the encounter if you don't share it. There is a message in it for the Church. I know you have carried this Word for a long time and have guarded it carefully with all your heart, but now is the time to reveal it to God's people."

When Pastor Sekove spoke these words, the Word of the Spirit came upon me and said to me, "Whatever he has said is from Me. Whatever he said, I want you to obey it. I have made him say these words. It is time for Me to reveal My Glory and Desire to My people. The time is now."

The interesting bit to this story was, that we were only obeying God's instructions which came to Sekove, Miriam, Marsha, Olivia and me. At that time Miriam and Marsha were not present for the release as God wanted Miriam to receive the document via email and pray on it and He wanted Marsha to receive an invitation although He knew Marsha was going to be busy that day. In our natural minds, all of these weren't necessary. We didn't understand the reason why God had it this way, including me. But as weird as the instruction was, they followed through with the directives that the Lord had given to me and I am honestly humbled by their willingness and very grateful that they trusted that it was God who issued those directives. And certainly, their obedience stood out and spoke great conviction to my heart. I was reminded again that what God considers important He treats also with deliberate directives, great care and significance, just like the 'John Thomas' instruction that ensured John should fly to Goroka on a very specific day.

Now at the table as Pastor Sekove spoke, then came *the Release*. It felt very much like Jesus telling John the Baptist, "Let's obey what the Father wants. We are fulfilling the plan of God for all righteousness." And even if John didn't fully understand why he had to baptise Jesus. I can only say, that God knows all things and He knew there would be a John the Baptist who would be there to baptise Jesus and in my case, He knew there would be a Sekove, Miriam, Marsha, and Olivia to carry out the Heavenly instruction to bring *the official Heavenly release*. What a great privilege it is to serve God.

There at the dining table, Pastor Sekove, Olivia and I after talking a bit more, we then sealed our concerns and deep contemplations with a prayer of agreement. We prayed with thanksgiving and worship and asked God to bless each of us who had obeyed the instruction. That included those present, those assigned to receive the document and those invited.

But before you read the details of the holy meeting prepared by the Lord, I would like to emphasise an important point. Please, consider with great seriousness that I desire no glory from man. It has taken a lot of yielding, and trusting the Holy Ghost for many years. There were many stretched-out periods of no momentum or acceleration from my earthly viewpoint. Yet, Heaven has always been on time and on point. I have waited twenty-one years to tell you about this dream.

I believe that in releasing this dream; to shout it from the housetops (Luke 12:3), that the great level of Manifestation and Glory equated in this dream will become our atmosphere and life in the Spirit, because the time is now. God wants to minister the reality and power of His desire to you and bring you into deeper counsels of the Spirit. May the fulness of His revelation knowledge be for you *the Great Tide of Revival* that must pour upon the land with a great gushing and fill every one of us. The Lord be glorified.

When you read the details of the dream I had received from the Lord and consider my reflections that follow, I have no doubt that you will gladly concur with my thoughts also; that I am only a man with many flaws, yet the desire and selection of God rest upon whom He has chosen. We are chosen, not of our own will but

CHAPTER 10 *The Great Induction & Anointing Service*

of *His own selection*. We are marked for Heaven's cause even amidst our own struggles.

I believe as I obey the Lord now to reveal the contents of the dream to you that I am fully released to step into the new which God has spoken of, and look forward to times of immense soaking and overflowing in God, with the congregation and household of the Most High. For when God appoints a season to you, He also ensures that everything He told you about it, will come to pass.

> "For when God appoints a season to you, He also ensures that everything He told you about it, will come to pass.

My life has been one mixed with blessings and setbacks, yet God in the Power of His love has reached down to me and has rescued and strengthened me greatly. For certain, He took my broken pieces and put me together. I consider myself the least among the ministers of God as I can testify to the fact that God uses broken and unwanted vessels and pours His Glory into them. There is no other god like our God who qualifies the unqualified, and cleanses the heart that comes to Him and seeks His Face—that is the Power of the message of the Cross of Jesus.

I am in tears as I write this. For I know the abundant work of grace manifested toward me. It is healing to my soul. That same abundant grace of God is like an outstretched Arm to the hopeless. For He gives them hope and courage when they are weak.

The Lord has kept me this far by His grace and mercy. For He knows how fragile our hearts are and He will hold us gently with open Arms, and at the same time, He is strong and mighty against the enemy for our sakes. He will lead us even in our own uncertainties. It is He who has considered us worthy to receive this gracious inheritance of Salvation, like that man on the cross beside the Lord. He chose Jesus and therefore became worthy to enter His Will. How magnificent is the grace of God towards us? It is the overflowing Love of God that has reached out to us to save us. For out of His own will did He beget us so that the testimony of His Love may also reach many like us; who may be lost in the world. For they too are appointed to receive that same call of salvation and reconciliation. What a mighty God we serve. For through His Son Jesus Christ, we are made whole. Therefore, if we must boast our boast is in Him who has worked a mighty work of transformation in us. It touches my heart exceedingly, to think that God would consider using any of us, who are by nature, sinful and unworthy of His Presence and Glory. Let the Excellency of the Power be of God and none of us.

Tears fill my eyes as I am overwhelmed by the *Agape Love* of Christ Jesus, the Lamb of God who has made us kings and priests unto God our Father; to Him be Glory and dominion forever, Amen (Revelation 1:5-6).

He is our Beloved; Jesus our Saviour and the Anointed One of God, to whom we owe our lives. And with the twenty-four elders, we bow down to worship and cast our crowns before Him who is worthy of all Glory; the King of all kings, and Lord of all lords.

2 Corinthians 4:6-7

For God, who commanded the Light to shine out of darkness, hath shined in our hearts, to give the Light of the knowledge of the Glory of God in the Face of Jesus Christ. But we have this Treasure in earthen vessels, that the Excellency of the Power may be of God, and not of us.

VISION: (Sunday 18th February 2002)
THE PRELUDE

It was in the early morning hours of Sunday the 18th of February 2002. I had spent the night praying and after that, I was taken hastily in the spirit, like what Ezekiel experienced. An angel of the Lord had picked me up and hurriedly carried me into the spirit realm. In the spirit realm, we travelled through what looked like a water well that led to a deep clear ocean. Amazingly, we were in the water and I could still breathe. That really intrigued me, because I was immediately conscious of my breathing as soon as we entered the water. As he carried me with tremendous speed, he then said to me, "I am sent by God who sent His Son Jesus Christ to die on the Cross of Calvary, and He was raised to life three days later and now sits in Power and in Glory at the right-hand side of the Father." As we travelled deeper into the ocean, he then asked me a question, "What do you want the Most High God; the Almighty One to do for you?"

I answered the angel instinctively as I had been seeking God's face concerning His calling for me, "I want to see God. I want to see His Glory. I desire for my prayers to be answered. I desire that He attend to me even in times of trouble. And I want so much to be used by God. I want to be His holy vessel."

The angel replied, "God has heard your request and will do what you have asked. He will come in Glory soon. His Glory will fall and His Revival is near. His great Power is about to be released on His people. So be ready. Be prepared; be ready."

I thought to myself, wow! what a wonderful vision. Am I really going to get my request? What a special message to receive too. The Psalms 37:4 scripture came to mind as we travelled on.

The Great Induction & Anointing Service   **CHAPTER 10**

Psalms 37:4

Delight thyself also in the LORD; and He shall give thee the desires of thine heart.

I quickly understood that God wasn't just taking me on a joy ride. There was a reason for the short trip. When we reached the bottom of the ocean, I found myself, again sitting on my bed and the angel was gone. I reached for my Bible that lay by the pillow and there I came out of the vision.

Wow! That was fantastic and totally out of this world. But I somewhat had mixed emotions. I felt unworthy and yet so privileged to have received such a wonderful encounter. Just when I thought you couldn't get any better than that, it seemed that conversation with the angel was only a precursor to the main event that would happen in a dream I would receive on the next morning; Monday the 19th of February 2002.

DREAM:
(Monday 19th February 2002)

THE GREAT INDUCTION & ANOINTING SERVICE

In the dream, I was met by the Holy Spirit (dressed as a powerful man of God) who came to me with His ministering angels following right behind Him. Without wasting a second, He said to me, "Son, do you know that the preparations for your Anointing-Ordination-Induction Service are complete and it is ready and waiting for you right now? We came to pick you up."

I could see the joy and excitement on His face as He said to me, "People all over the nation and the world are attending the ceremony. The Service is on at midday today."

So I dropped whatever I was doing and I followed the Holy Spirit and the angels to the Church building (The House of Worship) where the ceremony was going to be held. When we arrived at the building, it was a magnificent structure the size of three stadiums combined and was made of what looked like marble and the finest wood.

Alongside, the roads that lead to the Church dome were filled with people from shoulder to shoulder. These people came from all over the nation and the world, from all walks of life and were waving banners that glorified the Name of our Lord Jesus Christ.

When we entered the dome, it was filled with people. I noticed the colourful-adorned choir; dressed uniformly in red, white, blue, and gold. This was the choir of holy angels that stood at the choir section of the stage area, singing praises and worshipping the Lord. They sang on from the beginning of the service to the end with heavenly songs, singing unto the Lord.

The atmosphere was Heavenly, and I was lost for words; I couldn't comprehend the magnitude of this special occasion. I thought to myself, "Who am I? I am nobody, and unworthy of such honour. What is special about me that all of Heaven and Earth stood still for this one occasion?"

I prayed to the Lord, "Oh, God what is so special about me? For I am unworthy of such an honour; that You have stirred the hearts of Your people who have come from far and near to this holy occasion. They have come on this very special day to witness the Lord's Anointing upon me. I am unworthy to receive such an honour from Your gracious Hand. Gracious, Lord I say thank You sincerely. Not my will but Your Will be done, Amen."

And as I was finishing this prayer the Holy Spirit said to me with exceeding joy, "Look Norman; people from all walks of life, both great and small, have come. Great and mighty men, leaders of nations, even the mighty prophets of God, powerful evangelists and ministers of the world!"

I remained speechless as joy overwhelmed me and filled my heart because of the grandeur of the event; for it was beyond me. It's that special feeling you get when it is your special day when all the attention is on you.

Then The Holy Spirit led me up to the stage and directed me to my seat where I sat amongst the dignitaries (an exclusive VIP-only section). My special seat was closest to the pulpit where everyone could see me.

Then *the Anointing and Induction Service* began.

The Holy Spirit (now dressed up as the great man of God, in a silver and blue suit) was the Master of Ceremony for the occasion.

CHAPTER 10 — *The Great Induction & Anointing Service*

He explained to me that the clothes He wore meant THE FAVOUR OF GOD!

And as He took His place at the pulpit to speak, the Church became quiet; even the streets filled with the crowds as far as the eyes could see were quiet and a great silence and holiness filled the place. It was as if everyone knew what to do at that very moment and were in harmony through the *Anointing Ceremony.*

Then the Holy Spirit said to the Church of God in a loud voice,

"God has brought all of us here to witness and take part in the ANOINTING–ORDINATION–INDUCTION of our most beloved brother NORMAN MOREA TRENT SABADI. The Anointing Ceremony will be done this day to set him apart for God's special work and that is to:

- Be a minister to the nations of the world;
- To proclaim God's Divine Power and His Divine Nature to all human race on Earth;
- To set the captives free;
- To lose the bondage of the oppressed; and
- To bring healing and Revival to all in need."

The Holy Spirit continued, "Our Service here now is purposed for this reason; that God Almighty Who has called Norman by His grace—has ordained him and will anoint him to be the Carrier, Leader, and Servant of the great work which God has placed."

It was here that I began to understand why this service was being held. My ears were attentive to what the Holy Spirit said, and I tried to grasp the magnitude of *this Great Calling*. My eyes widened with wonder and my heart pounded faster with anticipation. Yet, a certain calmness gripped my being. It felt holy and peaceful at the same time.

Then after saying *the Ordination Affirmation and The Official Declaration of God* for the meeting, The Holy Spirit then led the

Church into the next part of the Service. It was time for the *Induction Prayer*.

First, the Holy Spirit prayed in a loud Voice and offered the prayer for the Ceremony, praying unto the Heavenly Father with holy Words of blessing.

Before the Holy Spirit could offer *the Prayer of Induction* for me and for the mission that God called me to, He asked the Church to rise and agree with Him in prayer.

The Church then stood up in unison and raised their hands toward me in oneness following the leading of the Holy Ghost.

An amazing tangibleness of the Power of the Spirit was present as I watched hands all across this great big sanctuary raised. I had never felt *a tangible Unity* like this before. There was such a holy silence; and great love, respect, and reverence for God's Presence saturated the place. I could feel the holiness and blessedness of God caressing my being.

My spirit was lifted to witness and you could see God's fear and honour filled the atmosphere throughout the grand dome and along the streets as far as the eyes could see.

Then the Holy Spirit walked up to me and took my hands into His and began to pray, "Oh, Lord God who created all things, Almighty One, the Most High God, there is none beside You. You alone deserve all Glory, Honour, Power, Worship and Adoration.

You reign over all things and Your Word is perfect and eternal. Gracious Lord have mercy on us and stretch forth Your Hands from Heaven, from where You sit on Your Holy Throne.

Lord God, let Norman see You Oh, Holy One (Matthew 5:8 and Hebrew 12:14);

Lord God may Norman see Your Glory and may Norman be Your habitation (John 14:21-23, Psalms 132);

Lord God, with every prayer Norman utters, let it be heard; let every cry that Norman raises to You be attended to.

May he find favour with You Lord. And even before he makes his request known to You, oh Lord hear the prayers of his heart and answer Norman speedily. Oh Lord, respond to Norman's prayers and supplications made unto You, answer him even before he asks of You.

Mighty and powerful God use him mightily in Your work, that he may be a sweet smelling fragrance to all humankind, and above all, unto You; that You may be pleased and that You may be glorified.

Oh, Lord God let Your light shine through him that he may be the light for those who are lost in the dark.

May the Lord Jesus Christ be seen in him.

Prosper Norman, and let everything he touches be prosperous;

May Your blessings rest on him and may success and prosperity be upon his life.

Bless his offspring and anoint them. Oh, Lord God, I pray that You will also prosper them (Psalms 112, Isaiah 44:3-5)."

Then the Holy Spirit led everyone into deep adoration and worship unto the Lord praying in many tongues and praying with intense intercession for about one hour. The singing and worship were beautiful. And the sweet-smelling aroma of prayers and worship filled the House of God. It was the splendidness of God displayed.

After the Holy Spirit concluded the beautiful prayer, there was once again a stillness and great silence in the Church. The air was unceasingly filled with the holiness of The Lord God, it was so pure.

The only sounds we heard were the wonderful, soft, and pleasing singing of the choir of angels adorned in beautiful colours, which stood behind the podium. They were singing the whole time, even during the prayer hour from the beginning of the service right to the end. I enjoyed this atmosphere and my heart was filled with love for the Lord God.

Now it was time for *the Anointing Ceremony* and great anticipation was in the air.

Then stood, one that was dressed in elegant priestly garments. He looked magnificent in appearance. At first; observing Him from where He stood, I didn't realise that this was the Son of God, Jesus Christ our Lord and Saviour.

It was only when He walked up to me, that (as I describe now); *Love, Peace, Holiness, Power* and *Glory* walked up to me.

He was dressed with many crowns placed within His main Crown, so elegantly adorned. His countenance was magnificent to look upon, filled with Glory that beamed as lights of many colours glowing brightly upon His being. The precious stones on His Crowns glistened as stars embedded into the Crown. His white and gold garment shimmered with the Glory of God.

Knowledge entered me in that very second and I knew I was in the Presence of the Messiah; the Great High Priest, the Captain of my Salvation and the Lord God of my life.

My heart soared and shook with reverence at the same time within me. To think that Jesus Christ, the King of Glory was in the midst of us and now standing before me, was far beyond what my simple mind could grasp.

The Glory and Power of God was so mightily upon Him my spirit cried out within me testifying and ministering to me the words, "He is the Holy One of God who has redeemed us by His precious Blood and by whom we are all called and sanctified to be holy and to walk in His Glory".

Now as Jesus walked up onto the podium and toward me, He spoke with a gentleness that possessed great authority saying,

"Norman Morea Trent Sabadi! Please get down on your knees before the Lord God! For all of Heaven and Heaven's angels and all who are gathered here, are now witnessing God's favour and mark of ownership upon you. Bow in reverence before the Almighty One!"

I quivered so evidently, with reverence before Him. And with trembling, I got down on my knees and prayed in my heart to God desiring in my heart that the Will of the Lord be done.

Then Jesus said, "Norman…(He paused) God Calls you and Anoints you to reach the nations with the Word of God. Preach His Gospel of Peace and Power."

(I have included a few scriptures as references here. Isaiah 43:1, Isaiah 61, Isaiah 42:1-11, Jeremiah 1:1-10, 1 Peter 1:1-16, Ephesians 3, Psalms 145).

Then the Lord Jesus laid His hands on me, upon my head and declared in a mighty Voice, "In the Name of The Father, Son, and Holy Ghost, I ANOINT you to be God's vessel!"

He then turned and looked over His left shoulder to three angels waiting to serve Him. The angels were dressed in a long brown tunic and standing slightly behind Him. They all had their posture bowed low before the Lord, and not a single moment did they raise their head to look at Jesus.

The three angels each stood with a jar of *Anointing Oil* by their side, in an orderly manner—standing one beside the other with their heads bowed before the Lord.

And each jar was about 80cm to 90cm high and about 25cm in diameter.

The first one closest to Jesus then picked up the first jar of Anointing Oil and handed it to Jesus.

The Holy Spirit later told me that the *Anointing Oil* was prepared specially for this Anointing Service. The jars had a unique design on them and were painted blue and white with fine gold and red linings perfectly marked in the design.

Then as the Lord Jesus took the first jar from the angel and turned to me, He then began to pour the *Holy Anointing Oil* on me while speaking Words under His breath.

(At that exact moment, the whole Church had already stood up and was in deep silent prayer as The Lord Jesus anointed me).

The Anointing Oil poured from the crown of my head to the soles of my feet, and it also went into my body and my whole being with my clothes was soaked with it.

I have never felt such Power flow through my being. The Power of God was heavy upon me, and it surged through my body like Fire multiplied thousands of times over.

It's ineffable and incomparable. No amount of descriptive words could express fully the Glory and splendour of His Power.

Then Jesus took the next jar of *Anointing Oil* and poured it on me again as He did with the first.

He took a third one from the third angel and did the same.

My being was on Fire, as the Holy Ghost filled me and His Power clothed me.

I was taken over by *the Dunamis of God*, and a profound *brokenness of the Holy Spirit* lingered in my spirit. I felt Glory on the inside and outside of me at the same time.

(The Holy Spirit then told me that each jar of oil poured out on me represented the Father, the Son, and the Holy Spirit, and *these Three are One*).

Words can't account in any way at all; it's indescribable. The Glory of God was so full upon my being nothing in this world can compare to it.

As tears streamed down my eyes, my spirit cried out from within me, with brokenness, "Lord I am Your servant. I am Yours. Take all of me!"

The aroma of the *Anointing Oil* was so sweet and so powerful it filled the atmosphere and the reverence of God was upon everyone that attended. The Glory of God was so heavy upon the place neither those who were in the Church dome nor those on the streets could speak.

Then the Lord Jesus declared in a loud Voice, "The floor upon which the Anointing Oil was poured and where I stand is holy grounds and no one is to walk on that floor where the Anointing Oil has spread and covered.

The Anointing Oil must NOT be wiped off the floor after the Service, nor is anyone allowed to touch it: for it is the Holy Oil of the Lord God. And Norman is not to be touched nor spoken to (right now) as the Fire and Glory of God now rests upon him."

Truly, Jesus Baptises with the Fire and the Holy Ghost. Nothing in this world can compare to the Power of God.

I was so broken and cleansed within my heart and my tears just kept pouring while I sat on my knees in complete awe and overtaken by God.

You probably can sense the depth of my wonderment. Words fail me even to this day to describe the *Kavod*—*the weight of the Glory of God.*

Gazing through the streaming of tears, I raised my head briefly to see as the crowd of saints began to slowly and quietly depart. They all looked so happy. Their reverence for God was evident. The meeting had ended and the Lord Jesus still stood there beside me. I noticed my elder sister Airegi Joan, a few rows back from the front, waving at me, and was so happy for me. I could feel her joy for me.

Was she, being a part of the dream, a sign from God for a future time? I believe so. But I should note the meaning of her name as a reference. I believe this is important also:

> 'Airegi' in our ancient primal (Molēgolē and Ririga) language (on my father's side) means POWER AND AUTHORITY—"*Lohia*" *lords or chiefs* (a name describing our

paramount chiefly lineage)—and Joan, is the feminized version of 'John' (from Hebrew: Yohanah meaning: GOD IS GRACIOUS! John was the one who came in the Spirit of Elijah before the Christ,

When I awoke from the dream, the Glory of God still rested mightily upon me, with great awe and brokenness. Tears coursed down my face upon my bed, as I worshipped the Lord.

The Lord is my Witness. Believe me or not, my whole bed was soaking with the *Holy Anointing Oil* from my head right down to my feet. I was thoroughly drenched with it and I also could smell the fragrance of the holy Anointing Oil in the room.

How does one describe this supernatural phenomenon? No human explanation could give a reason as to how the *Anointing Oil* in my dream was now on my bed and still all over my body and clothes.

I hurried off my bed and knocked at my parent's bedroom door. I then told Mum about the dream. (Dad was away for work and land matters in Port Moresby at the time I had the dream).

Mum believed it immediately and at the same time was in awe and wonder over what the Lord had just done. And much like Mary and Joseph were, she pondered on this thing in her heart. What would become of me?

Even to this day, I feel that Anointing so strong upon me. When the Glory of the Word comes into the room and rests upon my being.

Especially, when I get into deep prayer and worship, I am again, soaked in His Presence. The Power of His Word comes and rests so heavily upon me to *preach*.

And I have learnt that every time I open my mouth to preach, His Power becomes tangible, it changes the atmosphere I stand in. I have seen hearts burning before me with great conviction, and become captivated by the Fire of His Word; that great stirring which is the inspiration of the Holy Ghost.

Oh, that this will be for you too. I have nothing to gain from this. For I only want Jesus. I am so thirsty for Jesus. I want Jesus. I desire that the Glory of Christ be formed in you. That you become the people of His Glory. For *the Fire of His Presence* wants to abide upon us together and be in our midst.

Hallelujah! The Glory of the Word! Father, we praise You for the Anointing which is Your mark of ownership and favour upon us.

Oh, that Holy Calling, may it never let up till we are all overtaken by the fullness of God.

And like Paul, I declare the same tenderhearted thoughts; that I am the least amongst the Apostles. I am the least among the Ministers of God. I desire no Glory, but that the Glory of the Lord be formed in you.

I know that though I may feel unworthy, God has made me worthy. And though I am sincere and unpretentious, I must at the same time, be confident in the Anointing of God that rests to do His Will. The valiant God must win a mighty battle against the enemy. For He shall, by the Power of His Word, defeat all His enemies and subdue them under His Feet.

NOW IS THE TIME FOR REVIVAL. Now is the day of refreshing. For the 'Break of Dawn' is at hand. Let us enter into THE BLESSING OF OUR GOD with confidence.

To God be all Glory and Honour, Power and Praise for the Great Work He has called us to fulfil, Amen, Amen and Amen.

ANOINTED? BUT WHY ME? I AM NOT WORTHY...

Believe me, I have asked this question many times over the twenty-one years. That is a long time to be troubled over the Heavenly Dream and I have had no earthly counsel to help. But the Holy Spirit has patiently mentored me.

Sure, you have read about all the wonderful encounters of the Power and Presence of God. But what has that done to me as a person?

The lessons are too abundant to fit into one book. But I will impart what is necessary for this God-Assignment.

We have this holy treasure in our earthen vessels and this glorious inheritance has been paid in full by our Lord Jesus. For this reason, we do not belong to ourselves, but we belong to Christ. The excellency of the Glory and Power will remain God's forever. Ours is the blessedness of being considered worthy in His eyes. I can't fathom the depth of God's grace; that Jesus would count us as valuable and *selected* vessels marked for His Holy Assignment on Earth.

I have to admit, if I were to include all the parts called *'the sins I committed and where I failed,'* this book would be twenty times thicker, much to my shame and disgrace.

It would turn out to be more of my infamy and disgust rather, than my testimony of the saving Power of Jesus Christ.

But the truth is, I am wretched beyond help and without a doubt, the saving Power of Jesus, did break through the strongholds of darkness and redeem me so brilliantly beyond my own ability to comprehend. I am washed in the Blood of the Lamb. Knowing in my heart, that Christ was despised so that I could be accepted. This is a 'LOVE' I can't explain.

I know that the enemy will attempt to use my failures and past sins to accuse, discredit and bring disrepute to myself and the Work that God has already accomplished through me.

But, I stand to lose nothing. I have died to the world and have chosen to give myself fully to Christ. That is what grace can do—I too was saved by that *Amazing Grace*.

My one desire is to gain Christ and only Him; and to come into the full knowledge of Him, whom I love so dearly and have given my life completely to.

"Yes Jesus, none of me and all of You."

So, with boldness, I gladly proclaim that the *Finished Work of Christ is being perfected in us by the Holy Spirit Who abides in us.* For in our weaknesses, not only is His *Strength* made perfect in us, but His *Word* also is made perfect in us who believe in Him. Because His Word is His Joy and Strength.

I testify with all boldness that the Power of God is in our weaknesses and God's Voice is louder there. Because that's where He finds brokenness and a contrite heart. That's the true offering that the Lord delights in. He looks for brokenness and contriteness.

> "The Finished Work of Christ is being perfected
> in us by the Holy Spirit who abides in us.

Oh, that we will behold His Glory together and be given fully to the Holy Calling of our Priesthood in Him. For we are the sheep of His pasture and the remnant of His first love.

> "The Power of God is in our weaknesses;
> God's Voice is louder there

I am overcome with emotion because of the amazing grace bestowed upon us. For The Lord shall show us the path of life; in His Presence is fullness of Joy. And at His Right Hand, there are pleasures forevermore (Psalms 16:11).

Jeremiah 31:3

The LORD hath appeared of old unto me, saying, Yea, I have loved thee with an everlasting love: therefore with lovingkindness have I drawn thee.

Why then does the Sovereign God choose fallen man even if none of us are perfect? That, right there, is the actual message of the Gospel of our Salvation: the redeeming Power of our Lord Jesus Christ. God commended His love towards us, in that, while were yet sinners, Christ died for us (Romans 5:8). Paul wrote to the Christians in Rome and said (Romans 5:1-5), (paraphrasing here)

> "We have peace with God through our Lord Jesus Christ; that by faith we have access to this abundant grace—yes this unmerited favour and undeserved blessing.
>
> We are glad when we face tribulations, knowing that our tribulations build in us patience, experience and hope. And that hope gives us confidence because it is the love of God poured into our hearts and expressed in our imperfect lives by the Holy Ghost, who was given to us to help us."

We have the Holy Spirit to help us through our weaknesses; to chisel and mould us by the Power of His Word working in us, and to reach the fullness that is in Christ.

I emphasise the importance of the Holy Spirit and the Word, made available to us by a New and Holy Covenant established by Christ's death, resurrection, ascension, and sending of the Spirit.

Great is our confidence in the God of our Calling. The trumpet of our most excellent and mighty Warrior—Conqueror; Jesus Christ who is able to quicken those who come to Him.

God wants us in His family. He desires our fellowship every day, just like He did when Adam was still in the garden. He will delight in you and fill your cup when you also find that special place to honour His magnificence.

God uses imperfections and flaws. If you're worried about them, be assured you were part of His plan a long time ago.

> " God uses imperfections and flaws. If you're worried about them, be assured you were part of His plan a long time ago.

Our faith in Christ doesn't make us weak at all. Instead, it gives us the courage to act even in the midst of our hardships, failures and trials; we act because we know He is near and His Word resides with us. For it is the Life and Word of the Spirit dwelling in us that grants us the courage to pursue the path to live boldly for God.

And if we are to take hold of the fullness of Christ Jesus our Lord, we must forget those things which are behind us now and go forth to those things which are before us. Hope, therefore becomes one, of living joy, in brokenness, yet with much assurance.

And when we pursue Christ, we find ourselves continuously being washed by the Spirit of the Word. Our struggling, sinful nature is dealt a mighty blow by the Spirit each day, as we surrender our weaknesses to God.

With that said, when you sit with me, you will notice, that I love good company and that I am a simple man. The only difference is God in my life. I am very much still as ordinary as you are; a man still full of blemishes, but I am becoming less of my old self, and becoming more like Christ as I fellowship with Him, each and every day.

My life in Jesus remains broken in unbroken fellowship before the Lord. I understand that the Glory of His Word is being formed in us, who have set our gaze upon the Anointed One and the brightness of His Glory Cloud. We have looked to the Throne of His mercies and judgements where the newness of God dwells.

It has been the work of the Holy Spirit in us to encourage us forward. We are exhorted to stay the course and go after Christ. We do not turn away from that great Love. Rather, we become elevated by the Hand of that abundant mercy, which is 'new' for us every morning. Great is the faithfulness of our God (Lamentations 3:8). Hence, we must press on to that wonderful blessing of the high Calling given to us.

Lamentations 3:22-26

It is of the LORD's mercies that we are not consumed, because His compassions fail not. They are new every morning: great is Thy faithfulness. The LORD is my portion, saith my soul; therefore will I hope in Him. The LORD is good unto them that wait for Him, to the soul that seeketh Him. It is good that a man should both hope and quietly wait for the salvation of the LORD.

THE ANOINTING
&
ABUNDANT GRACE

We can find many examples of the grace of God working to lead the saints in the Bible; both in the Old and New Testament.

Take King David as our first example. Although he was anointed by the Prophet Samuel as the chosen king of Israel, even after the Spirit rested on him, there were many trials ahead.

Note that God chose David by the condition of his heart and not by the outward perceptions of our human standards, nor by the righteousness of his own works.

David went on to slay the mighty Goliath and David also defeated many armies. Yet, he was nowhere closer to the throne. In fact, it was more the adverse than the expected. David didn't become king immediately after Samuel anointed him. He spent his early years running from King Saul. What a horrible predicament; to know that he was going to be king, yet the current king was pursuing his life.

But David had a deeper knowing of his calling only because the Spirit rested on him to affirm that call. When you know the Call of God upon your life, regardless of what you face, that Call speaks louder within your spirit and causes you to take courage with prayerfulness and persistence.

There is something so powerful when a person grabs a hold of the vision birthed in them. They run after it with courage. And this is how the Anointing upon David's life worked on his mind and heart.

The Anointing is able to work mightily in us whether it is in the storm or when there is calmness and peace. The Anointing will work in the green pastures and in the valley of the shadow of death; in chains and freedom.

That same Anointing was given to mark you out and set you apart for the Call. You can be confident that the Anointing upon your life is stronger than the forces of darkness and is able to keep you through your yielding to the Holy Spirit. The enemy, with much effort, may seek to detour and stop you from reaching the high Calling of your destiny, but even they are not able to hinder the Spirit of the Word burning in you.

Jesus gave us that powerful insight when He proclaimed, "The gates of hell will not prevail against you (Matthew 16:18)."

For the rulers of darkness know very well that when you understand your place in God, you become a formidable force for the Kingdom of Light. That holy place in God is not only our sonship by adoption but our priesthood in Christ. That place becomes evident when the Anointing speaks; it speaks. For it is the fearlessness and confidence of God displayed. It is heavenly assurance that no matter what the enemy throws at you, God is going to bring you through with a strong Arm.

David, in the midst of his trials, sought God unceasingly. Even in the darkness of the valley of the shadow of death, David's heart was unmoved but became stronger in the Lord; he remained steadfast in his worship and honour toward God. He learned to trust God in trials and tribulations.

At a certain moment of this undesirable crisis, it looked like favour was on his side (1 Samuel 24:2-10). As opportunity had it, he was given the chance to kill Saul in a cave (where David and his men were hiding). Saul went into that cave alone to relieve himself, not knowing that David was there. David's men knew this was the day God surely had delivered David's enemies into his hands. They said to David, (paraphrasing here) "Now is your chance to seize the throne."

But David couldn't because he respected and honoured the Anointing upon the vessel, more than his desire to seize the throne or save his life. David understood the purpose and weight of the Anointing that set him apart. It was of God, and not of man. That Anointing demanded more from him than just being king.

David wasn't moved. He knew that the same God who poured the Anointing on him was the same God who appointed Saul and would establish David in due time.

The Bible doesn't exactly say at what age David was anointed but we know by the written account that David was a strong young man; strong enough to take down a lion and a bear.

A few years later after Saul's death, David was anointed by the people of Judah and Israel as king. He was thirty years old when the people confirmed him as their king (2 Samuel 5:1-4). They were only confirming the true ordination that had happened years before.

Remember? God said to Samuel, I have found a man after my own heart (1 Samuel 13:14, 16:1).

Although David was a man after God's heart, he also wasn't a perfect man. Let's take a closer look at David's life story. Did you know David had six wives and two concubines? (2 Samuel 2, is a list of a few of them). Of the six wives, one of them was Bathsheba, the wife of another man named Uriah. In 2 Samuel 11:2-25, David plotted an evil plan to have him killed in battle so that David could take Bathsheba to be his wife. Six descriptions fit David's actions at this point in his life: a pervert full of lust, one who envied what belonged to his neighbour, a thief, a tyrant, an adulterer and a murderer.

David had sinned and no doubt, God wasn't pleased with Him. God's judgement came upon David's household, but God also forgave David because David had a repentant heart.

God's promise to David was to establish an eternal lineage—more so, the Messiah would come through David's lineage as a descendent of the Promise (2 Samuel 7:16). And although God judged rightfully, God also poured grace upon David because he repented and turned his heart to God.

David was a sinner. If we judged and decided on the appropriate candidate to fit the job, we wouldn't pick David—but God did. For it is by the selection of God that we are sanctified, and that selection has nothing to do with our human reasoning or imperfections. God surely chose a sinful man. But why David? As the Prophet Isaiah puts it, "God's ways and thoughts are higher than ours (Isaiah 55:8-9)."

And, "Incline your ear, and come unto me: hear, and your soul shall live; and I will make an everlasting covenant with you, even the SURE MERCIES OF DAVID (Isaiah 55:3)."

In other words, if David, is the measuring instrument for mercy, then you can take to heart that God knew you before He picked you. God chose you of His own Will. God's choice is not a selection based on your flaws but based on your heart. God wants you to rise above the weight of sin, and be free from the burdensome grip of iniquity.

Deuteronomy 7:9

Know therefore that the LORD Thy God, He is God, the faithful God, which keepeth covenant and mercy with them that love Him and keep His commandments to a thousand generations;

1 Corinthians 1:9

God is faithful, by Whom ye were called unto the fellowship of His Son Jesus Christ our Lord.

As you live in the liberty of the Spirit, then the nature of Christ, the second Adam, becomes more visible in you. For it is Christ who quickens our hearts and cleanses our souls by the Anointing and fullness of His Spirit upon us.

I am no exception either. My own journey is nothing short of a mess of disappointments and continuous failures. The words of Paul speak louder here, "For all have sinned and fallen short of the Glory of God (Romans 3:23)."

I have wondered why God would pick a wretched man like me. I now understand a little bit that this wonderful revelation of the infinite love of God is becoming in me the perfection of the Spirit of Christ.

There is that part of our lives that we keep secret from others. Nonetheless, that is not the emphasis of the Spirit. Although, He is aware of our weaknesses and shortcomings the Holy Ghost will still lead us to focus on the Intent of God for us.

I know myself and that I do not deserve any of God's goodness but that by the Blood of Jesus, God has allowed me to be a partaker of this great inheritance in Christ Jesus.

To me, I am less than the least of all the saints. And I am encouraged to pursue Christ. Perfection is in Christ if we are willing to go through the moulding of His Word and Spirit.

> " Perfection is in Christ if we are willing to go through the moulding of His Word And Spirit.

I don't deny that the Call of this Great Mandate and Anointing is beyond comprehension. I am only getting to know more about God each day. My contemplations have left me more unsettled than peaceful over the years; doubtful more than assertive.

Albeit, there is one thing I can declare confidently: we are called to bring Glory to His Name and that the Excellency of the Anointing and Ordination belongs to Him, and not us.

I am hopeful and more joyous in Him. I know, as a messenger sent by God, I must give an account of my stewardship before the Lord of all callings and Anointings. I recognise that by His grace my stewardship finds its deepest and most meaningful voice in my brokenness and willingness to be obedient to the Spirit. I can trust Him, who has taken my brokenness and will use it for His Glory.

LEARN TO EMBRACE YOUR WEAKNESSES

As I write this book, It's now 2023, and the Spirit has made me ready. My words have been shaped by a life continuously lived in the flames of the Spirit of God. There have been many high times and many low times, some of which I wish, I could press a button and simply solve. But no, God's refining is needed.

I have learned to embrace my weakness and not fight it. I am not saying to entertain that old man and his sinful nature. What I am saying is, we must let the full work of sanctification grace our lives. We can only live in the holiness of God by our continuous yielding to God.

The Apostle Paul was also faced with a thorn in the flesh. He said three times that he asked the Lord to take it away from him. But it looked to be that the thorn served a reason in Paul's life.

God is orchestrating His Will through our weaknesses. Although we might disagree, like Paul, God won't erase those shameful events that trouble our conscience. Instead, through our weaknesses, He keeps us humble, sincere and willing to follow Christ. (Note the bolded words)

2 Corinthians 12:9-10

And He said unto me, **My grace is sufficient for thee: for My strength is made perfect in weakness.** Most gladly therefore will I rather glory in my infirmities, that the Power of Christ may rest upon me. Therefore I take pleasure in infirmities, in reproaches, in necessities, in persecutions, in distresses for Christ's sake: **for when I am weak, then am I strong.**

You are not alone in the uncertainties and troubles that sin causes. Pick yourself up off the floor my fellow warriors of God. Become one given—yes, given to God so that the Power of Christ may rest mightily upon you.

David, after committing this terrible sin repented and was remorseful of his actions. He regretfully cried to be renewed and clean again before the Lord God. His remorsefulness was penned into what is now, Psalms 51:

The Great Induction & Anointing Service CHAPTER 10

Psalms 51:8-17

Make me to hear joy and gladness; that the bones which thou hast broken may rejoice. Hide Thy face from my sins, and blot out all mine iniquities. Create in me a clean heart, O God; and renew a right spirit within me. Cast me not away from Thy Presence; and take not Thy Holy Spirit from me. Restore unto me the joy of Thy salvation; and uphold me with Thy free Spirit. Then will I teach transgressors Thy ways; and sinners shall be converted unto Thee. Deliver me from bloodguiltiness, O God, Thou God of my salvation: and my tongue shall sing aloud of Thy righteousness. O Lord, open Thou my lips; and my mouth shall shew forth Thy praise. For Thou desirest not sacrifice; else would I give it: Thou delightest not in burnt offering. The sacrifices of God are a broken spirit: a broken and a contrite heart, O God, Thou wilt not despise."

CHAPTER 11

MY DAD RECEIVES A VISION

—

BEFORE THE THRONE

This one belongs to Me

Not long after the Anointing dream, then a Word came for me in 2002, that I would be travelling to Australia. I was in Grade 12 then.

But God was going to deploy an unusual plan, and one I would easily have disagreed with. The instructions for my next direction came through many dreams, not only given to me but from others. It was clear that the Lord wanted me to join the Papua New Guinean Defence Force (PNGDF).

God had to really convince me, that this was His directive, by making others see the same dream of me joining the defence force.

I didn't understand it initially, but I obeyed God. My cadet training was the pathway the Lord wanted me to take.

Unbeknown to me, this pathway that began in September of 2004, would find me in Australia, where I met my wife, Olivia, in April of 2007.

CHAPTER 11 *My Dad Receives A Vision — Before The Throne*

By the end of 2008, our son, Ethan was born. I had left the army by then and was now embarking on a new journey.

The strife and struggles, and to an extent; the waywardness of army life had left me with inner scars and wounds I needed to heal from. The stains of my sins were upon my heart and weighed on me with a guilty conscience. God was patient with me. Life in the PNGDF had pushed me into places I had not been before, and I was obviously exposed to the pleasantries and lusts of the world. I had one foot in the world and the other in God, but inwardly I wanted God.

I needed a deep cleaning from God again. The worst place to serve God is in a lukewarm state. That's like trying to sail a boat in troubled waters. But prayerfulness is the mark of a repentant heart.

> " The worst place to serve God is in a lukewarm state.
> That's like trying to sail a boat in troubled waters.

I didn't feel anything like an anointed man of God. Gradually, I began to make my journey back to the Lord. At the beginning of the year 2012, the Lord started stirring my heart again to take up the Call and pursue Him. Heaven's grace shined, and the ever-so-gentle God began to lead me down that glorious path of transformation that my heart sought after.

Olivia and I gave ourselves to fasting and praying intermittently and the more we did, the more of the things of the Spirit became manifested in our lives.

Afresh, I needed a jolt to launch to the deep. That great big push came in an amazing way again with God's full involvement. It started with me prophesying a Word to my dad at the homestead in Kapala in January of that year 2012. The prophecy was that something wonderful was going to happen for him on the first weekend of April 2012. I had seen in a vision, that two angels were posted at the entrance of the yard and they would be there till this event happened.

Well, I had forgotten about that prophecy and when the first weekend of April came, I was in the middle of completing an I.T course at the Canberra Institute of Technology. But God was leading. We just didn't see it at the time.

The prophesied event had finally come. On the first Saturday of April 2012, Dad was doing his usual early morning prayer when a vision from the Lord came suddenly to Him. After coming out from the vision, he called me and delivered the message to me. "Norman, are you sitting down? I need to talk to you, son."

"Dad is everything okay? You sound very serious."

"Yes, son everything is okay." Dad went on to tell me that while he was praying like he always does, he would pray for all his children (This was his usual prayer routine every morning). It was then that the Lord had taken him in a vision, into the Throne Room. And he stood on the sea of glass glowing with many colours, that was before the Throne of God. Then a heavenly screen appeared before him and there the Lord spoke to him about each of his children as one by one flashed before him. It was there that when the image of me appeared on the screen, the Lord gave him the command. "Let Norman go…This one belongs to Me!"

When the Lord had finished speaking to him, as soon as he came out of the vision, it was placed heavily on him to call me first and deliver that message. Dad never talks like that, and I knew He had truly been taken in the Spirit to see and hear the Will of God. I felt in my heart I was ready to take up what the Lord had assigned to me. But there was a problem, I didn't know where to start. The only way I knew was to become hungry for God again.

CHAPTER 11

My Dad Receives A Vision — Before The Throne

The year 2012—the year of the Second Baptism of Fire (That story is in Chapter 14 of this book). A great cleansing and quickening happened for Olivia and me that year. The light and peace of God entered our home and even our friends saw the change in us.

Genesis 35:2-3

> Then Jacob said unto his household, and to all that were with him, put away the strange gods that are among you, and be clean, and change your garments: And let us arise, and go up to Bethel; and I will make there an Altar unto God, Who answered me in the day of my distress, and was with me in the way which I went.

Because I spoke about my Anointing—Induction Dream in the previous Chapter, it would only be fitting for me to proceed further to tell you about the second Anointing Dream which happened on the 14th of January 2022. This time, it was completely different from the first. This one left me more in wonderment. But God knows all things.

That being said, it is important to note that we don't author visions and dreams, we receive them. We don't author prophecies, we receive them. I am prompted by the Lord Jesus to hide nothing from you but to reveal His desire for us.

> " God doesn't make a mistake about who He chooses, when He chooses, where He chooses and why He chooses. God has picked you and you are perfect for the 'God assignment.'

CHAPTER 12

MOSES ANOINTS ME A SECOND TIME BEFORE THE GLORY CLOUD

DREAM:
(14th January 2022)

A second time? Yes I know, all this seems to be too fictitious to be true. But as I said earlier, we don't plan these Heavenly encounters, nor do we ordain them, or initiate them by our own intentions and certainly not by our wisdom. Because they are not of man, but of God. Our destinies are all written in the books of God's Master Plan. And what we call prophecies are actually written records of events noted on Heaven's Calendar and made known to us as prophecies.

We are only fulfilling what God has already planned and ordained; every significant event of our lives is already noted in those Heavenly pages. As these events happen, a page of Heaven becomes ours. We are marked by God for happenings and

CHAPTER 12   *Moses Anoints Me A Second Before The Glory Cloud*

experiences we ourselves would never consider. But that is how our wonderful God works.

Jeremiah 29:11

> For I know the thoughts that I think toward you, saith the LORD, thoughts of peace, and not of evil, to give you an expected end.

Now to the dream—

In the dream, the Old Tabernacle sat in the midst of an Australian Suburb. The priests all wore smokey white garments. As I looked on, a priest was washing the High Priest's hands with a silver vessel at the door of the Tabernacle. Then the High Priest took the bowl from another priest. The two assisting priests stood with him.

Then together they entered through the door of the Tabernacle to the *Holy* Place and walked up to the Veil of the Most Holy Place.

The High Priest was ready to enter through the veil of the *Most Holy Place*. The assisting priests then held the vessel for him so he could push the dark-coloured curtains with his arms. He took the bowl from their hands and then proceeded on.

Then as he was entering, at that exact moment, I went from the person observing the scene to the one in the scene; I became that high priest as I carried the vessel and walked into the *Holies of Holies.*

While standing there, reverence mixed with curiosity filled me as I looked around intensively through the room. My first expectation was to see the Ark of the Covenant. I realised immediately, I wasn't in a room but in an open place.

It looked like I was on the top of a great mountain with a high rock face that had cliffs as walls. There to my left was an opening to the night sky.

There, the Glory Cloud of God thickened before me as I kneeled facing left to where the Cloud was. Then a strong and loud voice spoke (it was speaking from where the Glory Cloud stood), "Who dares enter the Holies of Holies, and is not chosen of God? Only the high priest is allowed in here!"

With my eyes still fixed on the Cloud of God, I noticed an image the shape of a great white bird (like a dove, but was as big as me), descending quickly into the place where I was. I became afraid that I would be killed if I didn't speak up, so I called out, as the bird or person approached the room, "I was anointed by the LORD in a dream (referring to the Anointing dream I had in 2002)" hoping that would give me validation to be in the Holiest Place.

Then as the bird landed at the base of the Glory Cloud, there stood a man in smokey white garments, similar to the ones I was dressed in. As he walked forth, from the Glory Cloud, I observed that he was about the same height as me. I immediately had a knowing that this was none other than, the Prophet Moses.

He approached me quickly, then stood to my left while I remained on my knees with my face halfway toward the ground and my eyes fixed on him. He wore a nicely groomed white beard; an oldish-looking man in his sixties (I assume he would have been older, but he looked younger).

Memories of my army sergeants came flashing back here because it felt like I was about to be toasted by my drill sergeant.

He had a serious look on his face but he knew what he was there for. He then looked down at me as I kneeled before the Glory Cloud; the Cloud of God stood steadfastly there in that high mountainous place and was very thick and dark. The flames of Fire were visible in the dark Cloud moving with great intensity.

CHAPTER 12   *Moses Anoints Me A Second Before The Glory Cloud*

The Prophet Moses said nothing to me but muttered a prayer under his breath, very much like our Lord Jesus did in the first Anointing dream.

He then placed his right hand on my head and spoke silently a prayer. And then he reached behind and grabbed a bottle full of *Anointing Oil* that was on a small shelf, (the bottle was about the size of a 700-gram tomato passata bottle). Then he proceeded to pour the whole bottle of *Anointing Oil* on me. It went from my head, down to my feet covering all of me including the garment I wore.

After he had finished Anointing me, he walked back to where the Glory Cloud was (He now stood to the left of the Cloud). While I looked on, the man of God began gradually ascending into the Pillar of Cloud. But before he was completely gone out of my sight, at once, I called out to him and asked him, "What will become of me after this?"

But he only looked at me and didn't answer. His countenance remained very fierce and solemn. He then vanished before me while the magnificent Pillar of God's Glory and Presence remained and filled that place.

Now at this point of the dream, I was still there but the scene changed.—

Now, I was in an old carpenter's workshop like the ancient Nazareth workshop I had seen in a documentary. There in the workshop were about two picture frames that hung on the wall where the Glory Cloud was in the previous scene.

Then entered a lady, from a door to the front (right side) of me and as Moses did in the previous scene, she also walked up to me. As she approached me, I noticed it was my old secondary school principal, Mrs Bernadette Ovê.

Moses Anoints Me A Second Before The Glory Cloud   **CHAPTER 12**

At this point of the dream, I felt I needed to make a mental note of her name in particular which afterwards, through a bit of research and inquisitiveness I found out its meaning:

- *Bernadette* - BRAVE & STRONG AS A BEAR:
- *Ôvè* - Wow: as in SOMETHING YOU ADMIRE. (From the Oro language of Papua New Guinea, because that's where Mrs Ove is from).

She then said to me, "You see there to the left wall, is where a portrait picture of me is hanging."

I looked but couldn't see the picture clearly as there wasn't enough light shining in the room.

I then left the place and was on the way to an area I wasn't too familiar with. Consciously, I knew I was going to another Christian brother's home and that this was my next stop. He was either renting or boarding at this particular place that was up on high grounds.

As I walked along the pavement, I still pondered on what had happened to me earlier.

"So that was the Old Covenant Tabernacle? What does it all mean; the man of God and the Anointing?"

I was quite overwhelmed by the experience. I thought about The Glory Cloud in the Holiest Place; that high mountainous point, facing through a cliffy face and how it opened to the beautiful night sky above.

I then arrived at the man's house, and I entered through the large sliding door and sat on this brand new comfortable grey couch. He wasn't there when I arrived but he had left the place ready for me.

The dream ended here. When I woke up, *the Anointing Oil* was still dripping down my head and along the side of my ears.

And like the first dream, the same phenomenon happened also in the second—the physical manifestation of the Oil.

I can try to add a thought of reflection here, but I truly have nothing to say. The first Anointing encounter being significant, had troubled me for over twenty years. How do you tell the story of such a powerful event except to tell it the way it happened? Considering this, what could I say about the second Anointing encounter? I believe that explanation will unfold at a later time as the Lord wills according to His Divine Plan. The LORD knows all things. I trust that all of this will be made clearer in the coming days. To God be the Glory, Honour, Power and Praise.

Concluding from the dreams that I have shared with you, I would like to now follow through with a deeper discussion on *The Anointing*.

The Anointing—

I begin this discussion by saying, that out of every God-event is a lesson of Heaven released to us on earth. God-events impart revelation knowledge to us. In them, we learn the ways and works of God. We learn through:

- observation,
- experience,
- participation,
- encounter,
- mentorship
- study and
- out of a humble spirit.

Hence, everything I teach in this book comes through these learning processes or avenues that I have noted in the bullet points above. So let's proceed with our discussion on *The Anointing*.

CHAPTER 13

THE ANOINTING
—
MANTLES & IMPARTATIONS

The Anointing is the Move of God

The English word for 'Mantle' is derived from the Latin word, mantēllum (covering or cloak), and is an outer garment worn usually as a sleeveless overcoat. The cloak worn represented status or an important office. Like that of the royal Mantles of kings and queens worn as a symbol of their authority.

Other words interchangeable with the word 'Mantle':
- Your Anointing,
- Your calling or office,
- Your appointed ordination.

Looking at the historical event of Elijah passing the double-portion of his Anointing to Elisha, the sign of it was the transfer of his Mantle to Elisha (2 Kings 2:1-15).

We understand from this, that the Anointing, although resting upon a vessel is also upon his garments. Whatever he wears is not

CHAPTER 13 *The Anointing — Mantles & Impartation*

only an outward symbol of his office or call but also a specific Power of God relating to the purpose and function of the Mantle, working through him. An example of this is when Elijah took his Mantle and used it to part the waters at Jordon. Or like the woman with the issue of blood, who touched the edge of Jesus' garment (Luke 8:43-48).

We have an Anointing because of the *Finished Work of Christ*. That Anointing is God's endorsement. It is God's Commission and Movement. The Mantle is a God-statement; it carries God's influence. The Mantle is an authoritative force, an established dominion with an abiding authority. It is manifested Power by which Heaven has direct access to Earth and through it, God has full control of the realms when the Anointing is in operation. The Mantle carries a greater dimension or realm of demonstration of the Holy Ghost. There is a certain level of boldness that comes with it.

Man can be gifted and talented, but the Anointing is God's gift and talent. You can't imitate God's gift. You can try to fake a miracle and get away with it but you can't fake the Anointing. There is a difference between enthusiasm and the Anointing. I would rather the disciples of Christ follow the leadership of His *unction* than have enthusiasts or devotees, seek to do God's work without His Spirit. You must become more than a fan and an admirer; you must become *a disciple of the Spirit of Christ*. You are either governed by excitement and optimism or your consciousness of the Spirit. The a*wareness of God* is where the Lord wants you to be. To know His Presence and His form.

To the one who walks by the still waters, the one who is thirsty for their God, they will find Him by and by when they yield to Him. But it is more than having our hands lifted and singing a song. It is more. It is when you go to a place in God, where *the*

Sound of His Voice matters more than the program of the Church service.

We come to an understanding of how to walk in our Anointing when we understand how to be led by the Spirit. This often occurs when the deep within you reaches out to the *Deep of God*—For the Anointing operates from that deep place.

It is a fountain of living waters springing up to eternal life within our inner man. That same fountain dresses us with the mighty Mantle of His Will and Desire. Yes, that Anointing upon your life is the grace of God manifested.

As I noted earlier, the Mantle is the Anointing, being that the Anointing is the cloak of the Spirit upon us. Some ministers view the Mantle as a separate working of the Holy Spirit to the Anointing. I see it as the same thing; just a different word to identify specific attributes of the Anointing.

If we simply went by the definition that I gave in the first three paragraphs we can see that the Mantle that fell from Elijah was the visible identifier or visible evidence representing that Anointing. So it is but one and the same thing.

Might I add: any person can wear a physical cloak. That doesn't mean an Anointing rests upon them. But for the servant of God that carries an evidential mark of the Power of the Spirit—which is that Anointing, whatever garment they wear comes under the endowing of that Power when it rests upon them.

The Anointing is the Power of God manifested. The purpose of any Anointing is to reveal God and do only what God wants. Hence, the Mantle being the representation of your Anointing, establishes the truth that it is not merely an impartation of a spiritual gift but one that is an appointment to a *calling, platform and position* of authority in the Spirit. Now that position is not an earthly one under our organisational structures. The calling, platform and position are from above.

CHAPTER 13   *The Anointing — Mantles & Impartation*

As the Body of Christ, we can share in the manifestations and operations of the Spirit, and the giftings of the Spirit are made available to everyone. This happens when the atmosphere of God is charged up for diverse giftings, faith and administrations of the Holy Spirit to work. The Holy Spirit always works with a willing vessel.

But when it comes to the Anointing, that is very *job-specific*. It Is not merely a gift from God, it is an *Office of Appointment, and one possessing authority in God*. That authority is not wielded by the will of man. Rather, it is the authority of the Holy Spirit upon a surrendered vessel.

That's why it carries a certain level of authority appointed only to that individual, to demonstrate God in that specific way. Every Anointing carries its own level of access in God, which is distinctive, specific and notable to that Anointing.

You can have three evangelists in the room but they each don't carry the same level of revelation, nor the same access and Power. That is because these three evangelists have different levels of access based on their appointed office as directed and ordained by God's purposes. From my observations, I note that often where there is a greater manifestation, this reflects the deepness of the relationship a person has with God. That's why in the Prophet Elijah's era, there were the sons of the prophets, and then there was Elijah. He wasn't like anyone of them. Although they were all prophets, none of them carried the same level of Holy Ghost demonstration as Elijah did. And Elisha became the one chosen to fill the *room or office of Elijah* (Note the bolded words).

The Anointing — Mantles & Impartation CHAPTER 13

1 Kings 19:16

And Jehu the son of Nimshi shalt thou anoint to be king over Israel: and **Elisha the son of Shaphat of Abelmeholah shalt thou anoint to be prophet in thy ROOM.**

I think of it like levels of access that come with the role. When you go to an army base, there are different levels of access; some have up to seven levels of access. Now depending on your job description, you are therefore entitled by governmental approval to have access to that level of security that comes with your office of appointment.

The same is true with the Anointing. That is why no prophet was able to operate like Elijah. That's why I said, *his Mantle was job specific.*

Now each level of government access, also brings with it, its own privileges, operations, permissions and influence. If you have access to the highest level of security, you also carry a very important role that ensures you are allowed only a certain level of function within its specified access. The office of your Anointing is very much like this too. That holy Anointing upon you is your platform and level of access by which you operate and minister.

Therefore, the kind of Heavenly demonstration and power that works through you is determined by the specific purpose of that Anointing that rests upon you. Your Anointing in operation becomes synonymous with you because only you are able, by the Spirit's empowerment, to do that specific task.

This brings to mind the story of how Aaron and Miriam, Moses's siblings, spoke against Moses (Numbers 12:1-16). They even said (paraphrasing here), "Does God only speak through Moses? Hasn't He also spoken through us?"

CHAPTER 13   *The Anointing — Mantles & Impartation*

That discussion was stirred up by the issue they had with Moses's wife; an Ethiopian woman. They became too focused on a minor issue, they forgot the broader purpose of the Call upon Moses's life. Talk about looking for things to use in order to accuse God's anointed ones (just an amusing point).

The devil plays this game very well even in the Churches today. He makes Christians gossip about one another and even speak condescendingly about the ministry of others. As critics, they are more focused on correcting errors but not in a way that helps to build the Body of Christ, but as a weapon of judgement used to condescend to their fellow brothers and sisters in Christ.

Sounds like a *competitive spirit of jealousy*, right? This is the work of the flesh and a spirit of error; one that God warns against (Galatians 5:16-21). If you have, in some way, made this error, I strongly urge you to repent before God. I often say this, if you are going to be critical about something, make sure to bring it to the Lord in prayer. Show that you care, by interceding for the person you are concerned for.

Back to the story—You know what happened next? *God heard it.* He heard Aaron and Miriam's slander and derogatory remarks against Moses, without his knowledge. God heard what they said behind Moses's back, and He spoke to Moses about it. He summoned Moses, Aaron and Miriam to come out and stand at the *Tabernacle of Congregation.*

Oh, you really must read it (Numbers 12:5-15). God was so angry with Aaron and Miriam. The Lord descended in the pillar of Cloud and stood at the door of the Tabernacle. And called Aaron and Miriam to step forward. He was going to correct their error. How fearful it is to fall into the hands of the living God (Hebrews 10:30-31). God was about to teach them a valuable lesson about His call and Anointing upon Moses. God said to Moses's siblings (paraphrasing here), "Listen to My Words. If there's a prophet among you, I will make Myself known to them in visions and dreams. But that's NOT the case with Moses. He is FAITHFUL in all My House. With him, I speak face to face: (from My mouth to His mouth and his to My mouth), a real conversation. I don't do it with hidden or cryptic speeches. And he has beheld My Form. I tell him My Words and he hears them exactly as I tell him.

Now, weren't you afraid to speak against My servant Moses?"

God's anger was kindled and when His Glory Cloud lifted from that place, immediately Miriam became a leper. That's when Aaron begged Moses to pray to God to forgive them. And when Moses *pleaded with God,* the Lord responded and instructed Moses to have Miriam placed outside of the camp for seven days and then she would be made whole again.

The Mantle or Anointing carries Heavenly recognition. It is the *Mark of God's Ownership and Favour* upon a man.

If you say you carry an Anointing, what you are saying is you belong to God—God owns you (1 Corinthians 6:19-20).

Thus, the Anointing resting upon you is *the Cloak of God's calling and Mark upon you.* It carries a very distinctive trait and marking notable and unique to the person that carries it. Your Anointing is your distinctive signature with you and God, customised by the Holy Spirit and carries its own personality and character traits.

There are different Anointings, and all of these point back to the One God and Spirit. For the One Spirit operates through all.

And because it is your call to a specific office. No one can fill your office until you have accomplished your assignment on earth. Only then is that office transferrable to the next carrier.

That's why you can't impart your office to someone else. But the Lord can allow the blessings, influences and privileges of your office to be shared. This is where the *impartation of the Anointing is applicable.*

CHAPTER 13 — *The Anointing — Mantles & Impartation*

The Lord God can take of your spirit (which is your Mantle) and grant an impartation of that to others, for His purpose. The working of this Anointing includes all the operations or gifts or administrations of the Spirit that function to minister God's will for His people (1 Corinthians 12:1, 4-11, 28-31)

An impartation, therefore, is a gift and blessing of that Anointing on your life, where others can have access to certain attributes and qualities of that Mantle.

This is what the Holy Spirit has taught me over the years. I have derived much learning by studying 'the Anointing dream' that I shared in Chapter 10.

In my early years as a new Christian, I noticed how you can get more than one impartation of Anointings from different ministers.

All this put together will form a special grace to operate in a unique Mantle customised by the Lord for you. These gifts and callings are irrevocable, meaning God will never take them from you (Romans 11:29). You never lose these blessings and gifts from Heaven. God won't change His mind about the Anointing upon you. But the issue is always on our part, not His. It's when a minister walks away from the gift and call of God, to go after their own desires and lusts.

You have probably heard a minister of God say, you can lose your Anointing: that is not scriptural at all. But if you become disobedient and walk away from the call, the Lord will be patient until you return to Him. Like the prodigal (or wasteful) son, your place, position and office will always be there for you.

The true concern here is rebelliousness toward God. Knowing very well that the works of the flesh work against the works of the Spirit of God, it will be that the Spirit can't linger or dwell there until you turn your heart back to God. If the Spirit of God departs from you, as He did with King Saul (1 Samuel 16:14), you must *come back to Him with repentance*. You can't expect to drink the cup of the Lord, while you drink of the cup of demons (1 Corinthians 10:21).

The Anointing is holy, and when you carry it, you must walk in absolute surrender to the Lord who has called you.

And if you have already received the Baptism of the Holy Spirit and Fire, then you have received your cloak (your Anointing). Remember, that Anointing is of God and none of you. That Anointing owns you now. You are given to the will of Christ to burn as His chosen ones. You have been marked by the God of Heaven with special favour and call. Uphold it with diligence and run your lane without fleshly restrictions. Be one continuously given to your call and discover the operations and privileges of your Baptism. Follow after the Spirit with all your heart and be obedient to the Voice of the Lord when He speaks to you.

THE ANOINTING

—

HIS WORD & HIS VOICE

The Anointing is not only His Power; it is also His Word and His Voice. And where His Word and Voice are, is also His Presence.

Like when the Holy Spirit moved upon the waters in the beginning. And When God spoke, His Spirit rested upon the Word of His Power and did according to the *Voice of His Word*.

Therefore, the Anointing resting upon you and residing within you will only respond to the Word of Power that rests upon you.

It is *the Voice of the Spirit* that the Anointing responds to. When the Spirit speaks, His Word is felt like Fire in your bones. That's *the grace of the Mantle:* when you are enabled, by the Spirit to know His

Word when He speaks and to become a witness for Him when He makes known His thoughts. This is where our yielding and obedience participate with the Anointing of the Spirit.

When the Anointing is present, the Holy Spirit through that Anointing teaches you how to discern and understand the ways of God, to know God, and to Move with God. With the Anointing is *favour*—favour with God and favour with man.

THE ANOINTING IS THE MOVE OF GOD

The Anointing is the Move of God. It's the working of the Holy Spirit of Revival. The Anointing is the Revival Fire of God burning within us. You need an Anointing to carry the Move of God; that Great Awakening of the Holy Spirit. It is the Revival Fire of our Lord Jesus.

The Anointing you carry is God's desire and ordained assignment on earth. The Anointing—The Move of the Holy Spirit, always burns in the hearts of those who carry His desire through their worship posture and obedience to the Voice of the Spirit.

The Great Awakening Movement will only come from that place where the Church has chosen to *host His Word* on their knees. It is not only a submission to serve, but a submission to take up the Mantle. You see the Glory can't be carried without knowledge. And the work of the Anointing is also to teach us the knowledge of the Glory. Your hunger is the correct response and attitude for Revival, but only the Holy Spirit can birth the Move in You.

If you want the Revival Fire of God, it's time you accept the importance of the Anointing, and acknowledge that without it, there is no Revival, and there is no Movement. When you recognise the Anointing, you are recognising God.

The Anointing — Mantles & Impartation CHAPTER 13

> "When you recognise the Anointing, you are recognising God.

The Wave of His Glory has already been appointed to the hands of those who have been faithful in His House. They are the ones who have not quenched the Holy Spirit and have not restricted the working of the Anointing.

And because I am confident in His Anointing, I am therefore confident in the Move of God. For I know that the Anointing upon a chosen vessel allows that person to carry the Word of Power with great intentionality and boldness in the Spirit. This leads me to say, that you have prayed for God's Revival, without understanding that He has already been in your midst by His 'Anointing.' The 'resident *Glory*' only abides in the one who carries the Word of Glory faithfully and obeys the Anointing that Moves upon them.

I emphasise again, that you can't have a Movement of God, without the *assigned* Anointing. Christ was anointed because the Spirit rested upon Him. The Move of the Spirit was manifested in the Anointing that rested upon Yeshua. That wonderful Anointing is the Power of the Spirit from Above that descended upon the Upper Room saints. They too were then anointed to carry, lead, and serve the Call of God upon their lives. They were baptised into that Fire of Revival because the Spirit rested on them. They too carried the Move of God as soon as they were endued with Power.

When will you see it? That the anointeds are here in our midst because the Spirit desires to Move in our midst; He desires to reside with us. For what other reason would He give you an Anointing?

God has already anointed Gideons and Elishas, and Josephs in our midst. God has positioned and postured saints like the hundred twenty of the Upper Room of Jerusalem, who are postured for Revival.

CHAPTER 13 *The Anointing — Mantles & Impartation*

We can't force the Anointing to manifest and deliver. Nor can we fabricate or imitate what belongs to God. That Power is from Above. The Move is of God and not of us. Our part to play is to yield to the Move, His part is to abide where we have made room for Him.

We are a *Move of God* because the Anointing has its way in us. We make room by our heart attitude toward God.

Some ministers teach about how to 'activate the Anointing.' But the truth is, you can't activate the Spirit; He activates you.

I think what they are really trying to say, is to partner with the Holy Spirit. You can partner with the Holy Spirit and allow Him to work through you. That's why prophets won't speak a word unless the Spirit gives them a Word.

If they speak ahead of the Spirit or speak their own words, then they will be in error of speaking a false prophecy. Here's a word of warning. If you prophesy a desire in your heart and make it sound like a Word sent by God; you are not prophesying what the Spirit wants—that's a false prophecy (Ezekiel 13:1-3). But when you prophesy, *the Word that comes to you* is free of your influence and self-ambitions. It has come to do whatever it has been sent to do:

- correct,
- rebuke and pull down,
- uproot and cleanse,
- Set free and heal,
- inspire and empower,
- build and strengthen,
- instruct and reveal,
- equip (mentor) and
- lead by the Holy Ghost.

True prophecy is when you utter only what God says, and not what you think God is trying to say. You don't formulate God's oracles for Him. *You say, verbatim—exactly what He says.*

That's why we cannot be swayed by what man wants us to say, we must be stirred only by what the Holy Spirit wants us to say. If someone comes to you and forces you to prophesy a Word to them, exhort them politely to wait till *He Speaks.* God must speak first, and then we speak, word for word, what He speaks.

If someone asks you to confirm the prophecy they received, I doubt that they even received a genuine Word from the Lord, but words they have made up to reveal their own desire.

The Anointing works by our dependence on the Holy Spirit. The Anointing works with our obedience. The Holy Ghost doesn't need to be stirred to work. It is we who need the inspiration of the Holy Spirit. We need Him. We can't create the Move of God with our enthusiasm. That's not the Anointing at all. But we can yield to the Move of God, which is the Spirit at work in us. Our obedience to the *Voice of the Anointing* is what brings the mighty works of God in our midst. We become *the Movement of God* by yielding to the *Movement of God.*

There are dead Churches around us because they have stopped letting the Anointing lead them. Instead, they have filled it up with programs, entertainment and motivational speeches. They tried to forge something that looked like the Move of God, and their fleshly efforts only imitated the Move, but they weren't really demonstrating with the Spirit's guidance, the real Move of God. They got exposed because their form of truth was only a form of godliness but it denied the *Power* thereof. They may fill your mind with words, but not the *Voice* of the Word. There is a vast difference between this type of minister and those who carry the Revival Fire. For the Revivalist, there is a place of empowerment *at the Cleft of the Rock.* The Revivalist is only effective because He is connected to the One who is able to work mighty works through him.

MORE THAN A SERMON

The Anointing of the Spirit works from a place of humility possessing holy insight and confidence. When you ignore the prompting of the Holy Spirit to flow with His message, then you rebel against His will. That is pride. God cannot use a prideful heart. Pride opposes the work of the Anointing. A true Anointing to preach operates out of the leading of the Holy Ghost.

As I said earlier, you can't imitate or fabricate the manifestations of God. It is not the giftedness of the orator that counts as the Anointing but the weightiness of the Spirit upon the Word that turns the hearts toward God. The Move of God is not just a good sermon. It is more than that. We elevate from a place where we are being preached to and preached at, to a people soaking in the preaching. The sermon flows from the Rivers of the gushing of the Spirit within us. At times, when the Spirit rests, it may not be a well-presented sermon from an oratorial perspective, but it is the open door for the Word to come and move in our midst.

There have been many fellowship meetings where we have witnessed the Word enter the room by only one *spoken revelation or when someone in the room yields under the weight of the Anointing present.* We lean into where the Anointing is, that is when we enter into the mighty flowing current of His Presence.

God holds His Word above all His Names. When the Lord passed by Moses before *the Cleft of the Rock,* God *proclaimed* the Lord God. God's proclamation was not just spoken words, but the tangible and visible manifestation of the Word in His Glory. It was the *Person, Form (or Appearance) and Power* of His Glory that Moses beheld.

Psalms 138:2-3

> I will worship toward Thy holy temple, and praise Thy Name for Thy lovingkindness and for Thy truth: for Thou hast magnified Thy Word above all Thy Name. In the day when I cried Thou answeredst me, and strengthenedst me with strength in my soul.

The same grace is given to us to stand at the Cleft of the Rock to behold Him. We now behold the fullness of His Word of Glory in the Person and Power of Jesus Christ; by the Spirit resting upon us.

The only way we can behold His Glory is to behold unceasingly, *the revelation* (rhema Word) conceived in our spirit by the Holy Ghost, That rhema Word is not only *a spoken Word* but a *revealed Word*. We are soaked by that revelation until it overflows and becomes Revival. Hence, Revival comes from the attitude of soaking in revelation. That revelation rests upon us like an Anointing Oil being poured upon our spirits to become one with the Word that washes us.

2 Corinthians 3:18

> But we all, with open face beholding as in a glass the Glory of the Lord, are changed into the same Image from Glory to Glory, even **as by the Spirit of the Lord.**

The Holy Spirit is our Helper—our Comforter Counsellor. As I noted earlier, He is the One that conceives and gives birth to the revelation of God in us. He will teach us when we lean into Him (1

John 2:20,27). He will show us if we turn our hearts to Him and set our gaze upon Him (2 Timothy 3:16-17). The Spirit is able to reach beyond where we have reached and do mighty things (Ephesians 3:20). He is able to do this by the Anointing He has placed upon us. The same Anointing that is upon us, is the Power at work within us. That holy Anointing is not the excitement of man, but the inspiration of God—-there is a difference.

It might look foolish, and sure there may be some uncertainty about Divine Instructions. But even human instructions can sometimes be perplexing and enigmatic.

When it comes to the *Word made flesh*, our spiritual disposition exceeds the earthly one. We are able to understand and walk in the Power of that Word resting upon us. Our intellect has nothing to do with this revelation. It must be understood and received with an attitude of surrender.

Another point to reflect on is, that God knows who you are before He speaks to You. He knows what your heart condition is before He makes known His Word to You. Nothing is hidden from Him. And if you are a man and woman after the heart of God, the Holy Spirit will pour revelation upon you. He knows you will hear His Voice when He speaks.

When God speaks, He's not affected by your frequency of thoughts. In fact, He will bring every thought under submission to Him, when His Word enters your spirit. That's when the Sound of His Voice becomes louder than the noise of the turmoil you may be in at that moment. That is the Holy Ghost sermon I speak of. The message that makes us yield and causes our hearts to surrender. That message is God's 'breakthrough' message because it carries the 'breakthrough' Anointing. That holy revelation draws us close to God and drenches us with His love, peace and joy. It is closeness with God and strength from the Spirit. How wonderful is *the Word Made Flesh*. How amiable are Your tabernacles, oh Lord of Host.

Blessed are they that dwell in *the House of Your Word*. Blessed is the man who finds *strength in You*, in whose heart are *the ways of God*. They go from strength to strength and every one of them appears before You *in true brokenness* (Psalm 84:1,4,5,7).

RESPONDING TO A 'GOD-APPOINTMENT'

When the Word comes into the room, that is a God-appointment. That Word then takes form in the heart of the one meditating upon it. Another point to note is that any Word received is A*nointing-specific.*

For example, *the word of healing* is given to the one *who carries an Anointing to heal the sick.* Then there are Words that have supernatural multiplication on them. Jesus carried the fullness of the Spirit's Anointing. He was able to yield to *the revealed Word of Power,* which by the Spirit, worked through Him to do mighty works. And when He spoke it over the basket of food, the fish and the bread, responded instantly to the Glory of the abiding Word and multiplied. I gave that example earlier also, regarding Elijah, who as the prophet of *Obedience,* willingly carried the *Word of provision* for the Zarephath woman. Therefore, the Anointing upon your life only responds to the Word that enters your spirit.

> " The Anointing upon your life only responds to the Word that enters your spirit.

That Heavenly Word is sent to accomplish its purpose (Isaiah 55:10-11). The Word that is sent, responds to the need in that place. When blind Bartimaeus asked Jesus to heal his sight, the Power of

Christ, came in the form of a Word, "What can I do for you (Mark 10:51)?"

There are assignments of God that are appointed to you by the Anointing or call that God has chosen for you. God's directives are your appointments. Just look at the examples in the Bible:

- Abraham was told that he would receive a son even in his old age and believed in the appointment of that promise.
- Aaron in a dream is appointed and directed to go to Moses to help Moses with the assignment of speaking to the pharaoh,
- Jehoshaphat was told that they didn't need to fight the battle but to follow through by going to the battlefield to witness their appointed victory over their enemies,
- Joseph and Mary were appointed to raise Jesus,
- John the Baptist was appointed to baptise Jesus,
- Peter, trusting the Word on Christ's mouth, walked upon the waters toward Jesus.
- The same Peter was told by the Word spoken from Jesus, to cast his net at a specific place assigned by the Word for a huge catch.
- The hundred and twenty disciples, by the Lord's Word, went and waited in the Upper Room for the Holy Spirit to come,
- Ananias was appointed to go to Paul so he could receive his sight and the Baptism of the Holy Ghost and Fire (even though Ananias was fearful of Paul, whose initial actions were to capture the Christians and destroy Christianity),
- Philip trusted the instruction on the mouth of the angel and hurried off to speak to an Ethiopian eunuch, and
- Peter saw a vision that confused him and was later told by the Holy Spirit to go to the house of Cornelius.

And the list goes on. These saints not only believed the Word but were willing to obey the Word. It was not a yielding to take the risk. Faith is not crazy. The faith I speak of is, *grounded in our knowing of the Word conceived within us*. 'Crazy faith,' is how the world thinks, but for the Church, ours is *an inheritance of Power* by the Spirit of God. We trust the *Word Made Flesh* when His directives come to us. We respond to the God-appointment embedded in the Word.

FAITH—A WILLING RESPONSE TO THE ANOINTING

God says 'Amen' to His Word for you. You are receiving a Word already agreed upon by the Father, Son and Holy Spirit, to fulfil its appointment. And for us, there is faith that reacts in *willing response* to the initiatives of God. When I use the word *'initiative,' I mean it originated from God and is authored by God.*

There is a faith that dwells with the initiative of God. That faith knows the Voice of the Word and is obedient to follow what the Word wants. I call this *knowing-faith, responding-faith—a willing response to God.*

Jesus possessed a *knowing-faith that came with willingness,* while those He healed, possessed a *responding-faith coupled also with willingness.* The Anointing works with the knowing-faith. Jesus' part was *obedience to the Anointing of the Spirit of the Word to heal.* On their part was *a willing response and willing obedience to be healed.* The Lord Jesus would often have a knowing that 'the Power to heal' was present (Luke 5:17). That knowing came from the Anointing abiding in Him (Acts 10:38).

As the body without the spirit, is dead, so a responding-faith without a willing response and obedience, is dead (James 2:26).

Simply put, mustered-seed-faith is obedience to the Word made flesh.

> Mustered-seed-faith is obedience to the Word made flesh.

As I said earlier, the modus operandi of the *Word made flesh* is to fulfil Divine intent. The Word becomes flesh by responding to a need, and the Anointing that carries the Word causes the 'need' to respond to the Anointing. I hope I didn't confuse you there. Re-read that statement again slowly. It is the full explanation of how Heaven's Will is accomplished on Earth.

But let's talk a little bit more about the *knowing-faith*. This particular faith responds only by obedience to the Lord and works in harmony with the Word of Power.

Furthermore, this faith works in obedience to the Anointing, and not outside of it. For example, if the Word declared is for healing, then the Spirit stirs up a responding-faith to touch the healing Power of God. Those who yield to that healing Power in that moment receive their healing.

The Spirit of God determines what Anointing must work at a specific time for God's specific reason. A specific Anointing is only present to meet a specific need.

I've seen these Anointings at work. When an evangelist is operating under that 'salvation-Anointing,' the Word burns with great conviction in the hearts of those who hear it. And when they surrender their lives to God in that moment they experience a true transformation. For those who encounter this evangelist's Anointing, they are never the same again—I am one of those.

DISCERNING ANOINTINGS

Now on the subject of discerning Anointings. One can only do this by the Holy Ghost. It is Holy Spirit awareness and knowledge made known in the spirit of a man who carries that gift to discern Anointings. Only the Holy Spirit reveals the Mantles to us because He is the giver of the Mantles.

Amazingly, for me, this discerning of the Anointings is a tangible experience, very much like beholding the appearance of the Word of Glory, as I described earlier. I understand it fully when these Anointings begin to work by the Holy Spirit in those yielded vessels of God, Hallelujah!

The prophet's Anointing, which is one I also function in by the grace and selection of God, is a powerful and prominent Anointing. When the Word of God comes mightily upon me, I am often clothed with *a knowing* of the Power that has descended upon me and a *knowing and understanding* of the Word revealed to me.

I always notice the weightiness or heightened confidence of the manifested Word in the room, when it comes. It comes very tangibly and with strong affirmation within my spirit, that there is no room for doubt. That's the *knowing-faith* working in the prophetic Anointing.

An evangelist knows his Anointing also. And likewise, the other offices of ministry. Again, I speak from experience, encounter, revelation and observation. You have to catch the training of the Holy Ghost in order to be proficient in the way the Holy Spirit works. Discerning the Anointings is a very important gift of the Spirit. It is needed for Revival; to identify the anointeds and the Anointing in our midst.

Every Anointing carries a *knowing-faith* to speak. The Spirit of God does not work in doubt and unbelief. He was given to us as the Spirit of Power, Might, and Sound Mind. So When the Word of the Spirit comes into a room, He comes to affirm and establish the purpose and desire of God.

In recent years, I've been experiencing a new kind of Anointing. It's not one I initially took to in my early days as a Christian, perhaps because of a lack of understanding of it. That Anointing is the *Anointing of Prosperity*. Immense criticism comes from Christians and heathens alike, who question its validity and trueness. But let King Solomon's example be enough to teach us that God also works in this area.

If God can make promises of abundance, then the same God can also pour that abundance. God blesses us not to forget Him, but to walk with Him (Deuteronomy 8:17-18).

We can also call it the *Joseph-Anointing*. The wealth He gives the *Joesphs* is for Kingdom assignment on earth. Even our Lord Jesus Christ needed a 'Joseph' to receive Him at His Birth and raise Him. He then needed another 'Joseph' to ensure His body was laid to rest in a tomb.

The first time it happened when the Anointing of prosperity entered the room, immediately I noticed my faith responding. That's as simple as I can explain it. I was in need of financial provision, and another minister carried the Word that possessed the Power to meet my need.

A point to note here is that whatever the need may be, there is a specific Anointing from God to meet that need.

Ephesians 3:20 perfectly describes this prosperity-Anointing (although it can be applied to other Anointings too). It is the Holy Spirit in us, who works above and beyond all that we think and ask for at that moment to deliver breakthroughs and wealth. He gives it to the hands of those who respond to it with the same *responding-faith that stirs their heart to act*. The same Anointing teaches your hand to be successful and directs your decisions. It is an administration and financial Anointing and with it, is the favour of God to manage and administer wisdom for finance.

These are just a few of the many Anointings available for the saints today, to operate in, by the Holy Ghost. May you find yours also, at the feet of Jesus.

I WANT TO MINISTER IN THE ANOINTING. WHERE DO I START?

It is the Holy Spirit who imparts hunger in you to pursue after His Anointing. Don't fake a yielding posture but be genuine in your pursuit of God. It's *your surrender and hunger for God* that meets the Power of the Lord of Glory. Let's expound on this thought.

How does one become a Minister of God? The starting point is when you accept Jesus as Lord and Saviour of your life. Then you grow, by continuous fellowship with the brethren and fellowship with the Holy Spirit.

Your *conversion* experience can cause you to testify to others about how God saved you. That testimony can lead others to Christ also.

From that salvation experience, you then progress on to pursue the Baptism of the Holy Spirit and Fire, as the saints of the Upper Room did in Acts 1 and 2.

You must first *wait* on the Holy Spirit to *empower* you for ministry. In the waiting stage, your preparation is filled with prayer, fasting, fellowship, worship, Bible study, breaking of bread, and communion.

The *intent to* wait is our posture. It is the prerequisite for the endowment of Power. This preparation phase grows into continuous experiences of soaking in God's Presence which then begins to release the mighty working of the Spirit through the prepared vessel. Just be hungry for God. He knows when you are ready. He will clothe you with Power at the appointed time. Seek closeness with Him.

Closeness with the Word and Spirit is a necessity because God is forming a good and holy thing in you.

> " Closeness with the Word and Spirit is a necessity because God is forming a good and holy thing in you.

When you find yourself praying about everything all the time, you're on the right path. Your worship then goes from an outward expression to a deeper desire to connect with God every time you yield, or should I say, tune in to God. These moments of soaking also bring Rivers of revelation and breakthrough, that cleanse and build your inner man and release the supernatural of God into your life. That's when that Holy Fire from Heaven descends upon you to empower you.

It is the Holy Anointing of God given for the work of the ministry. When the Anointing rests, your appointment begins.

Genuine hunger qualifies you for an encounter with the Living God (Jeremiah 29:12-13). If the disciples were endued with Power from God to be witnesses, then we also must wait till the Power from on High rests upon us and anoints us to be mighty witnesses for the Gospel of our Lord Jesus Christ.

THE MOVE OF GOD IS ALREADY IN YOU

The *Move of God* is the *Work of God*. It is the *Kingdom of God* manifested here on earth. As I mentioned earlier, the Anointing is the Movement; an Anointing becomes a Movement because the Anointing carries the Movement and is the custodian of the Movement. You need an Anointing from God to carry God's Revival. If the Anointing preaches good tidings, sets the captives free, binds up the brokenhearted, opens the prison to those that are in bondage, and proclaims the acceptable year of the Lord, then we need the Anointing.

We must be anointed for the Move of God. Every Anointing mentioned in the Bible was a 'God-Movement.'

God will never give you the Move of His Spirit until He first calls you to the Move. That Mandate becomes your *anointed purpose* — *the destiny you are called to fulfil on earth.*

The Anointing reveals the Father's love for His people.

The Anointing upon your life is Holy Spirit's approval to work with you concerning the Move of God.

I hear saints and ministers talk to me about the *coming Move of God* but don't realise the Move of God is already in them. It is that mighty Anointing resting upon them. For by it, the Lord will do great and mighty things. The Move can't come without an assigned Anointing. The Mandated Move is *carried* by an Anointing. It is *led* by an Anointing—The Mantle. The Move is *served* by an Anointing— The Heart for the Move.

It is good to intercede for the Move of God. But we can be forever interceding unless God sends a vessel to bring that Move. Two things an important to note here.

- The Move only will come through a *Vessel*, called and anointed for the task of carrying, leading and serving the Move.

- The Revival must be preached, will be preached and shall be preached.

You can't carry oil without a jar. Likewise, you can't have a Move without a Vessel who is chosen by God to bring the Move of God.

Only the Anointing, resting upon a vessel, enables that vessel to carry the 'God-assignment.' It is the Anointing that qualifies you for the appointment. When we make room for the Anointing, we make room for the Revival.

Our Lord Jesus is the Chief Apostle and Revivalist of the Move (Acts 10:38). He was anointed for the Move of God. He came *Preaching the Move—The Kingdom of God (Mark 1:14-15).* He is our example of why we must *wait for the Spirit and walk with the Spirit.*

Jesus told the disciples to wait in Jerusalem till the Holy Spirit endowed them with His power. Only then could they be true witnesses, carrying the Gospel of Peace and Power by that Holy Baptism upon their lives. They needed the Baptism of the Holy Spirit and Fire in order to carry, lead and serve the Move of God.

And if you are interested in Revival, learn the requirements for the Move. Be compliant with a Revival-mindset. And what is that mindset? It is an unceasing desire to be at the feet of Christ and to behold His Glory at *the Cleft of the Rock.*

The Anointing serves the purpose and desire of the Presence of God. If you want a Move of God, then you must also want the *Presence of God.*

OBEDIENCE—OBEDIENCE—OBEDIENCE

The Anointing upon your life is the permission granted to you. That Anointing is carried by your obedience and commitment to God. It is your appointed office to work under the leadership of the Spirit so that 'God-assignments' and 'God-directives' can be fulfilled through you. An example: is when Moses parted the Red Sea with *The Rod of God*, by *obeying* God's instructions. The sea didn't part because Moses had great faith. It parted because He *was obedient* to the *command* God gave him.

Therefore, we the people of His Presence are also the people of obedience to His every Word.

There was one time when I started to preach. I was led to preach about 'the Mantle.' Being led by the Spirit, I called out, "The Mantle has fallen. But who will pick it up?"

I was not facing the congregation but I faced the wall to the left of me. I noticed the Anointing lingering there, so I focused my attention on where God was, rather than being distracted by what was happening in the room. It looked weird, but I maintained my posture. And the more I focused on the weightiness of the Word lingering there, the more the Presence of God came, and He filled the Room. My obedience, was in that moment, God-focussed and not man-focussed.

Moses did the same here. The desperate noise of the people of Israel didn't help at all. But Moses called out to God and he got focused on the Word of God, before him.

Exodus 14:15-16

And the LORD said unto Moses, Wherefore criest thou unto Me? speak unto the children of Israel, that they go forward: But lift thou up thy rod, and stretch out thine hand over the sea, and divide it: and the children of Israel shall go on dry ground through the midst of the sea.

William Seymour, the preacher— was the chosen 'Fire starter' and carrier of the Azusa Street Revival. He also came under a mighty Anointing of the Holy Spirit to proclaim mass healings with *one word* by that same Anointing. His *obedience to the Word in the room* was exemplary.

Seymour, in obedience to the Holy Spirit, would place a wooden box on his head when he prayed. Although, he was ridiculed by others for doing that; they didn't understand why Seymour carried out this strange act. Seymour was doing it in obedience to God. His obedience to God was more important than trying to please the critics of the Move. It was a choice to either be just a *good pastor or a God-pastor*. His heart was after God, more than just ministry.

It was the reputation of the Glory that rested that was far more important than the reputation of a seeker-friendly preacher. And while that Glory lingered, many were healed, delivered, baptised with the Fire of God and sent out with great Power to witness.

The Prophet Moses's instructions for the great workings of God were conveyed by God through the *Wooden Rod* in his hands. To Moses, it was the *Rod of God* (Exodus 4:20) used to instruct the miraculous and supernatural on earth. For Pastor William Seymour, that instruction came in the form of a *wooden box* upon his head. Again, God conveyed the Power of Heaven through *his obedience* to have that box sit on his head. These wooden elements were used to make simple, the instructions-to-obey. Just obedience and nothing more than that. I did say it earlier, but it's worth saying it again here. That's what mustered-seed-faith is—obedience to the Voice of the Spirit. And you can't have a Move, without *obedience to the Voice of the Move.*

> " You can't have a Move, without *obedience to the Voice of the Move.*

Like Pastor Seymour, there have been many who have walked in the Fires of Revival by their obedience to the Word of God and the Leadership of the Holy Spirit. The authority and Power that flowed from these vessels came from their submission and obedience to the Spirit of the Word.

And now it is our turn to be obedient to the Voice of the Word. The responsibility to carry, lead and serve the Move lies in our obedience. Will you pick the up Mantle for the Move? Will you be given to His Voice and His Word? God wants to abide with His people again. And He is looking for a 'Glory Carrier.' Will you be that one who will say yes to the Move, by yielding to the Spirit of the Move? God calls you to the *place of obedience; that place at the Cleft of the Rock, that place of great revelation and true worship.*

And just as the Rod was in Moses's hands, and the Box that was upon William Seymour's head, may your *posture of worship and complete surrender* be the instrument that God uses to enter a room. May the *Rod* that was in Moses's hands, and the *Box* that was upon William Seymour's head, speak to you a greater and deeper lesson, by the Power of the Spirit that dwells in you.

Because only a *vessel of obedience* and *discipline* will carry God's glorious Move. 'Obedience' is their discipline.

> "Only a vessel of *discipline to obey,*
> will carry the Move of God

Let the passion of Christ burn as the Fires of transformation that must rest mightily upon His people and cause our hearts to come before the Glory of our Father. I resound those powerful words, "Oh, *Daughter of Zion;* the Lord calls you because He knows you by name and you belong to Him."

CHAPTER 14

A SECOND BAPTISM WITH FIRE BY JESUS

He shall baptise you with the Holy Ghost and Fire...

I mentioned in Chapter 11, about my father seeing a vision from God on the first weekend of April 2012. He was taken into the Throne Room of God and was given that wonderful message from God. He called me up immediately to deliver the message.

It was time to take up *the Rod of God* again. It was time to take up the work of the ministry and be obedient to the Anointing. My hunger for God began to grow again. This desperation for God would again, draw the splendour of Heaven to me in a way I had not anticipated.

It was now the end of May 2012. I sat to watch a David Herzog segment on Sid Roth about the Glory and my heart was exceedingly stirred. I didn't want to miss out on the Move of God anymore. I didn't want to be the one looking from the outside and seeing others enjoy the blessing of the Move. I no longer wanted to

CHAPTER 14 — *A Second Baptism With Fire By Jesus*

be a spectator of the Move. I wanted in on what God was doing. I wanted to be a part of what David Herzog was speaking about.

I looked at the time and it was going towards 3:00 p.m. The winter season had just arrived, so it was cold in the house. I then asked Olivia to watch the kids for me and that I would be praying in the room, seeking an answer: I was determined to get a response from God. At that time I thought, would the Lord do it again? Was His gift and calling truly without repentance?

I picked my notebook, filled with all the encounters and visions and dreams, since 1999. I figured it would make sense to remind God of His prophetic Words and the promises contained in the notebook. I based this thought on Habakkuk 2:1-4. I thought, if I was going to get God's attention, it would be to observe *the visions that were written down.* I planned to knock on God's door boldly until there was a response. To seek His face diligently until He answers. Jeremiah 29:12-13 sat in my heart. I knew this was what I needed to do; to seek God with all my heart, till I found Him.

I remember praying to God that afternoon in this manner, "God if You will not come and touch me and set me on Fire, then I will find a way to come to You."

"What a brilliant idea, right? To seek an audience with the Most High: the all-powerful God." - Norman Sabadi (quite amused at my mindless effort). My desperate and audacious prayer was either going to be a stupid idea or the exact thing that God required. Indeed it was a gutsy, but heart-to-heart, honest prayer. I smile to myself thinking about it now, because who in their right mind asks the God of all things, the Powerful God of Glory to come to them without considering the ramifications? But because I was so hungry for Him. Hunger for God had gripped me again like it did many years prior. Now the deep within me was calling out to the *Deep of God.*

I placed the 'Visions and Dreams' book on my chest and the Bible on top of it. And I prayed again, "God if anything of these that You gave to me, if it means anything to You, You will come and tell me Yourself. If You truly meant everything about what You said and about Your great Anointing and calling, You come and tell me Yourself. Jesus, if You won't come to me and touch me, then I will find a way to come to You and touch You."

Matthew 5:6

Blessed are they which do hunger and thirst after righteousness: for they shall be filled.

The time was approaching 5:00 p.m. now. I prayed intensely in tongues and kept repeating my audacious petition to God.

I remembered all the encounters that had happened over the years, and tears rushed down my face. I became repentant and my heart longed for Him again. Oh what a wonderful thing, when hunger in you becomes brokenness that touches the heart of God.

Our deepest encounters with God are always often ineffable and inexpressible. But I will do my best to describe what happened to me.

I then fell into a deep vision. I knew I wasn't in a dream, because I knew I was still awake; conscious and very much aware of my surroundings.

In the vision, I was now standing at the Kapala Homestead, in Gabagaba Village, PNG (our family home). How did I get here? Was I transported by the Spirit?

But as I looked around me, a bush 'fire' that was about twenty metres high, had already engulfed the neighbours' yard and the grasslands across the road from our yard.

CHAPTER 14

A Second Baptism With Fire By Jesus

My brothers, James and Bogana were with me, and as they were about to run from the Fire, I reached out to them, almost subconsciously, and grabbed the back of their shirts to stop them and said, "Do not run, The Lord is here!"

I thought, what did I just say? Well, it was my spirit that spoke, and my mind was playing catch up here. And because I said this, I looked up to see if it was true and standing at the entrance to the property (about thirty-five to forty metres from me) was a man about six feet, three inches tall. He was the blazing Fire; His whole being was the flames of Fire. He burned like the burning bush but never burning up.

I realised immediately that He was the cause of the Fires that engulfed the area. I knew who this was. Jesus was now standing and His body, poised in my direction.

Then Jesus hastened Himself and began to walk hurriedly toward me. That burning man; a man who was 'the Fire,' was now walking with intent toward me. I quivered with fear and reverence. I thought to myself, "What have I done? I am surely going to die now. Because I audaciously asked the Lord of Glory to come to me and that if He didn't come and touch me and set me on Fire, then I would find a way to come to Him."

And in that moment, I didn't know what to do but yield. I got down on my knees and raised my hands toward Him. I thought, "If I am going to die, I might as well surrender my all to the Lord now."

His fiery countenance was soon before me in a matter of seconds and He reached down and grabbed my outstretched arms with a strong grip and lifted me.

And I screamed in pain, for my life, "Aaaahhhhhh!"

The Fire of Christ consumed me. The Fire burned, like thousands of volts of electricity and Fire combined. It wasn't the pleasant experience of the gentle touch we receive when hands are laid upon us.

Although, it felt torturous to my being, at the same time it was glorious. That thirty seconds of Fire consuming my being, felt like forever. I remembered John the Baptist's words,

Matthew 3:11

> I indeed baptize you with water unto repentance: but He that cometh after me is mightier than I, Whose shoes I am not worthy to bear: He shall baptize you with the Holy Ghost, and with Fire:

Then Jesus let me go, and I was filled with His awesome Glory and Power. It didn't hurt anymore. He made my body to be able to accommodate the Fire that now burned all over me and inside of me. I looked down at my arms and the rest of my body and quickly observed myself.

My brothers were still there behind me and stood about an arm's reach from me. With Jesus standing next to me, I turned to them and Jesus immediately spoke to me and said, "Release the Fire upon them."

I reached out and grabbed Bogana's arms and I did as Jesus commanded me. He was instantly filled with the same Fire of God and prophesied saying, "THE REVIVAL HAS BEGUN," pointing to the streets and houses in Emerald, Queensland.

I made a mental note of the place, not knowing that it would be the very place, of our first *Revival Assignment in Australia*.

A bit of background to this: Bogana had just arrived in Australia from PNG, and was residing in Emerald, a small mining town in the Central Highlands Region, in Queensland. So his appearing in the dream was God prophesying that first assignment. The Emerald Revival would later start in May 2013.

CHAPTER 14 — *A Second Baptism With Fire By Jesus*

Then Jesus commanded me to pray for James (my twin). And I did exactly as I did with Bogana, but James looked stuck in earthly and fleshy matters and was consumed with bitterness, hate and unforgiveness. I wondered why he hadn't responded like Bogana did.

Jesus instructed me to do it again, and this time the Fire upon my body glowed like golden glitter all over me, upon my flesh and skin. This made me think of how the Ark of God, and the Rods that were used to carry the Ark were made of wood and covered in gold—a similitude of how we as earthen vessels (the wood), are clothed with Power (the gold). The other interesting thing was, that the Staves that were used to carry the Ark, once they were inserted into the rings of the Ark, would remain and never be removed—again the resemblance of man anointed by God, and their Mantle remains upon them till they complete their assignment and journey on earth (Exodus 25:13-15, Romans 11:29).

Back to the story.

So, I grabbed James's arms the second time following Christ's instruction and I spoke the Word again, "Receive the Holy Ghost Fire, In Jesus' Name! Fire!"

This time, it got on him and his eyes were opened and he began to prophesy.

Later, I asked the Lord what James meant in the dream. Was it for Papua New Guinea (PNG)? The Holy Spirit then explained to me that yes, there would be a time approaching, in the near future, when I would carry out the assignment to take that Revival Fire to PNG. That assignment is now at *the break of dawn* as I write this book for you. I am so excited and I look forward to testifying about it in my next book, if God wills.

But it also has another meaning. Because I care for my twin very much; I know I would be willing to lay down my life for him.

The Lord said to me, "You will love, embrace and carry My Move, the same way you love your brother."

I was deeply touched by this heart-full gesture and profound insight from the Lord.

Also, James in the dream, represents the state and heart-condition of the Church. God will heal and set the Church free from the spirits of bitterness and offence that have inflicted havoc in the Body of Christ, and left many lives in ruins.

So, I came out of the vision and the room was no longer cold but so very hot like an oven. I rushed to the door of the bedroom. The heat was so intense, I was sweating with the Power of God still running through my being.

Olivia was shocked when she saw me open the bedroom door hastily, and my countenance looked different. I had been overtaken completely by the Revival Fire of God.

Hallelujah! I was restored. I was made whole. For the Lord Jesus had truly kept His Word and came to me and burned me so powerfully, with His Holy Fire. There was no room for doubt anymore.

The Lord Holy Spirit then led me to hit the walls with my Bible, a strange act, you might say, then He said to me, "Get ready to leave this place."

The administrative aspect of the Revival assignment was now in progress. Heaven was on our case, and soon we had to leave our comfortable two-bedroom home, in September of 2012. We went and briefly stayed at Olivia's mum's house. She lived in another suburb of Canberra. Afterwards, we then boarded briefly at a family friend's place, before heading to Emerald, Queensland.

Coming to the end of November 2012, we knew we had to obey God, to go to Emerald. Following a specific direction, that was in a later vision, Olivia and I with our two kids left for

CHAPTER 14   *A Second Baptism With Fire By Jesus*

Emerald. Ethan was three years old and Jazmina was about one and a half years old.

Bogana had opened his arms to us, in the time of our need and asked us to come and stay with him. What Bogana didn't know at that time was that, God was the instigator behind our temporary, dislocation and itinerant situation. God was prophetically aligning us to fulfil the *Emerald Revival Mandate* that would come in May of the following year, 2013.

CHAPTER 15

THE EMERALD REVIVAL (MAY 2013 TO APRIL 2014

This is God's Will

THE EMERALD REVIVAL!

What an amazing experience it was. God told us there that during the Revival, we would learn, "The good and bad of Revival."

The good would be the blessing of Revival. The bad was the persecution, bitterness, offence, criticisms and misunderstandings that would rise because of the Move. Some things lay at the bottom of the dirty pool and would require the Revival Fire to expose them and cause that ugly mess hiding under 'the masked niceties' of Church life, and bring them to the surface to be dealt with by the Holy Spirit.

The Emerald Revival would not only be our first assignment as a couple but also our training for future Revivals. There was a sense of new beginnings and adventure in the things of God, in the air.

I remember as we drove to Emerald, we shared the driving on the way up. On a certain part of the trip at about 1:00 a.m., we had

CHAPTER 15   *The Emerald Revival*

just passed a small town called Gilgandra, in New South Wales. Olivia had taken the turn to drive and I lay my head on a pillow to get some sleep. Then a vision flashed before me, which had Joyce Meyers in it. In the vision, Joyce Meyers stood facing me and said, "This is God's Will!" I woke from it and remembered the Lord had said to me, "I shall align you to My Glory!"

When we arrived in Emerald, Olivia and I began to fast and pray at the beginning of the year 2013. This fasting would trigger a series of events that amazingly were all linked prophetically to each heavenly visitation I had encountered in the past years. The appointed times for the 'vision notebook' I mentioned earlier, had begun to unfold. Patience or long-suffering, for the Move of God is part of the necessity of our discipline to carry the Move. We can't hurry God, but we can trust God to lead us.

> " Patience or long-suffering, for the Move of God is part of the necessity of our discipline to carry the Move.

Our forty-day fasting, really geared our hearts and minds for what the Lord was about to do in Emerald. It was also our first ever forty-day fasting together.

We found a Pentecostal Church there. I remember on that first day when we met the Pastor of the Church, the Holy Spirit said to me to let him know that Revival was coming to His Church. I went, "Holy Spirit, we're strangers here. I don't know how he will take the Word." But I was obedient.

I was glad that the Lord had prophesied Revival for Emerald. God knows the place and the people to whom He has chosen to receive His Fire and Restoration. The Love of God is intentional. I love that God can position us in a way, often we ourselves are not aware of that alignment. The Mandate of Revival does bring with it a great blessing and God surely was going to do that for the Pastor and the Church in Emerald. Hallelujah! Revival is the pleasure and lovingkindness of God manifested to us. When we become frail and unsure, God's Spirit becomes for us the boldness of His love to lead us and show us the way forward. His Word was proclaimed now all we had to do was be patient with when it would happen.

Then later, in early April 2013, during fellowship time with the Holy Spirit, the Spirit told me to go to the Pastor again, and to say to him, *"The Wind of The Spirit* is going blow into Emerald, in the month of May 2013."

The Pastor's response was, "It's interesting you say that because the theme for the month of May is Worship."

Well, there you have it. Worship: as I have been teaching to you in this book, is at the heart of Revival and is the Divine Call of our priesthood in Christ.

I still remember that last weekend of May 2013; which was also the first anniversary of the Baptism of Fire, I had received from Jesus.

As we worshipped that Sunday night, the Lord told me to announce that the angels of Revival were on the way. Just minutes, after that announcement, the Wind of the Spirit came. A tangible feeling like that same Fire from Jesus poured like hot water into my chest and began to rest heavily on my body. I looked up, and the people began to come under the Power of God, from one end of the room to the other. The whole auditorium had come under the Power of God. Hallelujah! That same night, the Lord had come to Emerald, and the blessing from Above had found Himself a place to meet with His people again. The Mighty Wind of Revival had come to us.

Many were so overtaken by the Holy Spirit, that the ushers had to extend their duties by driving them home. What a glorious event.

But as the Move picked up, so did the persecution. All things considered, God was at work and we were there to do only what God required of us. During our time there, I learned a lot, and the Lord was teaching us quickly. New friendships were formed out of the Fires of Revival. God was truly moulding and shaping us for the work of the ministry. There were many wonderful moments of encounters, and so many wonderful *Holy Spirit* lessons gained during the time of the Emerald Revival. Some of which I will be able to impart to you as subheadings in this Chapter. The first one: *Prophetic Triggers*.

PROPHETIC TRIGGERS—THE LESSON

Prophetic Triggers, or as the Apostle Peter defined it specifically as 'Moved by the Holy Ghost.'

2 Peter 1:20-21

> Knowing this first, that no prophecy of the scripture is of any private interpretation. For the prophecy came not in old time by the will of man: **but holy men of God spake as they were moved by the Holy Ghost.**

Many interesting and wonderful things happened in Emerald. A particular event was one Sunday after service. A young man approached me, to ask me an interesting question, and one that never crossed my mind before. It was more like a string of questions regarding one subject: the 'Prophet's Mantle.'

"Brother Norman, how does prophecy work? Teach me what the prophetic Anointing and gifts are and how to operate in them. How do you know when a prophetic Word is present and ready to be released? I like the prophet's Mantle and I want to know more about it."

No one had ever asked me that question before. I quickly asked the Holy Spirit to help me with the lesson. I thanked the young man for his question and told him this would be the first time I was answering a well-put string of questions regarding the prophet's Mantle and prophetic giftings of the Spirit of God. As I paused for about a minute, the Spirit of God then formed the answers. "Prophetic triggers."

"What? What are prophetic triggers?" He looked puzzled and I needed to elaborate.

The Holy Spirit was in on the subject right away and began to pour what we needed to know.

Your five senses of sight, hearing, taste, touch, and smell are the gateways to the soul and spirit of a man. They are gateways to the spirit realm (where thoughts, visions and dreams operate). Through the senses, we communicate with the spirit realm.

The Spirit of God, therefore, uses these gateways to release His Word so we can receive it. By this I mean, we receive the Word revealed by the Holy Spirit, into our body, soul and spirit.

A prophetic Word can be released from the Spirit to us, through touch, and that becomes the point of entrance for the Spirit to enter into the natural realm. I told him a story of another Christian brother. The Lord had told me to tell him that God had a Word for him the next Sunday. But I also had no idea what that Word was. Come that Sunday and after Church, he hurried up to me to receive the Word. I was like, "Holy Spirit if there was a time I need you to be real, it's now because I have no Word for this man."

Sure enough, when I reached out to shake his hand, and as the palm of my hands made contact with his, a Word from the Spirit was instantaneously released. *The handshake* was the prophetic trigger that the Holy Spirit used.

This helps us to understand why you would read often in the Bible, mainly in the Old Testament when prophets would say,
"The Word of the Lord came To Me."

1 Samuel 15:10

Then came the Word of the LORD unto Samuel, saying,...

I love it when the Word *enters the room.* The Lord can use anything to trigger the release of that Word.

A trait of this gift is the ability to discern, by the Spirit, *the weightiness of the Word* when He comes to you to speak.

What happens in a prophetic trigger is fascinating and it is certainly a gift that every believer should desire.

Another point to note is, that all your senses are engaged with that Word when it manifests. It captures your attention and stirs in you faith to utter what your spirit hears. The weightiness of the Word can be felt like a river flowing within, accompanied by a deep knowing.

Then comes the 'delivering part,' where the Word lingers with Power on your being until you open your mouth to speak it. You are then prophesying, being *Inspired or moved by the Holy Ghost.* You speak it forth only in the way it has come to your spirit man, not adding your own words, but proclaiming what you see, hear and feel.

Now 'the weightiness of the Word' also varies from Word to Word. This is determined by God and how He wants you to receive it. It can be a Word for you or it can be a Word for someone else. That person doesn't necessarily have to be present when the Word is received, as long as you are there in that moment to receive it, through that prophetic trigger.

God transmits, and we receive. God authors it, and we proclaim it. As is the way of God, the Word of Spirit comes at its appointed time; not on man's appointment but on God's time. So you can't force a prophecy, nor can you force the Anointing to work. Only your yielding and availability to the Spirit is required.

The Word arrives like a pilot of an aeroplane communicating with the air traffic control tower. The pilot informs the tower that he is preparing to descend and land on the runway. The air traffic control tower has to be on the same wave frequency to receive the transmission from the pilot. In this illustration, we are the tower and the Word is the Aeroplane about to land.

The only difference in this example is that man cannot control when and where the 'Word' lands, man is only the receiver of its approach and arrival. Quite the opposite from the natural, it's the Pilot (God), that tells the tower when and where the Word will land.

But God is our Pilot and Captain of His Word. He decides when to land and which air traffic control tower (vessel) should be receiving His transmission for landing. So yes, we must be on the same wavelength as the Holy Ghost so that we can receive what He has for us and for the Body of Christ. For the Word of God is the Will of God (Romans 12:1-2).

That was certainly a wonderful lesson to share. That lesson has allowed me to mentor many, by the Holy Spirit, to discern *the Word of Revival* that enters a room.

Prayer:

May the Spirit of Prophecy and the Mantle given unto the Prophets, be also yours, to those who have been called into this faithful place. Precious Jesus, grant us the blessing of Your Word. Hallelujah! Great is our God and greatly to be Praised!

CHAPTER 15   *The Emerald Revival*

THE CLEANING ROSTER THAT TURNED INTO A 'GOD ENCOUNTER'

The experience I am about to share with you also happened during the time of the Emerald Revival. Olivia and I, being new to the Church, gladly gave our time to serve as volunteers at the Church. We decided to help with the cleaning roster. Some Saturdays, we would turn up to help others clean, even if we weren't rostered down. We wanted to be a blessing to the saints there.

The cleaning itself was always the standard; it began from the entrance to the coffee area, then to the kids' area, the men's and ladies' restroom, and ended at the main worship auditorium. It was a joy to give our time to the Lord in this manner.

This one particular Saturday, we had arrived early at about 7:00 a.m. at the Church building but the others hadn't turned up. Olivia and I went straight into the cleaning anyway.

I had finished doing my bit and was now in the main auditorium. I finally got to the front seats and turned to the stage to begin wiping down the pulpit and whatever else that needed a quick wipe over. It was normal practice for me to leave my footwear at the front seats and walk barefoot on the stage. This, I did, to give reverence to God, and to show honour to His instruments of service, where His Word was preached and where the worship band led.

It had nothing to do with religious practice. It was just my way of appreciating and reverencing the LORD. Don't be caught up with a practice, rather be a minister unto the Lord with reverence in your heart because you love Him.

Oh, how I love His Presence. How I so want to be in His holy place always. I loved being in the place where we worshipped God

—all the more, it was an opportunity for me to clean the podium with a joyous heart. The more I cleaned there, the more His Presence *thickened*. Yes, God's Presence is everywhere but when we host Him in a certain place with a certain posture, it becomes a special and tangible moment with the Lord.

Each time, I would pray and worship Him after I finished wiping down the instruments and the pulpit. There, I felt the gentle hand of the Holy Spirit embrace me as I got to the pulpit. The sweet Presence of the Lord overwhelmed me with joy and moved me to tears. His Presence was so powerful and overwhelming, I lay there at the base of the pulpit broken before the Lord.

When this happened the first time, I spoke with Olivia about it on the way home. She then said, "Well, I see God is doing something wonderful to you there (referring to the base of the pulpit). Perhaps we'll do every clean that way from now on. You clean right up to the podium and I'll finish with the other areas."

And so on the next Saturday's clean, it happened again and that beautiful Presence of the Lord lingered. I just sat in it and worshipped God the whole time. Olivia had finished her part of the cleaning, and when she came to the auditorium, she found me praying and weeping before the Lord on my knees. A sweet Presence blanketed the area as she sat with me.

This time we took no thought about the cleaning roster. We were going to be there because the Presence of God was upon the place, and we wanted to be soaking there.

So on the fourth clean, something more wonderful happened. This time, as I got to the base of the pulpit, that wonderful Presence of God began to envelop me again as it did in the previous times. His passion and desire gripped my heart. With my face to the floor before the Lord and with many tears, I sang softly and spoke to Him, "Lord, I love Your Presence."

I remembered how the Psalmist had said, "As the hart panteth after the water brooks, so panteth my soul after Thee, O God. My soul thirsteth for God, for the Living God: when shall I come and appear before God? (Psalms 42:1-2)."

Another passage from the Book of Psalms came to mind:

Psalms 27:4-5

One thing have I desired of the LORD, that will I seek after; that I may dwell in the house of the LORD all the days of my life, to behold the beauty of the LORD, and to enquire in His temple. For in the time of trouble, He shall hide me in His pavilion: in the secret of His tabernacle shall He hide me; He shall set me up upon a Rock.

As I wept before the Lord once again, I said to the Lord, "It feels like I've been here before. Like before I was born, I have been here before. That's a weird feeling."

The mystery of endless time in God seemed to speak something far greater than my mind—Identity and destiny communed with me and I responded thoughtfully, "Before time was ever formed, and before everything came into being, I knew You and You knew me. Lord, I have found You, I have found You."

It felt like I had found a missing part of me. I had discovered purpose, not as a stranger, but it was a long-lost missing piece of me. My heart knew this place: I belonged to God.

Then the Spirit of God spoke to me in a gentle Voice, "Norman My servant. You are My great preacher. You are My great preacher."

I then thought it would be right to explain my place more perfectly to the Lord, "You mean, I am Your preacher."

"No! No! You are not just My preacher, you are My 'Great' preacher. You are My 'Great' preacher." I was corrected and I accepted without questions.

As the Spirit spoke these Words, they surged through my body with torrents of His *Revival Anointing*.

Very much like the Prophet Jeremiah (Jeremiah 1:4-10), God was speaking to me about my ordination and calling in Him. Jeremiah said he was only a child and couldn't speak. But God said to him (paraphrasing here), "Don't say you're a child. I am sending you to speak for Me. And I will be with you. I will put My Words in your mouth and you will speak to them. Don't be afraid of them because I will be with you."

I gave myself to Him at that moment and worshipped the Holy Spirit there before the pulpit.

I was only meant to wipe the surface of the pulpit, but this became *my burning bush encounter* again and reminded me of His Fire that had consumed me in that blessed vision back in Canberra.

The 'PULPIT ENCOUNTER' as I call it, expressed that God has always wanted to have fellowship with man. Ever since He started with Adam in the Garden of Eden (Genesis 3:8), the Lord has not stopped meeting with us.

God doesn't just set you on Fire and send you forth to be a witness. His *Fire, which is the Voice of His Word, continues to commune with you, for the rest of your life.*

> " God doesn't just set you on Fire and sends you forth to be a witness. No, His Fire, which is the Voice of His Word, continues to commune with you, for the rest of your life.

CHAPTER 15 — *The Emerald Revival*

The Father works to guide you into your calling and to prepare you for the tasks you were ordained for, before the foundations of the world.

It may take years, but trust the Spirit, and lean upon His Words faithfully. For in due season, you shall see it all come together like a perfectly fitted puzzle. The Holy Spirit must mould you, and train you for the Call, even after you have received the Baptism of the Holy Spirit and Fire. Because we are meant to grow from Glory to Glory in Christ Jesus. We are meant to continuously behold the Glory of God (2 Corinthians 3:17-18).

Your *calling* requires your willing heart. Your calling is not your career—it is not an earthly office. It is what you were *ordained for and born to do.* And if you're in Christ, The Holy Spirit can help you discover your purpose in Him.

Our Heavenly Father really loves us. He loves us so much, that He is going to be there for us every step of the Way. But there has to be a willing participation and communion with Him.

While you continue the journey of life here on Earth, God, by His Spirit abiding in you, will continue to reveal many different aspects of your Mission Statement and Mandate.

If you study the life of Abram, who then became Abraham, you will see this exact pattern in which the Lord revealed more each time He met with Abram. On the occasion, when God cut a covenant with Abram, He then changed Abram's name to Abraham.

I love how God continued to affirm His promises to Abraham. Each encounter grounded Abraham's faith deeper and deeper into God and God recognised Abraham as His Friend because that faith became Abraham's anchor of fellowship in God (James 2:23). The same God wants to do that also for you and me as we draw near to God.

Back to the story... A few weeks after the 'The Pulpit Encounter,' we then had to travel back to Canberra to sort out storage and transport to deliver our household items to Emerald. On the way there, about three hours into the drive, the Presence of the Lord filled the car as I worshipped Him. The Holy Spirit then repeated the same words He had said to me at the pulpit of the Church, "Norman, you are My 'Great' preacher. You are My 'Great' preacher."

Again, that same heart-to-heart experience saturated me. But I wondered why the Lord had repeated it to me. The Spirit knew what I was thinking and spoke to me, "Whenever you hear Me say this, it means you will be preaching in that place where you are travelling to. This is My way of saying I have ordained a speaking engagement for you, where you will speak to the people for Me. And although you have not arranged one, I have already arranged one for Me, to speak through you, to the people."

A God-assignment always follows a willing and surrendered heart.

When we got to Canberra, a few days later, we went along with our friend Julie to a mid-week service at the Seven Streams Church International.

As the worship went on, we sat in the back row of seats. Then as the young and vibrant Pastor Tinashe, stood up to preach, he noticed us there.

A quick behind-the-story: I had sent him a prophetic Word about three months before, via email. I assumed that he had received the Word with a humble heart. For starters, we hardly knew each other, but God was speaking and I, being obedient to the Holy Spirit, delivered that Word faithfully.

The Pastor paused briefly and gave a casual greeting to us. In that same second, the Spirit spoke to me instantly and said, "This is that moment, My 'Great' preacher, this is that moment."

The Pastor then beckoned for me to come and greet the Church and speak whatever the Lord had put on my heart. Olivia and I were amazed. God did say it on the way to Canberra and here we were walking in those very words. We were humbled and honoured before the Lord.

So I walked up to him to greet him. He then handed the mic to me and asked me to share something with the Church. As he was passing the microphone over to me, the Spirit had already increased upon me with a Word. That same tangible power of the Fire of God was present and ready to be released there again.

The Revival Anointing came upon me and I began to minister in that short ten minutes. The Power of God was released upon the floor of that room and prophetic Words were given. This helped the Pastor and the Church greatly.

Afterwards, with an abundance of kindness in the Pastor's heart, he assisted us with administration for our vehicle to be serviced before we took to the highway again back to Emerald.

Hallelujah! What a mighty God we serve. Not only does He prepares *the place* where His Words must be spoken, but He also provides for His servants' needs.

A few days later, we stopped over at the Canberra House of Prayer (C-HOP) to see Hilary. She was glad to have us join them in the prayer session on Friday evening.

That night, again, the Lord's Spirit spoke to me, "I have opened the door for you here also, My 'Great' preacher. You shall be ministering here tonight."

I only listened and knew in my heart, and when the time came for the main prayer session, God moved mightily again. While the prayers went on, Hilary then called for me to share a word of encouragement with those who had attended the meeting. The Spirit of God, like before, came upon that place, as I testified about what the Lord was doing in Emerald. The Presence of God became so heavy, that He knocked Hilary back into her seat.

Great encouragement filled the place, and our hearts were warmed by the sweet Presence of the Holy Spirit. God truly knows how to meet us even at our lowest point. For His strength is made perfect in our weaknesses.

Prayer:

> Holy Spirit, I pray that you will pour upon us your great Revival. We yield to Your Presence and know that You are near when We call.

"GO TO ROCKHAMPTON
&
THERE I WILL BLESS YOU"

The Emerald Revival had gone on for about a year (May 2013 to May 2014). So much had happened spiritually for so many people. We saw many victories and we encountered battles too, which we dealt with through prayer, fasting, and mentorship.

Whether, we were judged, criticised, misunderstood, called names, or written off, there was equally a wonderful grace to minister and there was acceptance from others; and a desire to grow more in God. These are all the traits of Revival.

One Sunday, in May of 2014, we were getting dressed to attend Church, and the Lord said, "Your work here is complete. You are not to attend the Church anymore."

This was a difficult instruction for me. God never gave us a reason why we weren't to attend Church Service anymore. But

CHAPTER 15 — *The Emerald Revival*

Olivia and I obeyed. We had already come to a place in our walk with God, knowing very well that it was always better to trust God, even if we didn't understand it. We had a discussion and concluded that the Lord would reveal all these things to us later. God knew something and it wasn't necessary for us to know at that time.

A few days later, as we drove to the shops, the Word of the Lord came to me again, "Go to Rockhampton and there I will bless you. And in blessing you, I will bless you with a great blessing. Establish the base of My Ministry—Church there. Raise My Children for me (referring to Ethan and Jazmina). I will also instruct you to deal with the spirit of witchcraft there."

It felt very much like how God called Abraham (at that time his name was still Abram) to go to the land where God was going to bless him (Genesis 12:1-3).

Again, by the leading of the Lord, we took a brief visit to PNG to spend time with family and do some ministry work. After five months there, upon returning it was time for us to make the transition to Rockhampton.

Yet, we weren't just going to leave without releasing a prophetic blessing over my brother, Bogana and his wife, Sheena. Theirs, is a powerful testimony that requires another whole book of its own. Sheena wasn't too well and wasn't able to conceive. She had been through so much medical help and even the doctors didn't want to give her high hopes. What looked impossible for man, was certainly possible for God. The God of Heaven looked down and saw Bogana and Sheena's prayers. The Lord saw their hearts and granted them according to His Word, the blessing of the womb.

Today, they have two beautiful daughters, so precious and close to our hearts. Much to our joy, we share every happy moment with them every time they visit us in Rockhampton. And very much like the Shunammite woman, who made room for the Prophet Elisha, to house him (2 Kings 4:8-17), God had done the same for my dear brother and his wife.

A great rain of blessings always comes to them that follow after God's heart. When you are faithful in the little things, God will reward you in a special way, and even you will know the difference.

Matthew 10:40-41

He that receiveth you receiveth Me, and he that receiveth Me receiveth Him that sent Me. He that receiveth a prophet in the name of a prophet shall receive a prophet's reward; and he that receiveth a righteous man in the name of a righteous man shall receive a righteous man's reward.

Prayer:

Lord Holy Spirit, we make room for You. We bow before You and lay our lives down at Your Feet. Mighty God, we have seen Your wondrous works and believe together that we shall see more. We are confident that You will do great things with us because we are Yours. Oh, Spirit of God, thank You for filling our hearts with Your Presence. Thank You, for the Joy of serving You. We honour You with all of our hearts. Amen...

CHAPTER 16

EXPERIENCING THE GREAT MOVE OF GOD 'THE ROCKHAMPTON BLESSING'

An open heaven happens when God comes to speak

The following are testimonies and lessons gained from the start of what I call, 'The Rockhampton Blessing' or 'The Rockhampton Promise' after our move from Emerald in June 2015, right up to the writing of this book in 2023. We have taken hold of these words and believed what the Lord spoke over us, "Go to Rockhampton and there I will bless you." The journey gets more amazing as the Lord reveals more of His plans for the Great Move of God to us. This Rockhampton journey includes assignments the Lord has given to us for Cairns City, Queensland, Australia.

With this, I start here by saying, "What God ordains, He Leads." We are living in such a potent and Heavenly-ordained time and era. The season is right and ripe for the Move to reach many because the Power of God is hovering over places where hearts are receptive to the Spirit. These blessed words come to me as I sit in His Presence again, "For Your Glory, I will do anything."

My attention is continually drawn to *the Cleft of the Rock*. That holy place of encounter and revelation. What a holy and breathtaking moment it was for Moses; to behold the appearance of the Glory of God. The *Voice of His Word,* Who came to the garden of Eden to commune with Adam, was the same Voice, now communing with Moses. Oh, Glory! It speaks to me profoundly an encouraging thought; that the Call of God is without repentance. Regardless of the level of struggle or difficulty, the *Mercy* and *Truth* of God remain faithful to all generations.

God is raising a whole generation of valiant and humble ones, who have desired to be at the place by the Rock, which is Jesus. The hour of God's awakening is at hand. It is the hour of His abiding Word upon us and in our midst.

And, I must adjure you to focus on *the Word that carries the Promise. For in the Word is the Promise.* Anyone can preach, but when the Glory of the Word preaches, He changes the atmosphere to release *His Agape Love and His Mandate*. The Great Move of God is here and God is with us and in our midst. For the visitation of the Lord will be a great visitation, and the abiding *Power of His Presence* will rest upon us as *the Dew of Heaven* upon Mount Zion.

WHEN GOD COMES TO SHAKE A CITY

It takes Holy Spirit Noise to shake a city. That noise begins in the heart of the *Fire Carriers*. God shakes a city in such a way, His Presence is felt as a blanket over that place. That's when the vessels of God, who carry an Anointing, are led by God to conquer a territory. That Anointing upon the saints has the Power to break demonic stronghold over that city or region. The saints conquer, being led by the Spirit and NOT by earthly ambition or fleshly conquest.

However, for Satan to have continuous control over a city, he must ensure to keep the deception alive, mainly toward the Church. The devil achieves this by keeping the Church inwardly focused. Given this thought, we notice the Churches of that city then are more concerned with their own organisational growth and functionality, than to pursue any heightened level of fellowship and communion with God. A lukewarm Church is a comfortable Church. A comfortable Church doesn't care for the Move of the Holy Ghost.

God addresses this problem by causing hunger in the hearts of the few. The Sovereign One deploys more than a strategy, He equips and empowers the praying Church that mobilises to see and enter the Move. That gathering is instigated by the Holy Ghost.

And the demons know very well that when a Church begins to stir up an attitude of prayer, word and worship, this Church becomes a dangerous force against the enemy. The Power to encounter change becomes evident in the ministers that have not only travailed in prayer but have soaked in an ocean of revelation from the Holy Spirit. That's how a Move is conceived and birthed.

The birthing of a Move is a spiritual phenomenon that has the Markings of the Lord of Hosts. He is the Author of The Move. When the Tide of God enters a city, He raises the level of revelation and equips the saints for victory. A Church aligned with the Spirit of God has the Power to influence the atmosphere of the city.

Like when Jerusalem came under God's influence when the Spirit fell upon the hundred and twenty saints in the Upper Room. On that same day, three thousand souls came to the Lord with their hearts burning with great conviction by the Spirit of the Word upon Peter's mouth (Acts 2).

CHAPTER 16   *Experiencing The Great Move of God: 'The Rockhampton Blessing'*

HOST ME A CONFERENCE

—

THE 'GOD CALENDAR'

It was now early 2018. Again, I was in a time of prayer and worship when the Lord spoke to me and said, "My Great preacher, My servant, Host me a conference."

God always stretches us outside of our comfort zone. At that time, we only had four families serving under 'The Place Where He Speaks.' Was I to tell the three ladies; Pastor Timena, Sister Marsha, and Sister Joyce, with their families that God wanted us to host Him a conference?

God was serious about it and I wasn't going to disobey either. Up to that point we had only been doing house fellowship on Wednesday evenings and prayer nights on Fridays.

We weren't a mega Church. We didn't have any musical equipment or ministry assets to facilitate a conference.

But God showed me the Gracemere Hall, near where we lived. He wanted us to host our first conference there. I first had to announce the plan to host the conference to the faithful saints.

As the three ladies look back at that event now, they laugh to themselves with joy because their initial reaction was one of shock and uncertainty; it was expected though seeing, we didn't have the manpower, nor the resources to pull it off. This was also going to be our first ever held conference as a Church ministry.

That Wednesday when we met, I then announced to them, "God told me that we are to host a conference for Him."

"What?

"God said what?"

The third asked,

"Are you sure, Pastor Norman, that you heard from the Lord?"

"I am hundred percent sure."

Sister Marsha then added,

"Whatever the Lord wants, I am ready."

You should have seen the look on their faces. Stunned with wonderment, they each sat to digest the very thought that we were to host a meeting for God. It was too much to consider at that time, and this wasn't just going to be a house meeting, but a conference.

Yet, God knows whom He calls. He knows about you, even before He has handed the assignment to you.

I gave the women time to pray on it and to get back to me. Sure enough, God's Spirit visited each of them in their time of fellowship and prayer and each responded with a confident, Yes.

Olivia and I have been so blessed to walk with these sisters of the Lord and we have experienced both the good and the bad together. We have learned much through the process of hosting God—lessons like waiting on God, which is fundamental to our lives in God.

There are some lessons you won't learn until you go through the training process that produces the lesson. There are areas in your life that God wants to increase and promote you in and the only way to do that is to bring you through the practical aspect of stepping out and following His lead.

Then God began to add to the group. Our hearts were stirred. Just months before the conference, God began to bless us with musical instruments, Church banners and much more, right up to the final week of the conference. I was working at that time, and the Lord multiplied my work—because I was paid by the job and not by the hour. With that increase, the Lord led us to be able to cover the cost of the meeting and made sure we were ready for the conference.

CHAPTER 16   *Experiencing The Great Move of God: 'The Rockhampton Blessing'*

If ever you were a part of 'The Place Where He Speaks' team preparing for an upcoming conference, you'd note this one thing; that we chose not to go ahead of the Holy Spirit. God chose the location and time and we turned up to His meeting. We learned early, to let God call the meetings. He chose the date, He chose the speakers and He even chose the theme for the conference.

There were occasions where we had to wait right up to the last week, for God to pick speakers for the meeting.

We had seen God Move in powerful ways, and we had learned that God was at work and our part was to follow His lead.

This is actually a very difficult thing to do—waiting on the LORD. Most Church ministries would have already picked their speakers and the location months in advance, and preliminary announcements made then. But for us, it was fasting, praying, worshipping God and seeking His face every single day leading up to the meeting.

And there lies the difference between a God-ordained meeting and a meeting initiated by man.

Sounds scrupulous. My previous experiences with God, caused me to carry out the will of God in this manner.

Nonetheless, God still honours man to a degree, but only to that degree of your waiting and yielding.

But if you truly want God to come without limits, you must give *full control* to God. This is the fountain from which the great Revival and Awakening of God flows.

No assignment is without a challenge. But God provides for His assignment because He knows whom He has chosen to carry this assignment. Sure we might not be fully equipped from an earthly perspective but God will make us ready to carry the assignment.

CHAPTER 16
Experiencing The Great Move of God: 'The Rockhampton Blessing'

I picked up some very special 'Revival Gems' through the five conferences we have hosted for God since 2018. I would like to share some of these precious 'Revival Thoughts' with you.

WHEN YESHUA'S MANTLE RESTED ON THE PREACHER'S WORDS

The testimony I am about to share stirs my heart with joy. It's a unique experience. Again, I will do my best to be as clear and concise as possible.

In the year 2018, we attended the funeral of a precious man of God. Before we got there, I was prompted by the Spirit that I would meet a particular minister of God, and the Lord would point him out to me. At the funeral service, there were a lot of ministers present. But I noticed a certain man who carried an Anointing that was visible. The Spirit then indicated that it was him. I then prayed to the Holy Ghost, "If this is that man, make a way in this gathering that I will get the opportunity to meet him."

Well, God did. During the funeral reception at the Rockhampton Baptist Church grounds, I was having a chat with another minister when Bishop Ned Gabey walked up to us. He was looking for that pastor standing next to me.

On introducing himself, Bishop Ned, then by the unction of the Spirit jumped straight into sharing a word. It felt like the right moment and the Power of the Word was present. I was standing then with Olivia and Sister Marsha. We had been in the company of these kinds of Holy Ghost conversations before, so we leaned in immediately and listened to the man of God.

The minister started with the words, "A season of harvest lies in the seed that you are about to sow. Multiplication comes from

CHAPTER 16   *Experiencing The Great Move of God: 'The Rockhampton Blessing'*

the seed that you nurture. It is not the size of your congregation that matters. It is what you carry in obedience to God that matters."

I could feel the Holy Spirit grab hold of the inside of me as he spoke. Olivia and Marsha paid close attention to the Word. They urged the man of God to speak further.

"David was a man after the heart of God. David moved God with his worship. And God loved David's worship so much. The same David loved the Presence, it was all that he knew. God had a great plan for David's life. God wanted to promote David. God gave David the position of king so David could carry the influence of the Presence at a higher level than where he was.

David only influenced the sheep at that time. But God wanted David to bring a nation under that same influence, to worship God in Spirit and in Truth. Now the Presence went from just a field level to a national level and a global level. And all David did was love the Presence of God. David loved the Presence but God wanted to give him the position."

Bishop Ned didn't know that in that same year, the Lord had instructed us to host our first conference. We were embarking on a powerful call from Heaven to *host His Presence*. So, I told the bishop I would give him a call to come and preach at the conference. And soon the months became days and the conference had started.

Bishop Ned was appointed to share on the third day of the conference. He preached a powerful narrative style of message combined with momentary pauses to bring revelation to the story. It was the story of blind Bartimaeus who cried to Jesus at Jericho (Mark 10:46-52).

Now, as Bishop Ned came to the part where Jesus had stopped to answer Bartimaeus's request, in that exact moment as he uttered the words, "What do you want that I should do for you?"

The bishop's voice wasn't there anymore but a different voice spoke. It was the Voice of our Lord Jesus. I mean literally!

I can't tell you exactly how I knew this, but it was. I had never encountered anything like this before. I, being a *Word-Carrier*, knew that this was a dimension of God, completely new to me. It was the Voice of our Lord Jesus. My spirit knew Him immediately as He spoke.

But interestingly, whatever I was asking for appeared to have leapt out of me and met Christ's Words. My request was granted as soon as Christ said, "What do you want that I should do for you?"

Pastor Sekove shared it this way regarding the weight of those words, that God was giving Bartimaeus an open cheque. Just like how He asked Solomon, "Ask what I shall give thee (1 Kings 3:5)." The next day, the Lord opened the door for me far beyond what I expected.

It was in that first conference also, that Bishop Ned had blessed and commissioned the Church's new pulpit and named it, "The Burning Bush." As he spoke the Word, the power of the Spirit was heavy upon the place, and weighty upon us as we received the blessing of the Spirit.

Why did the Lord name it 'The Burning Bush?' I only came to that knowledge after our seventh conference that we hosted in late July 2023. When we hosted, 'The Elders Prophetic Conference' in Cairns, it was on the last night of the conference that I came into a full understanding of why the pulpit was named 'The Burning Bush.' Its name carries the message and representation of *the purpose* of the Burning Bush which is, 'God's appointed meeting place where He comes to meet with man and to speak with him.' That appointed place is made holy by His Glory resting upon that place. And in that moment of encounter, God Baptises and Commissions His chosen vessels with His Revival Mandate for His people. Hallelujah! It is in that place that God marks His vessels

CHAPTER 16   *Experiencing The Great Move of God: 'The Rockhampton Blessing'*

out by placing His Power upon them to do His Will. That Power is *His Mantle* for Revival. The Upper Room, where the one hundred and twenty met and remained in communion, was commanded by the Lord. Just as the Burning Bush was for Moses, the Upper Room was the Burning Bush for the one hundred twenty disciples. It was in that holy place that His glorious Power from on High rested, to place 'a distinctive mark' on His burning ones. They were marked as carriers of the Move. That 'mark' was the *seal of the Holy Spirit* resting upon them. They were sent out with the Fire of Word burning in their hearts and resting upon their beings. We learn from this first example and that of the Azusa Street Revival, that every Revival requires a Mandated Carrier—Leader—-Servant of the Move of God.

Now that I have explained that part of the story let's go back to the events after our first conference in 2018. Two months after that first conference, in December 2018, the Word of the Lord came to me while I was praying at the base of our newly blessed pulpit. The Holy Spirit said to me, "Norman My servant, host Me another conference. For I have much to say to My people." And God repeated this three times to me.

We then hosted that second meeting in the last week of May 2019, in obedience to God's directives. Again, we invited Bishop Ned and his wife to come and minister at that second conference. This time the theme was, 'Arise and Shine.'

I remember, also that my mum had joined us for this conference (She and Dad had come from PNG to spend time with the families here in Australia).

It was the third evening of the conference and the bishop was on for preaching that night. He was surely on Fire. He preached for about five minutes then realised he had to announce the title of the sermon. So he paused, flipped open his notes and read, "This Is Your Season To Arise."

And the second time again, I heard Christ's Voice and the same powerful Revival Fire that I had become very aware of, came upon me mightily. Christ again was sitting on those Words and the bishop's voice was turned off and the Voice I heard was the Lord's.

The Power of God fell where I sat and rested upon me. It was also like the same hot water burning sensation that I experienced in the Emerald Revival of May 2013. I have continued to experience that burning in my bones—Oh the Revival Fire of the Lord, Hallelujah!

I leaned forward and very nearly fell to the floor because the Fire was intense upon my body. But I made sure to stay glued to my seat till the end of the message.

The Word was ripe in the hearts of those in the conference room and the bishop extended the invitation for prayer at the altar. The funny part of this story was, that I chose to get up and help 'catch' for Bishop Ned, as he went through the prayer line, but I couldn't hold myself up either. What a help I was (humorously musing over it again).

But as the bishop finished, I was already on the floor lying prostrate before the Lord.

Initially, I was on my knees but the Holy Spirit challenged my worship posture. God wanted to know if I was really serious about His Revival Fire. Not that He doubted me, for He knows our hearts. But God's Spirit mentored, encouraged and challenged me in a way that stirred my heart. He said to me, "If you want this; if you really want what I am about to do in this place, you will show it to Me." And I knew exactly what He was asking of me. I knew I had to show it to Him. I had to become like Moses at the cleft of the rock, who made haste and bowed himself low before the Glory of his God. The Glory had descended already and was upon me as the mighty Power of God all over my being. God was asking me to introduce Him to the others in the room by my *posture of surrender before Him. That's when discipline becomes worship and commitment becomes love for His Presence.*

My spirit knew exactly what the Holy Spirit was asking from me. I went from a posture of kneeling before the Lord, to lying prostrate on the wooden floor of the conference hall, in complete surrender to the God of Glory. I would've been there on the floor for about twenty minutes or so. And I recall, as soon as I got off the floor, Heaven was already in the room—The Presence of the Lord was heavy upon me and He was with me.

That night a mighty Move of God broke out in the meeting and the Glory of the Word flowed from the front podium to the back of the room. Wherever you stood in the room, the Lord would touch you there. That mighty Revival Fire burned and the outpouring poured into the next day and went on for another 2 months.

Think about it, all of these happened only from one Word spoken by the appointed preacher. In this instance, it was Bishop Ned Gabey.

I must note, that he wasn't aware of this at all. I later had to testify to him about how Jesus kept resting on specific words that he had preached in the sermon which the Spirit had him minister to the people. I described to him, that the Voice of Christ was evidently resting upon specific words, and this happened while he was preaching. He listened intently with awe and realised the Spirit was truly focused on the specifics and God moved in response to those words. It was God who had authored and directed the sermon in the mouth of the preacher.

We all play our part in hosting the God of Glory. Whether you are aware of this or not, your willingness is everything to God. You may not be the preacher in a particular gathering that you have attended but that doesn't stop the Holy Spirit from pouring the Glory of His Word upon you. If the bishop's part was to deliver the

Word, my part was to hear the Voice of the Word that rested upon the message he preached. And the excellency of it all belongs to God.

One thing's for sure, we learned that to host God a conference, was to *host His Word*. When the appointed time came for the Glory of the Word to enter the room, it was that manifested Word that had later descended upon me suddenly during the conference and was the Power of God resting upon my being to be released to the people.

I also learned another valuable lesson from this experience. And I have carried that valuable lesson wherever I go. I learned that if you are attending a conference appointed by God (whether you are hosting it or not), go with an expectation to receive from God. And go also with an expectation to release what you receive. Be ready to receive. And also be ready to give.

CHAPTER 17

THE REVIVAL MENTORSHIP - ANOTHER LEVEL

When the Spirit Moves in our midst

 WORD OF ENCOURAGEMENT FROM THE SPIRIT:

Humility is often dressed up in many different ways. Even in a suit and tie. But the humility of God carries with it a significant mark of inheritance that bears the Name of God on it.

You have to be hungry for it, to be in it. When they say jump into the River, that is the only way you will know the blessedness of that River. Be humble and jump in.

You have to be humble enough to carry the Glory, and humble enough to recognise your need of Him also.

It's not about the fact that you've been in ministry for twenty years (Whatever that number is for you) God honours the work you have done. It's about making His Glory our Home. God shall descend mightily upon His people with a Baptism of Fire. I believe you are ready for it.

But soldier of God, it's not time to bow out of the race. Generals of the Most High, the Trumpet of God is blowing and

CHAPTER 17   *The Revival Mentorship - Another Level*

you must put on the Mantle of your calling. Take up the Mantle of your calling, for God is not yet finished with you.

ARISE!

It's not time to turn to the left, nor to the right. It's not time to delay because you're stuck in a sea of thoughts. I am sorry that I speak this way to you.

But the Children of Destiny will rise in the Unction of their God. You are that Generation appointed to see this Glory and He will come upon you magnificently.

Take off your sandals when God invites you into the Glory of His Presence.

Know that God has not missed His appointment. He will meet you at the appointed time.

Hold up the Rod of God with a strong arm. For a great victory is about to be won. Let others hold your hand up with you. Jehovah Nissi is with us.

Submitted with humility before the Lord of Glory and the ONE whom I behold at the Cleft of the Rock.

GOD IS THE AUTHOR OF REVIVAL

Every year God does a new thing. And like the previous years, many encounters also happened in 2022. These encounters add to our, revelation knowledge in Him. Here's one I want to share with you.

In January 2022, I was preaching in our Gracemere home in Rockhampton. It was our normal Sunday Service. The meeting was held in the dining area of our home. We sat the pulpit—'the Burning Bush,' to the centre of the room. And the Spirit led me to preach on the story of the Prophet Elijah repairing the Altar of the Lord on Mount Carmel (1 Kings 18).

I began by saying, "The Word of the Lord came to Elijah at the appointed time (verse 1)."

It was time for the Lord to heal the land, and bring the rain upon Israel again. But first, God wanted Elijah to tell King Ahab to send a message to gather all of Israel and the prophets of Baal; four hundred and fifty of them, to meet with him up at Mount Carmel.

The place they were to meet was at the site of the broken-down Altar of God.

The Word was deposited into Elijah. It sat upon the Mantle He carried. Elijah's first words to the people of Israel were, (paraphrasing here) "How long will you be stuck between two decisions? If the Lord be God, Follow Him, but if it's Baal, then follow him. And no one said a word to him in reply (verse 21)."

This was a spectacular showdown between the idols that Israel worshipped and the Living God. Then as the story follows, the prophets of Baal were told to build their own altar and then call on their god to answer by sending fire on the altar.

The challenge was—whoever's God answers with Fire let Him be God.

Note, that the whole nation was gathered to witness this. This wasn't a small gathering at all.

Now the important lesson that you also must note in this event is that Elijah was only doing this because the Word came to Him. Elijah received *the Word*. It was the Word that called the meeting, not Elijah. The same Elijah could've, out of the goodness and devotion of his heart, gone at anytime and repaired that Altar and offered a sacrifice. But Elijah didn't call that meeting. It was God who did.

Elijah could've built the Altar in Jerusalem but no, that wasn't the place either. Because the place was also chosen by God. We note also that the Word of the Lord came at *the appointed time.*

God is the One, who picks the place, He picks the time, He picks the vessels, and He picks the ministry (or what is to be done in that place).

CHAPTER 17

The Revival Mentorship - Another Level

> "God is the One, who picks the place, He picks the time, He picks the vessels, and He picks the ministry, that is, what is to be done in that place.

After saying these words, I paused again as the Holy Spirit downloaded more of the message into my spirit.

I then presented a familiar scenario for everyone in the room.

Here's the Scenario—

There were three Churches, each with different sizes and therefore varying in influence and operation also.

The first Church was a mega Church with a five thousand-member congregation. A big platform indeed. The second Church was of moderate size with three hundred members. Still a good size. The third Church only had twenty members.

All three sent invites to you (By this time, I pointed to Sister Timena). The Lord then said to attend the third Church, although that small Church's request came to you last. But the first Church was adamant that you should go to them. They offered to cover your transport, your meals, your accommodation and any other requirements. Think about it, they had the platform and this would extend your influence greatly. The second Church was on the phone to you as well. They wanted in on the request and were also pressuring you to come to them first. The Pastor of the little Church knew you were a busy person, but they still put forward their request too.

You then went to prayer, and while on your knees, you were asking God which one should you go to.

But God had already answered you on it—He told you to go to the small Church because He had a Word for them.

I then directed the question for Pastor Timena to answer for everyone in the room.

"Pastor Timena, which one would you go to?"

"It would be the One that God chose—the small Church."

Yes, that was the correct answer. If God is the One to pick the place, time, vessel, and ministry, then we obey what God wants.

But today, Churches and Ministries call a conference, choose a big place to meet, they give the conference a theme and look for the most anointed and most influential preachers to come and speak on that platform. But the Move belongs to God and not man. God's *Voice* is not in man's *Noise*.

We often call Elijah, a great prophet of faith and a fervent prayer warrior. No doubt he lived his life completely given to God. But we don't ever call him *the Prophet of Obedience*. Yet, that is who Elijah really was. When you study his entire life, you see that the real reason why Elijah was a great prophet, was because *He obeyed the Voice of the Word*.

He was a true Revivalist (as I described in Chapter 9); a Word Carrier, a Burning One, who was Sent *to preach and demonstrate* the Revival of God. The meaning of his name even proclaimed it— There is one God whom I serve: my God is Yahweh!

Friends, *obedience is the predominant trait of the Revivalist* and is also a requirement for the Move of God. Along with it is humility, and the desire to please God.

I have poured out my heart to you in this book and have devoted myself to the Anointing of God to write this book for you. I have imparted teachings where the Spirit has directed me. But the only way you will truly learn is by *catching the Revelation of God*. When you pay attention and become obedient to the Voice of the Spirit, you come into the acquisition of the Divinely inspired Word. And when the Word burns in you, that's when *the received Word* becomes in you, *the Revealed Word*. When your acquisition of *the Abiding Word* becomes in you the manifestation and demonstration of Power and of the Spirit. I can teach it, but you must catch it. It's not enough that the message sits only reaches your ears and remains only as a message. God wants to teach you in His way so that you can come into the Knowledge of His Glory.

1 Corinthians 2:1-5

> And I, brethren, when I came to you, came not with excellency of speech or of wisdom, declaring unto you the testimony of God. For I determined not to know any thing among you, save Jesus Christ, and Him crucified. And I was with you in weakness, and in fear, and in much trembling. And my speech and my preaching was not with enticing words of man's wisdom, but in demonstration of the Spirit and of Power: That your faith should not stand in the wisdom of men, but in the Power of God.

The message was flowing very well. Unbeknown to me, a *Suddenly* was about to happen in the room. I was totally unaware that God was about to demonstrate that message right in our midst.

Then the Spirit said to me and I obeyed, "Say this to them,"...

"I, Norman Sabadi, cannot give you Revival. I am not the author of Revival. The Move of God belongs to God and God alone. I cannot in any way at all bring you Revival. I cannot initiate, nor manufacture by any means, the Outpouring of the Spirit, because it doesn't originate from me. I, Norman Sabadi, cannot give you Revival. God is the One who gives you Revival."

And as I said these Words, being led by the Holy Spirit, suddenly, the Glory of the Lord came mightily upon me and in an instant the meeting place was filled with the Revival Fire of God. The weight of His Presence knocked me to the floor although, I had only been about twelve minutes into the message. God had come and there was nothing else to say.

The Power of God hit the room like a lightning strike. The Mantle of the Revivalist sat upon the room and every one of us came under the Spirit's influence in that very moment. There in that meeting, God revealed callings and giftings to each and every person who attended the meeting—while I lay on the floor completely helpless, and under the Power of the Spirit. That's a God-meeting when we make room for what God wants. That's a God-meeting when He takes over and all of what we call normal gives way to *His normal.*

Prayer:

> Oh, burn in us, Revival Fire. Burn bright and let Your Light beam radiantly through us. Let it be not of a man, but only You Jesus. For You are the Lover of our souls. Oh Lord, You have turned our hearts to You. And we rejoice in the Glory that You pour out upon Us. Oh, burn in us—REVIVAL FIRE, BURN!

REVIVAL CHASERS Vs FIRE CARRIERS

I have met individuals who are enthusiasts for God: fanatics of the Move of God, and cheerleaders of the Presence of God. I call these people 'Revival Chasers.'

They are very much like 'storm chasers'—They pursue the Glory Cloud of the Move, but they have never been baptised in the Revival Fires of that Cloud. They have chased the Move enthusiastically but have never caught the Move. These are the individuals who love the *Touch of God,* but never go beyond that and become *Fire Carriers.* And sadly, they are still stuck in the stories of previous Moves of God, but have no fruits to show for Revival; they have not carried the Fires of those Revival

Movements forward to future generations. All because they were only Revival chasers.

Our heritage as *Burning Ones* was born out of the Power of the Spirit and the Word, and we aren't just visitors of the spectacular. We were born out of the *Fires of His Revival Anointing*.

If you are going to carry the Move of God, it's important, that you learn not to follow man. If you're going to understand the Move of God, don't listen to those who have never carried the burden of the Word, and have never encountered or ministered in the intensity of the Revival Fire. And just because someone has been in many Revival meetings, doesn't mean they understand what it means to *Carry the Move*. They may be an experienced cheerleader but not a well-seasoned Fire Carrier—there's a big difference.

The fanatic can burn with a passion for God, but the Fire Carrier burns with the Word of God's Passion—there is a big difference!

God wants to mentor Fire Carriers. These are those who will catch the Fire with humility and willingness and take it to wherever they came from and become the Fire Starters in their own Family, Village, Suburb, Town, City, State, Province and Nation.

Catch the Move! Catch the Fire of the Word! It's one thing to teach you about the Move. It's completely another thing for you to catch the Move by being hungry and obedient.

The Revival chasers have enjoyed being under the shade of the Tree of the Revivalist, but have never picked its fruits to plant. Sadly, they never became carriers, because they are still stuck in the mindset of a cheerleader. They have chased the Glory of the Word, but don't know how to submit and surrender to the Word. They are big fans of the Revivalist, but not disciples of the Word that he carries.

And why is Revival mentored? Because it's not just noise and excitement, which are some of the byproducts of the impact of Revival. Revival seeks to establish growth and maturity in Christ. Revival is God abiding in our midst to teach us the knowledge of His Glory until we come into the fullness of the stature that is in Christ.

And to teach us this knowledge, God also has to teach us, what is NOT the knowledge of the Glory. He must show us what is fake and artificial, so we can tell the difference. And the most effective way He does this is by exposing us to the authentic Move of God. We become so well-trained and accustomed to the real Revival Fire, that we can discern the fake noise of the fanatics and cheerleaders when they show up.

These Glory chasers are good storytellers of the past Revivals and long for those days again, but they never progress into the knowledge to carry the Glory. It's good to be a great storyteller. But it's even better to be a witness for Christ, under the Anointing of the Revival Fire of God.

Catch the Move and be a Fire Carrier!

PROPHETIC WORD ABOUT OFFENCE

PROPHETIC WORD (15 November 2020):

These are days of prophecy. For these are days of the Spirit. And His children will prophesy. Yes, they will prophesy.

And I shall take your sons and your daughters and they shall prophesy. For the cup of the people have been empty.

But I shall send amongst them my prophets and prophetess'; my young ones. I have trained them with My hands. For they are young with the vision of God and fresh with the Anointing of My Spirit.

CHAPTER 17 — *The Revival Mentorship - Another Level*

And in the fullness of my Anointing shall they prophesy.

Are you a person of courage? Willing to run with the Word of God?

Some Churches are shaking hands with the devil. Come out from among them.

Satan has shot a major arrow. Listen, listen. It's called the arrow of bitterness and offence in the Church. And we as the Church must stand up against the Spirit of bitterness. You will find it in the streets, in the families, you will find it even right up at the pulpit of the Church and that is where the corruption is happening.

Therefore, wash your hands clean (says the Lord). For an hour you do not know, I will come and visit My Body, and be amongst people. And My *Shekinah (dwelling) and Kavod (Glory)* shall be amongst you again (says the Lord).

Then shall they fear My Name, as it was spoken by the Prophet Isaiah, from the west, and His Glory from the rising of the sun. And they shall bring upon My Altar and acceptable offering.

Let him who has ears, hear what the Spirit is saying to the Church.

I'm going to be direct again. I have seen bitterness and offence destroy marriages, families, ministries, and Churches. You probably have known and seen these happen too. Do you know how the great Azusa Street Revival ended? It was because the same brother Seymour, the *Revivalist* used by God to start and carry the Revival, became offended at his assistant pastor because of a minor doctrinal issue, and locked the doors to the building with a padlock. Offence can destroy movements. Offence can violently hinder the work of the Spirit.

> " Offence can destroy movements. Offence can violently hinder the work of the Spirit.

We deal with offence by the Spirit of grace, forgiveness, humility, sincerity and a desire to serve the oneness of Christ.

I hear ministers preach about lying down in green pastures but when they get home, bitterness has gone to bed with them. They preach about the King's table, but the table of their dining room is occupied with a record of wrongs.

It's the paradox of hypocrisy, to preach about love but still have an offence lodged deep within the heart. That offence, my friends, is the thing that is hindering the Move of God from coming fully into your life, your city, your village, your suburb, your state and your nation. Get rid of the offence and the complete healing will come.

That ugly spirit of resentment wastes no time stealing the joy in the hearts of those who have been consumed with prejudice, criticism, rage and hate. It has, without their permission, effortlessly robbed them of their peace. They have fallen for the bitterness trap set up by the devil and are bound by animosity. That same spirit of resentment and friction desires nothing but to cause division and does not stand for Revival.

Some people live their relationships based on *a record of wrongs and rights,* or as I put it, *good books and bad books.* This kind of individuals usually have a deep-rooted hurt still with them from a past event that is still affecting their current relationships. They have not been healed from that past hurt.

If that's you, Christ offers you freedom through the Power of His Spirit to set you free, right now.

Forgiveness, and 'forgetting the wrongs,' bring breakthrough and restoration. Bitterness is holding you back from the open door that the Lord wants you to enter. But, Revival is at hand. And God wants you to take it with both hands, to own it, and to invite the Revival Fire into your home.

CHAPTER 17 — *The Revival Mentorship - Another Level*

Make Him Lord of your home, and watch Him turn things around so quickly that the healing of your family becomes the overflowing effect of the healing of a whole city, and you are very much a part of the healing of the whole nation—but it starts with you. Will you let Him into your heart today?

The Spirit of Prophecy has come for your breakthrough and your new beginning is now at the break of dawn. He has come for you and will contend for you with the Power of His Word and Spirit. He desires to help you *heal the Altar of your heart*. When you let go of yesterday, that's when today truly begins. *The New begins*, when the old no longer has control over your life.

2 Corinthians 5:17-18

> Therefore if any man be in Christ, he is a new creature: old things are passed away; behold, all things are become NEW. And all things are of God, who hath reconciled us to Himself by Jesus Christ, and hath given to us the ministry of reconciliation;

DOES REVIVAL OFFEND YOU?

Especially, as we come into the Move of God; the sustaining aspect of the Move will come down to us watching out for the spirit of offence and ensuring it does not get to our hearts.

We must allow for *Grace* to have its way in us so that the finished work of Christ may be complete in us, who have laid it all on the Altar before God.

Our hearts made whole in Christ, is that acceptable offering God is looking for.

The 'spirit of bitterness' is that dangerous arrow, that the enemy has shot at the Church at all levels. This is been used to inflict great deception and a fatal wound. Satan has aimed this devastating arrow at governments of nations, institutions, families and individuals, with the attempt to destroy anything to do with God, seeking to bring to an end the message of the Gospel of Jesus Christ.

This 'bitterness spirit' has taken many forms today. You don't have to look far to find it; on social media, and traditional media.

How can the Church be effective in walking in the Glory of God, when we too are entangled and bound by strife and offence?

Matthew 15:18

But those things which proceed out of the mouth come forth from the heart; and they defile the man.

Matthew 6:14-15

For if ye forgive men their trespasses, your heavenly Father will also forgive you: But if ye forgive not men their trespasses, neither will your Father forgive your trespasses.

In Matthew 11, John the Baptist was in prison and he heard about the *Move of God* going on through the promised Christ—his cousin, Jesus.

John sent two of his disciples to Jesus and they came with only one question from John, "Are You the One (meaning the Christ) that should come? Or should we look for another?"

This question intrigues me. Why? Because, the Holy Spirit had already confirmed that to John at the River Jordan when John saw the Spirit of God descend like a dove upon Jesus and he even heard the Voice from Heaven saying, "This is my beloved Son, in Whom I am well pleased. (Matthew 3:13-17)."

John was the one who insisted Jesus baptise him, but Jesus encouraged him to carry out the baptism because it was what the Father in Heaven wanted.

So was there a change in John's heart? Was there something more John was expecting Christ to do? You might have a different revelation on this.

But, here's what I see in it. I believe John wasn't asking this for himself, he was asking this for those who were going to listen to Jesus' response to that question. That question had everything to do with the Revival—the Move of God that Christ Jesus was carrying to fulfil (Note the bolded words).

Matthew 11:4-6

> Jesus answered and said unto them, Go and shew John again those things **which ye do hear and see:** The blind receive their sight, and the lame walk, the lepers are cleansed, and the deaf hear, the dead are raised up, and the poor have the gospel preached to them. **And blessed is he, whosoever shall not be offended in Me.**

From what I see, Jesus was giving a *testimonial report* or as we call it, *a praise report* to John.

John was in prison, and that testimony and praise report would have encouraged him greatly.

Jesus concludes that response with an unrelated subject to His answer, "Blessed is he, whosoever shall not be OFFENDED in me."

Jesus was in no way implying that John was offended. What Jesus was really saying is, many were expecting the Move to come in a certain way. They thought that Christ would start a revolt and emerge with a mighty Israelite army to fight back the Romans and establish His earthly kingdom. If you read the rest of Jesus' talk after that question, that's actually what Jesus was addressing. And He went deeper on the issue—He was addressing it to the naysayers and spectators of the Move.

That unrelated statement was for the critics and those who didn't think He was the Christ because they expected something else. Because they had judged the Move and were looking through the wrong lens of their preconceptions and prejudice.

That's the same with the Church today. When the Move doesn't quite line up with our expectations, we resent others who *show off* their Revival blessings, instead of seeing it as a testimony.

We are easily offended when God starts to use someone we wouldn't even consider, worthy to carry the Move. We like our concept of the Move, but we ourselves haven't yet entered the Glory. Just like the pharisees, we stop others from entering into that blessed Movement of God (Matthew 23:13). We preach Revival, but we stop those who try to Move in the Spirit in our midst, only because they don't fit what we require. Our blindness has caused us to become void of what God requires. We have become stagnant and unable to discern the Move.

But the real issue may be the log in the eye—that needs to be removed with repentance and humility. This is a hard pill to swallow but you need to hear it.

Looking back on that 'Matthew 11 talk,' Jesus noted that the critics even judged John, saying he had a devil because John was too blunt with his rebukes. The same *misguided interpreters of the Move* looked at Jesus and said he was a gluttonous winebibber and a friend of sinners (Matthew 11:18-19). They scorned the message by scoffing at the messenger.

But Jesus hits home with four points in that teaching. Let me point them out to you:

- Spiritual Wisdom justifies her own Children. Meaning, if you are led by the Spirit of God, you will be able to see what God is doing. The same Spirit of God working in the Revivalist will stir you up with agreement and a desire to see God Move.
- The least in the Kingdom was greater than John the Baptist; he was the *Elijah-movement* that came before the Christ. This means, when it comes to the second *Elijah-movement*, it would be the one before the Second Coming of Christ. This Movement will be carried by those who are the *least in the Kingdom*. They are not about titles, positions and accolades. They are the ones who have laid their lives down to carry the *Voice of the Word, which is the Voice of Revival*.
- This revelation will be given to the simple in heart. They will be given access to conversations that only Jesus and the Father have.
- Come to Me and find *Rest. Christ is the Rest,* who removes the burden from us and He is the fullness of our inheritance in God.

When we judge the messenger, we become unwilling to listen, uninterested and unresponsive to the message they carry to deliver to us.

We are in error, in judging the holy and anointed message that has come from the Most High. We failed to discern that the Spirit of God was at work. Because of that, we have brought a spiritual drought upon ourselves. I strive diligently to understand: was it all because our expectations and requirements weren't met? We were offended when God used the simple in Spirit to do mighty works in our midst.

But, the Lord told me in a prophetic dream on the 03rd of April 2005, that "It will be the poor in spirit who will command in My Glory."

Matthew 5:3

Blessed are the poor in spirit: for theirs is the kingdom of Heaven.

The fullness of the Kingdom of God belongs to those, who have chosen to make room for God. They will see God work through His signs, wonders and miracles because they have reached out to the Lord of Glory with all their hearts. They have yielded and answered to the Holy Calling and have surrendered their hearts to the Mighty Move of God. They have come with brokenness and a contrite spirit. The Spirit has touched their hearts and their repentance is genuine and sincere. Blessed are the eyes that see and perceive, and the ears that hear and understand (Matthew 13:13-17).

Prayer:

Dear Lord Holy Spirit, please forgive us for judging Your Move. Please cleanse us of our own fleshly thoughts and ideas about the Move. And Give us a fresh Baptism and a fresh Revelation of Your Revival Fire.

We are here Lord. Our hearts are ready. We want more of You. And we lay aside the weights that may easily cause us to be drawn away from You. And we come confidently before Your Holy Presence and before Your Throne of abundant Grace and Mercy.

We are ready Lord Jesus. Come and have Your way in us.

SONG OF GLORY FILL MY HEART

2 Chronicles 5:13-14

It came even to pass, as the trumpeters and singers were as one, to make one sound to be heard in praising and thanking the LORD; and when they lifted up their voice with the trumpets and cymbals and instruments of musick, and praised the LORD, saying, For He is good; for His mercy endureth for ever: that then the House was filled with a Cloud, even the House of the LORD; So that the priests could not stand to minister by reason of the Cloud: for the Glory of the LORD had filled the House of God.

A PSALM TO THE LORD:

Song of Glory, come fill my heart. My spirit longs for Your embrace. Beside the still waters, I lay me down; calm, by the rivers of Your abundant Grace. There, I find rest and hope. I am revived by Your Words of Life, flowing from the depths of Your Spirit to mine. Again, that beautiful exchange, ineffable, but so brilliant. I bow my heart before Your splendour and I sing with You, oh Holy Spirit. For the song You Sing is filled with Your Anointing Oil. Song of Glory, fill my heart, and let my cup overflow. In the fullness of Your Presence, my soul delights. Till all shall see the Power of My God, who has chosen to abide in our midst forever, Amen.

God wants you to experience the blessing of His Presence. God wants to reveal His Glory to you. His heart and purpose for you is to be in the midst of His People. The dedication of the first Temple reveals this wonderful truth to us (2 Chronicles 5:13-14). So much power is displayed in the event of the Glory filling the Temple that King Solomon and the people of God built for the Lord. The DEDICATION SERVICE for the Temple became a memorable and most blessed of occasions because the Glory had come and filled the Temple. The purpose of the Temple was to Host the Presence of the King of Glory. The name Bethel (meaning the House of God) was truly established as Solomon, the priests and the people became one in their hearts toward God. Their worship expressed God with deep sincerity. We can see from this example that the Glory descended upon those who were gathered in one accord and were ready to receive their God. Indeed, the Glory is drawn to your oneness with Him. The oil of God only pours where there is 'one accord' (Psalms 133). When the Baptism of Fire fell upon the Upper Room in Jerusalem, where the saints were gathered, their hearts were also in one accord in that place where the Power of God fell (Acts 2:1-4). There is power in oneness. The power of the Church is in our oneness with God and with one another. True oneness is in God.

'The Cloud of His Glory Filled the Temple:' These words captivate my heart in a very deep and profound way. I am moved by the Spirit as I meditate on the wonders of the Glory Cloud and the Beauty of His Presence. This should be the desire of God's people. The Presence of God is our confidence and our hope. God is our delight and our everlasting joy.

With that said, I am going to be scrupulous again. You might think this is more for the worship team and the worship leaders, but I know it's for everyone. I continue to see the Church making this mistake. We keep choosing the wrong song, even after the Holy Spirit has already stirred our hearts to sing a particular song. Instead, we are more confident about our list and follow through with it, rather than be led by His prompting. It's more than just the type of songs we sing. It's about when we sing it from the heart and in such a way that it draws the Glory of God upon us. We have our list of songs, but the Holy Spirit wants to lead us to the right songs that draw our hearts into one accord before God.

Indeed, I see the full display of emotion and heart when in worship; which are attributes that are important in a heart-to-heart worship, but I am talking about something more deeper than that. If you want His Presence to come into the room, you must go beyond just singing a song. You must tune your hearts and ears *to where the Spirit is singing and where the Spirit is speaking.*

You can hear Him singing the song in your spirit and you can also know when He speaks because you can tell where the Anointing is resting and where His Presence is heaviest. You're certainly going to know because your heart will be drawn to that place.

Usually, when I tune into that song (or the frequency of God), I will often tell the worship leader and the musicians to repeat that song, because the Spirit is resting on it. I do this until a Word from the Spirit enters the room. This is what I spoke about in an earlier Chapter, about avoiding the song list, and instead following where the Holy Spirit is flowing. I am sharing this out of experience. The Spirit is ready to flow and move in our midst. All we have to do is trust Him.

You might ask, "How will I know if the Spirit is resting on that song?" When your heart wants to sing more of that song. It's the song of the heart and the true expression of what your spirit wants to say to God. The Holy Spirit helps you to identify that song to take you to that place. Because He knows your heart better than you know yourself. He knows what you need. He knows the song.

You can feel the definite mark of His Anointing lingering on that music and song. When it happens, don't change songs, stay on that particular song. That's where the Spirit is. The weight of His

Anointing gently resting on that song is the Holy Spirit's way of saying, "That's the song I want you to sing."

In that moment, that song is no longer just a song, but a melody of elevation in the Spirit and a current of the Anointing flowing, it's a *Place in God*. He raises the platform and turns up the level of Holy Spirit flow in that room when you stay there. *That's where He is Speaking and that where He wants to work.* In this heart-to-heart worship, your spirit becomes aware of the Holy Spirit and your heart prefers Him in that precious moment. There the song list must give way to *the song of the heart*. Because the heart is now singing *the song of the Spirit of God*. It can be a song in tongues or a completely new song from the Spirit.

It doesn't mean that all the other songs are not as effective and not of God. No, it just means the appointed song is now being sung at the appointed time, in the appointed place. God is very specific here. And if this challenges you, I ask you to put aside any form of resentment or incredulity.

Now there have been times when the Spirit didn't need any song at all. Just silence, and the sound of people praying and weeping before Him. God doesn't need our sound because He can make His Own sound. And that sound is the Glory of the Word that enters the Room and becomes like fire in the bones of the anointed.

The main emphasis of raising this point is to teach you how God prefers to enter the room—God will only come to a prepared Altar that is responsive to the Voice of the Spirit.

Then there have been occasions where, He didn't want us to start with a song, but start with a prayer, or with communion, or with preaching and sharing. That's also what I talked about earlier, where you refuse your program and enter into *God's purpose and program*.

CHAPTER 17 — *The Revival Mentorship - Another Level*

You can't force into a program what God wants to direct by His purpose. You can't supervise and limit what God wants to mentor and elevate. Where you put limits, God desires liberty. Where you control the lighting, God has His own light to illuminate the hearts.

When you press into His Presence, you're striving. But when you hear His Voice and follow, you're resting—There is a difference.

You might want to create an atmosphere with your smoke machine, yet God can create His Own—He is the Glory Cloud. What you want to order, God would rather orchestrate and bring healing, deliverance, miracles, signs and wonders. He is God and there is no other besides Him. Oh, let the Lord have His Way. Let Him Sing His Song and you follow His lead.

CHAPTER 18

THE POSTURE THAT BRINGS & CARRIES THE GLORY

Worship is purpose, not program.

The following revelations in this Chapter, are lessons I received from the Cairns Revival Conference which we hosted for the Lord, in May 2021.

The lead-up to the first Cairns meeting was what I call, a hidden prophecy. It became clear to me after the Lord outlined what was required for that meeting. The Holy Spirit spoke to me to host Him another conference and this time it was to be in Cairns City, at the Shangri-La Hotel ballroom. A 'Gideon Callout' was to precede the Meeting.

God surely has Glory lessons lined up for us, as we follow His lead. Again, it was in a Bishop Ned sermon, when the Spirit spoke these words, "Worship is Purpose." I lingered on those three words, as the sermon went on. The Holy Spirit was saying something very important and it was to the Body of Christ.

CHAPTER 18 — *The Posture That Brings & Carries The Glory*

The next day was Sunday. We joined Bishop Ned to attend a service with a ministry in the city. I was then given the opportunity by the hosting pastor to greet the members of the Church. That Word from the night before burned within me. I knew it had been placed on my heart to share to the Church family that morning.

How could I resist or restrain the Spirit of God? These revelations are given to help us draw near to God. Often revelations from God convict people in different ways, based on where they are at. Some will hear it as a strong rebuke, others will hear it in their spirit as an instruction, and for some, it will correct them, and for others, it will refresh and inspire them.

2 Timothy 3:16-17

> All scripture is given by inspiration of God, and is profitable for doctrine, for reproof, for correction, for instruction in righteousness: That the man of God may be perfect, thoroughly furnished unto all good works.

I see this time and time again, every time a revelation from God is released in the room. And when that same revelation is shared, out of it often flows multiple revelations. The Holy Spirit ensures that revelation meets the needs of every heart in the room, from the greatest need to the least need—He always works that way.

That's what happened on that Sunday morning as I shared those words, "Worship is Purpose, not program. When you enter into God's Purpose, then you will see His Program prepared for you."

Take our Lord Jesus Christ, the Head Apostle and The Chief Revivalist, as our example. He always listened to His Father. He always followed His Father's program, because that program was *Divine Purpose flowing through Jesus*. It became His life and His ministry. He was governed and led by the Commission of the Father upon His life. The Glory of the abiding Word of His Commission burned mightily in Him.

Revival, being God-controlled and God-led, becomes a reality for us when we have decided to follow the heart of God.

If *Worship is Purpose, this purpose governs our posture.* Worship is the posture that attracts and hosts the Glory. I have told you my stories in the earlier Chapters to show you this. I hope that these testimonies have given you insight and allowed you to also discover God, by participation, experience, encounter and revelation.

'Worship Posture', is to have a particular way, approach or attitude towards God that aligns your heart with God's heart.

What does your heart really want to say to God? That's what worship means—from the heart.

True worship, comes from the brokenness of your spirit. This brokenness is able to discern and become aware of the Holy Spirit. Our adoration toward the Holy Ghost only pours from a place of awareness. That awareness comes from our desire to surrender to God.

If our Church programs are hindering us from expressing true surrender, then they hinder us from encountering God.

Your posture also resonates with the place of your calling, whether you realise this or not. Take Queen Esther as an example. She bowed low when she came before the king. She didn't give him bad attitude. She humbled herself before him, in order to win his favour and the goodness of his heart. Only then, did the king reach out the sceptre of his approval to offer Esther the opportunity to speak the desire of her heart (Esther 5:1-3).

The same is with God, our King. He also is looking for our posture of submission and desire for Him. For the Father seeks such to worship Him (John 4:23-24).

CHAPTER 18 — *The Posture That Brings & Carries The Glory*

For us to see a continuous and increasing flow of the Revivals of God, we must be given to a lifestyle of unceasing surrender.

Our worship posture also is spiritual positioning and partnership with God. That's why in Revivals, you will see more healings and miracles, and signs and wonders because God has come and made His Home in those who have adopted the posture that hosts His Presence.

Are you seeking change for your family, your city, your neighbourhood, your village or your nation? The Power of change lies in your worship posture;

Psalms 33:12-15

> Blessed is the nation whose God is the LORD; and the people whom He hath chosen for His own inheritance. The LORD looketh from Heaven; He beholdeth all the sons of men. From the Place of His habitation He looketh upon all the inhabitants of the earth. He fashioneth their hearts alike; He considereth all their works.

Elijah was God's *prophet of obedience*. He was led by the Spirit of the Word to repair the Altar of God. And the mighty God was drawn to that offering of willingness and obedience; God sent *The Fire of His Revival* upon that repaired Altar.

The same is with our hearts—which is the Altar of God; when we have prepared ourselves for Christ to ignite us with His Power, Peace and Passion. The Lord then sends the Baptism of His *Word upon us and into our hearts*. And in heart-to-heart worship, the Fire of the Mighty God is kindled.

The land will experience healing when the people and their leaders choose to repair the Altar of their hearts and obey the Holy Spirit. 2 Chronicles 7:14, is talking about a restored Altar—your heart. It is the Altar of *His Visitation and Abiding Power*.

God is giving you His personal invitation to partake and participate in Heaven's desire, through your obedience and willing response.

Families are going to be made whole because one person chose to respond to the desire of the Ancient of Days.

But what if bitterness resides instead of wholeness? Then the Altar will remain dysfunctional and wounded. And while the Altar remains in ruins, the land will continue to suffer.

I speak the truth. If you still have bitterness or offence in your heart, that posture of bitterness is taking part in the gradual degradation and destruction of a whole generation. If this is you right now, this attitude is far from the grace and mercy of the Cross of Jesus, and void of the resurrection Power of God. Bitterness is poison to the heart. But the Word of God is cleansing and wholeness.

The servants of *the abiding Word;* the prophets of God, were men and women of unbroken worship. Their Altar was accepted before the God of their worship. This precious worship toward God pours from a heart not broken in ruins, but *'broken in wholeness'—where healing, sincerity and love for God gushes forth.* That brokenness is the sweet-smelling fragrance that gets God's attention.

Brokenness is what draws the 'Suddenly of God.' The *Rain of Heaven* follows when the Altar of ruins becomes the repaired Altar of wholeness, ready to receive the Fire of God.

Indeed, the *Worship Posture* lead us to know the Heart of God.

Matthew 6:10

...Thy Kingdom come. Thy Will be done in Earth, as it is in Heaven.

CHAPTER 18 — *The Posture That Brings & Carries The Glory*

The worship posture is the posture and attitude that hosts the Revival Fire of God. It's not a man-controlled worship. The Spirit helps our heart to come to that place. This posture goes beyond lifted hands and singing along with the worship team. I am talking about a worship that flows out of brokenness and sincerity toward God.

I often say that our Sunday services should be called 'Surrender services.' Because our brokenness before Him matters more than we realise. Where there is no surrender, there is no encounter with the grace of God. In our surrender, we repent, ask for forgiveness, forgive others, and give ourselves completely to His leading. We wait, and we wait and we wait, until *He Speaks*.

James 4:7-8

> Submit yourselves therefore to God. Resist the devil, and he will flee from you. Draw nigh to God, and He will draw nigh to you. Cleanse your hands, ye sinners; and purify your hearts, ye double minded.

Worship is not a program: not humanly generated as religious work. It was never intended that way. True worship is always from the heart. It is our higher calling in God.

THE VOICE IN THE WILDERNESS

When Revival comes, He is like a stranger in the land; a stranger with no name and one who does things differently. This Holy Voice in the wilderness comes with Heavenly intent to be in our midst. How we respond to that Voice is important. There is one governing truth we must understand in order to receive His Voice;

only God can author and authorise His Move. He will pick us—we don't pick ourselves. He is the Voice in the wilderness, that has no labels, no branding, no denomination, no banner and no titles accept one—He is the Power from on High.

I speak in this manner because, God doesn't want us to get the glory for what He authors and delivers, and for the Move that He ignites and leads. The excellency of the Power belongs to God. A good example of this is when God told Gideon He was only going to need a few to win the battle. God didn't want the people to think they really didn't need God in the first place and that their own hands had saved them.

The Holy Ghost knows whom He is looking for. It will be a generation that isn't given to worldly ideas and methods. It's wasted effort if we try in vain to build the city but God is not in that workmanship (Psalms 127:1). God's way is far more splendid than ours. The Way of the Spirit is far more excellent and impactful.

Psalms 127:1

> Except the LORD build the house, they labour in vain that build it: except the LORD keep the city, the watchman waketh but in vain.

Many Church leaders are praying for Revival but they will be challenged to accommodate the authentic Move because it will demand a shift in their paradigm and doctrine. For sure, Revival will also expose our errors, not to destroy us, but to heal us.

For when the *Wind of the Spirit* blows into a city, in the appointed time, God will bring refreshing and renewal upon the people. Then the old wineskin of our old ways must give way to the 'New' that is in God. For the old wineskin of religiosity is unable to accommodate the New Wine of the *Refreshing of God*.

And a *Wave of the Spirit* cannot be carried if God doesn't assign a *Wave Carrier*. God will raise Revivalists to carry the Glory. Will you be one of those chosen individuals who will say yes to the Glory of God?

GET FOCUSED—WILL YOU HOST HIS WORD?

When the Revelation of His Word of Power, ABIDES.

Psalms 9:1-2

> I will praise Thee, oh Lord, with my whole heart; I will shew forth all Thy marvellous works. I will be glad and rejoice in Thee: I will sing praise to Thy Name, Oh Thou Most High.

The Prophet Samuel was greatly grieved by King Saul's rebelliousness and disobedience. Samuel was so disheartened over it. Many Pastors can feel this way when the sheep under them go astray from the Lord.

But God needed to shake that grief off of Samuel and get him focused on the *New Word*. The prophetic nature of Revival invades in a very powerful way to remove the grief from you and get you focused. The Word of Power received becomes a tide of inspiration that quickens the heart to focus on the breakthrough at hand.

A New Sound had attracted God out in the fields of Bethlehem. And it was coming from a young shepherd boy named, David. It was *David's worship* that drew the appointment of the Anointing to him, and the time had come. David's worship had caused the Prophet Samuel to come with *the Word*.

Samuel got focused, and filled the horn with Anointing Oil. The Word sat in Samuel—He was now carrying it for God's chosen vessel. The purpose and appointment of that Word was to reach David. It was to be released upon David.

And as I alluded to earlier, the workings of your ordination were given before you were formed in your mother's womb. Before you were formed, God knew what type of worship you were going to pour out unto Him. He made you fearfully and wonderfully as an instrument of worship for Him. He prepared in you everything that was needed to bring His Presence and to bring His Word.

The appointment was set from the day He thought about creating you. He formed you in your mother's womb so He could prepare you to walk the appointment of your Anointing.

No working of the Holy Spirit is without the Word of God. It is because the *Word came, that we received.*

THE WORD WAS SENT.

Hence, healing is only available when the Word of Healing is present. Breakthrough only happens when the Word of Breakthrough enters the room, and because we made room for the Spirit of God through our worship.

And the Anointing you carry, is that access and grace by which God responds favourably to. Because the Anointing of the Spirit works with the Spirit of the Word. While on this point, I emphasise that you can't separate the Spirit from the Word. To talk about the Spirit is to talk about the Word and to talk about the Word is to talk about the Spirit.

That's why I said, the Spirit will only respond to the Word. I love the workings of the Anointing. For the anointed preacher, when the Anointing to preach comes upon them, their words become impactful in the Holy Ghost. The Spirit places a message in them to preach it in the way the Spirit wants it delivered. The Holy Spirit also enables the preacher to discern, that the Anointing to

CHAPTER 18 — *The Posture That Brings & Carries The Glory*

preach is present. It is that discernment that releases the Power and Revelation of the Spirit.

While on the subject of discerning the Word, the story of the two disciples on the road to Emmaus came to mind. They were talking about bad news; the prophet Named Jesus of Nazareth had been condemned to death and crucified just before the Sabbath. They explained to the stranger that had joined them, although their eyes were not able to discern that it was Jesus who they were speaking to.

But it was when Jesus opened His mouth and began to teach them about what was in the Scriptures concerning the Christ, that their hearts began to burn because the eyes of their understanding were opened. Jesus, the Anointed preacher was with them.

The Words on Christ's mouth, quickened the spirits of the two disciples. And what Christ was really doing was correcting their focus and stirring their worship to host the Word—He has risen!

Oh, hallelujah! It was prophesied that death would not be able to hold Him down, and the grave would lose its sting. Now the Risen One was walking with them, who were inattentive and unsuspecting of His countenance. While they listened to Him speak, unaware that the reality of the Power of God began to envelop them because they got focused on the Word of Power and they said to one another, "Our hearts began to burn when He spoke."

God also wants to correct our focus so we can see and behold the Glory of the Word. When we Host His Word, We Host His Presence—His Word is His Presence. It is the Word that proceeded out of the Mouth of the God of Glory Himself.

When Abraham focused on obeying God, The Lord *became Jehovah-Jireh—God Provides, and the covenant-keeping God.*

Abraham hosted that Word by believing in it, for it contained the seed of fulfilment which remained in his spirit until the appointed time. Then the due season was approaching. God sent His angels to visit Abraham to declare the promised Word, "Sarah will conceive."

That's when the impossible became possible.

The same was also with Jacob when he worshipped the Lord God of Bethel. God proclaimed to Jacob, (paraphrasing here) "I am the God that made an Oath and Promise to you at the Place Where I spoke to You, Bethel—The House of God."

God was Jacob's *Elisheva*—My God is an Oath.

How about Hannah? She too received something from the Lord. When Hannah worshipped, She got focused on the God of His Word. *God became for her, the Healer of her womb and the Remover of the reproach. God became the fruit and the joy Giver.*

He became the Word of Faithfulness that was received and conceived in Hannah's *Faith*, before she received it and conceived it in her womb. Little did she know, that a prophet was conceived on the inside of her, and that blessed child would later become the Prophet Samuel, who would also carry the Word that was conceived on the inside of him.

When Moses worshipped and lifted up the Rod of God in obedience to God, *The Lord became Jehovah Nissi—The Lord our Banner.*

I am saying, get focused on the Word of Power. Get focused. When Joshua got focused, *God became the instruction for the breakthrough and the God who brings down a mighty wall.*

Will you get focused?—Will you Host His Word?

When Gideon worshipped, *the Lord became the Valiant One that gathers a chosen army for victory.*

When Jehoshaphat worshipped, *the Lord of Hosts, became the God that fights for me.*

When Solomon and the Israelites worshipped, *the Lord became the God of His Glory Cloud that filled the Temple; the God of the Place Where He Speaks.*

When Elijah repaired the Altar and worshipped, *the One and Only True God, became the God that answers by Fire, and the God of His People.*

GET FOCUSED!

The disciples got focused and obeyed Christ. They went to Jerusalem and waited on the Promise. Then came the glorious day of the Spirit's descent and *The Lord became the God who baptises with the Holy Ghost and Fire.*

Oh, that you will join this list of saints, and host His Word in your surrender. GET FOCUSED! There's no secret formula. Just surrender and obedience to the Word that enters the room.

Revival is God's answer to the one who possesses the posture of Worship.

> " Revival is God's answer to the one who possesses the posture of Worship.

If we are to be a people of His Presence, we must also be a people, able to discern the Word of Power.

When Heaven's Glory rests upon and resides in earthen vessels; these *Broken Vessels* release a *Divine Sound*. And In that Divine Sound is *the Healing River (Ezekiel 47)*. Everything that River touches comes to life.

But God is looking for a willing vessel that will let Him mould and shape them by His Word. It is really God's invitation to an opportunity to transform a family, a city, a nation and a people—if you will get focused and host His Word.

The fulfilled Word in us is God's pleasure. When God is pleased with you, His appointment reaches you.

The Posture That Brings & Carries The Glory **CHAPTER 18**

Two examples come to mind here:
- The Prophet Samuel carried the Word for David—*One after God's Heart.*
- John the Baptist carried the Word for Yeshua—*This is My Son in whom I am well pleased.*

Even our Lord Jesus had to help John get focused (paraphrasing the narrative here), "John, the Word is inside you. We both have to fulfil the Word that you carry; that you've been hosting right up to this very moment. John, we have to obey the Word the Spirit of God put in you."

John got focused, and his obedience to the Word released a Divine Sound. Jesus and John both carried and hosted the Word in *oneness and agreed together that it needed to be obeyed* and this brought the River of Heaven into One Place—The Spirit had descended mightily upon Jesus.

The Anointing of the Spirit has handpicked you to fill you, empower you and send you. It is *the appointed Dew of Heaven that enters the room;* there, the Lord has commanded His blessings (Psalms 133:1-3).

And for the Upper Room saints, they were in one accord when the Dew of Heaven came in the form of *the Wind of the Spirit and Baptism of Fire.* And the smell of that Fire began to burn. The sweet smelling fragrance, was the *New Sound, the New Sound, the New Sound!*

> "
> ..In His favour is life: weeping may endure for a
>
> night, but joy cometh in the morning..Psalms 30:5—
> SO GET FOCUSED!

CHAPTER 18 *The Posture That Brings & Carries The Glory*

WHEN DAVID DANCED

A time came when David planned to recover the Ark of God and bring the Ark to Jerusalem. At that time the Ark was still in the house of Abinadab, who lived in Gibeah (in Judah), which was about six kilometres north of Jerusalem (2 Samuel 6).

And because David loved the Presence, He wanted to host the Ark of God, in Jerusalem. But he tried to do it, using a cart (representing man's pattern or idea of how to carry the Presence), and that mission was a failure. The Ark of God was temporarily hosted in the house of a man named Obededom, a Levite.

The Ark of God wasn't made to be carried on a cart, it was made to be carried on the shoulders of the *Ministers of God.*

In 1 Chronicles 15:11-16, we read about how David called the priests and the Levites. And he told them to sanctify themselves because they would be carrying the Ark of the Lord God of Israel to Jerusalem, to the place where David had prepared to receive the Ark. David told them that their first attempt was a failure only because they didn't do it in accordance with God's order, according to the way God had instructed Moses (1 Chronicles 15:13, Exodus 15:13-15). They thought they didn't need the Levites to carry it, so the Ark was put on a new cart. God breached upon them and Uzzah was the one who lost his life as a result of it.

They had to get it right this time. So the Levites, were to bare the Ark of God on their shoulders with the Staves included (Exodus 25; 13-15). David went further to appoint singers and musicians to be a part of bringing the Ark of His Testament to Jerusalem.

The Ark of the Lord God represented the meeting place between God and Man.

CHAPTER 18

The Posture That Brings & Carries The Glory

Exodus 25:22

> And there I will meet with thee, and I will commune with thee from above the mercy seat, from between the two cherubims which are upon the ark of the testimony,...

This sets the stage for the continuation of our discussion about, 'Hosting the Word.' This time we want to capture the essence of that lesson in David's story.

You see, when you host the Word, the Word is going to be real with you, but are you going to be real with the Word? Because God is going to call you into uncomfortable places. But you need to let go of your crown, and cast it at the feet of Jesus. You need to let go of your status and reputation, if you desire to carry His Presence. You need to stop drowning in bad news and begin to focus on the Word.

God is the greater reputation and when He rises upon you, He's going to heal your family, your city, and your nation. When you are called, you are called. Rise to the Voice of your calling. He is near to mightily deliver you and direct you in the path you should go.

David became desperate for the Presence. He was Hungry for God. He didn't like that Obededom was getting all the blessings because the Ark of God was in Obededom's house. Holy jealousy came upon David. He wanted the Presence. Think of it, for three months, Obededom had the blessing of God poured on his home because He was a good host and steward of the Ark of God's Presence.

This is the climax of the story: The Ark of God's *Meeting Place*, didn't depart Obededom's house, until David decided to correct His worship posture—David danced before the Lord.

CHAPTER 18 — *The Posture That Brings & Carries The Glory*

The Priests who carried the Ark, followed behind. Yet the Ark of God's Presence was waiting for His chosen king (the man after God's heart) to respond with the correct worship posture. The Ark didn't move until David and the Levites became authentic before the Lord God.

David knew this worship; in fact, he did it as a shepherd boy. He would play his harp and dance and sing unto the Lord. Now that same anointed man of God was leading a great procession of worshippers and priests, to Jerusalem. The purpose of that kingly anointing that he received earlier as a kid now made sense. David was to show Israel that to worship God, you had to do it with all your heart and also honour the pattern God has ordained for His Presence.

And the influence of his Anointing and leadership rested upon the people while he danced before the Ark of God.

When a pastor becomes hungry for God, that same hunger will become contagious among the people. It takes Holy Ghost influence to impact a nation. It takes Holy Ghost impact to bring change. Change is God's language. But the *fiery Ones, the hungry Ones must become desperate for the Presence again.*

Oh, Hallelujah! When the Fire burns, change comes. A new day rises upon a people that have entertained the *Kavod (Weighty Glory) of God. When you choose to host God, expect a mighty blessing to follow. That blessing will impact everything in your life.*

Reflecting on David's story, we can see the lesson that applies to us. The same heart that moved God as a shepherd boy was now moving God's heart again, but now as God's king and God's messenger and vessel of honour before the people. The sincerity in David's heart accommodated the desire of God. He became hungry for the Presence and demonstrated authenticity before the God of his blessing and influence. And you also are God's chosen generation and God is calling you to take up the Mantle with authenticity in your hearts.

> Obedience and surrender are holy responses.
> They align with the desire of God.

Not everybody celebrated the bringing of the Ark of God into Jerusalem. Not everyone's heart was in alignment with David's. While David danced, Michal judged and despised him in her heart. She ridiculed him for dancing publicly, girded only with a linen garment. To Michal, it was a shameful and undignified act. But for David, it was a heart-to-heart worship and dance before the Lord God who had appointed him to be king over God's people. Because of Michal's abhorring of David's worship before the Holy Ark of God, she was barren till the day of her death. We also must be careful not to judge those who worship God in Spirit and in Truth.

But for those who choose to worship God like David did, sure, earthly eyes and ears will judge and despise, but God will not deny nor reject those who honour His Revival Fire. For He is the God that comes to you, at the break of dawn. He will honour those who honour His Presence and the Glory of His Word. For His Presence is Holy Evidence of Change.

> The Presence is Holy Evidence of Change.

WORSHIP

-

A BEAUTIFUL EXCHANGE

Surrender leads to soaking. And from the soaking comes the overflow. That's when God is manifested.

Jeremiah 31:3

The LORD hath appeared of old unto me, saying, Yea, I have loved thee with an everlasting love: therefore with lovingkindness have I drawn thee.

Oh, that my soul shall behold the wonders of my God. Oh, that I would dwell in the House of my God forever.

King David put it so profoundly (Psalms 27:4-5),

"One thing have I desired of the LORD, that will I seek after; that I may dwell in the House of the LORD all the days of my life, to behold the beauty of the LORD, and to enquire in His temple. For in the time of trouble He shall hide me in His pavilion: in the secret of His tabernacle shall He hide me; He shall set me up upon a Rock."

A transaction happens while you worship the Lord. While your adorations are poured out to God, there the Presence also saturates your being—that's a beautiful exchange.

When your spirit finds its rhythm and melody to lift up the Lord. At the same time, your spirit has entered into a place of *soaking*. Your attention then is drawn into one place onto one person—-the Lord Jesus.

That posture before God is where the sweet-smelling fragrance of your worship ascends to the Throne of God. Like the Altar of incense in the Holy Place. You find yourself sincerely giving your all before God, with spirit, mind and body. When God breathes in the sweet savour of your worship, God also releases His desire into your heart—that's a beautiful exchange.

God doesn't want you to compare your experience with someone else's. He just wants you to drink of the overflowing cup of His Spirit.

How wonderful is that beautiful exchange? When the Anointing of God mingles with your worship and pours like Rivers upon that place.

For the *Sweet Aroma of God shall come; He shall descend from on High and fill the place of His desire and Habitation.* And He shall pour out His Spirit at the place where He has appointed, and with the *burning ones* which He has called by name. They are the *Fire carriers of His Word*. These are the Revivalists. He will not use any other to carry that Holy Mandate, for it is precious to Him. He knows whom He has called and appointed. And upon that Holy Place shall God make known His oracles, and the wisdom and knowledge of His Glory. There, shall His *Aroma of worship* be.

We have heard the call to come up to *the Cleft of the Rock*. It's when worship becomes a *place in God* and not just a *song*. And our hearts, in that moment, experience that beautiful exchange between the Glory of God and our Earthen Vessels.

> " We have heard the call to come up to
> the Cleft of the Rock; It's when worship becomes
> a *Place in God*, and not just a *song*.

And in that beautiful exchange, the work of the Spirit is active to bring us into remembrance of all the Words of Christ. Our hearts

CHAPTER 18   *The Posture That Brings & Carries The Glory*

begin to burn, and our spirits soar. For we are there with Him and nothing else will do—we just want Him.

Prayer:

We just want You Lord. We want You. We would rather seek Your Face and encounter You, in that beautiful exchange.

CHAPTER 19

THE PLACE WHERE HE SPEAKS

We are called to host and reveal His Presence

have followed the trail of *His Presence* from when I first received that Holy encounter and experience. I have followed the leading of the Lord, and have tried as much as I can to do so, both in season and out of season.

There is no comparison to that one pursuit; *the pursuit of His Presence*. Sure there have been times when I wasn't conscious of Him, but He was conscious of me. I wondered how God was there in the darkest places of my life and still remain my fortress. How so, when I couldn't see the supreme might of His grace at work in my life, and yet He remained faithful. God is eternally faithful and abundant in mercy.

He has continued to be there in my life as *Jehovah Shammah— The Lord is there*; and *The El Elyon—the great God Most High*, watching and guiding the way.

I am sure you feel the same way too.

CHAPTER 19   *The Place Where He Speaks*

Because of His Presence, we know His Name, just as He knows us. We know His *Voice* and *Heart* for us because we delight in Him.

All of this is made possible and established in God, because of the finished work at the Cross of Jesus, where Mercy met Truth, and Righteousness embraced Peace.

Psalms 85:8-13

I will hear what God the LORD will speak: for He will speak peace unto His people, and to His saints: but let them not turn again to folly. Surely His salvation is nigh them that fear Him; that Glory may dwell in our land. Mercy and Truth are met together; Righteousness and Peace have kissed each other. Truth shall spring out of the earth; and Righteousness shall look down from heaven. Yea, the LORD shall give that which is good; and our land shall yield her increase. Righteousness shall go before Him; and shall set us in the way of His steps.

Prayer:

Lord, we give ourselves to You; over and over and over again, until we are completely consumed by the Spirit of Your Word. We choose to surrender to You and yield until there is none of us and all of You. We desire to be Your servants at *the Cleft of the Rock* where we can hear Your Voice and see the form and fullness of Your Glory.

THE BIRTHING OF THE PLACE WHERE HE SPEAKS

It was the night of Monday 24th November 2014. The Revival in Emerald had been fulfilled according to God's purpose and now we were seeking God for direction.

While Olivia and I worshipped, the Word of the Lord came mightily upon me and caused me to go down on my face and lay prostrate on the floor.

Then the Lord spoke to me and said, "You shall Name My Church, My Ministry and My Building 'THE PLACE WHERE HE SPEAKS.' This Commission and Mandate belong to Me. For I am the God that will speak to My people at that Place; 'THE PLACE WHERE HE SPEAKS.' And a brother will say unto another, come brother and let us go up to 'The Place Where He Speaks' for there shall we hear what the Lord has for us. The mother shall do the same with the daughter. For one shall speak to another and say, come let us go up to 'The Place Where He Speaks.' For there shall we hear God's desire for us. And they shall be of every tribe and tongue, every nation, both young and old, who shall say to one another in their own language, come let us go up the Holy Hill of God, to 'The Place Where He Speaks' and there we shall rejoice in the Voice of our God and become one with His Glory and Presence. There we will hear His Voice and His Words for us."

There I saw a vision of a grand dome to my right with the Words, 'The Place Where He Speaks' published above the front entrance to the building. And to my left, a beautiful garden. Twelve large rounded stones sat at its entrance and a great big bird as the emblem that hung over the entrance of the gate to the garden. The image of that bird is now the Logo of the Church-Ministry and Commission, 'The Place Where He Speaks.'

THE UNFOLDING MAGNIFICENT REVELATION OF THE PLACE WHERE HE SPEAKS

God is my Witness. We actually didn't know what God meant. At the time when I received this, Olivia and I were on our knees together to acknowledge the Word of the Lord. Since that night, we have carried the Mandate, and desire of these Holy Words and will do so, to the end.

If you asked me then what 'The Place Where He Speaks' meant I could give you an answer but not a full answer. I too, was discovering the meaning and depth of the Words of the Lord.

Together with the *Church family*, I have journeyed the years experiencing *the Fires of Revival*, and have soaked in meetings where the Glory of God rested on us and upon the room. Some of these stories, I have shared with you in the earlier Chapters of this book.

I speak to you as one longing continuously to be overtaken by, and drenched in *the Glory and Fire of the Holy Spirit*.

I have come to that understanding that Revival is about *God abiding in our midst*—And when He is in our midst, He will speak to us.

Now I am completely clear on it, that God wasn't referring to *an organisation;* a man-structured ministry, labelled as one, according to man's concept—with board members and a constitution. Although, we have these earthly administration in place, we do not hinder the Heavenly Administration.

'The Place Where He Speaks' is not a man's doing. It doesn't belong to me. This Holy Mandate belongs fully to God. It is the *desire, and Commission of God* given to us, vessels of this earth, to carry what is Heavenly. The origin of all ministries is from the Throne of God.

And to fulfil certain of these obligations here on earth, God has to make His *Mandate, Desire and Commission* again, a little lower than the angels of Heaven. Much like He did with Christ. God didn't think it was robbery, not in the slightest, to reduce its value, nor to cause it to conform to worldly perspectives and legalities. In God's will, *the Heavenly Constitution* overrides the earthly one. The heart of God is clear on it, that it should remain as THE WORD MADE FLESH IN OUR MIDST—This is what 'The Place Where He Speaks' really means.

Psalms 8:4-6

> What is man, that Thou art mindful of him? and the son of man, that Thou visitest him? For Thou hast made him a little lower than the angels, and hast crowned him with Glory and honour. Thou madest him to have dominion over the works of Thy hands; Thou hast put all things under his feet:

The Holy Spirit was surely working in the writer of Hebrew (Hebrews 2:9-13) because when he wrote on Psalm 8:4-6, he breathed new insight into it. This time it included us:

> But we see Jesus, Who was made a little lower than the angels for the suffering of death, crowned with Glory and honour; that He by the grace of God should taste death for every man. For it became Him, for Whom are all things, and by Whom are all things, in bringing many sons unto Glory, to make the Captain of their salvation perfect through sufferings. **For both He that sanctifieth and they who are sanctified are all of One**: for which cause He is not ashamed to call them brethren, Saying, **I will declare Thy Name unto My brethren, in the midst of the Church** will I sing praise unto Thee. And again, I will put My trust in Him. And again, Behold I and the children which God hath given Me.

CHAPTER 19 — *The Place Where He Speaks*

The *Word made flesh*, was the same Word made a little lower than the angels. Likewise, The Word; coming from the Spirit, may comply only to a certain degree to the restrictions of our earthly bodies, but is not bound by the constraints of our own limitations.

In addition, the *Word that He Speaks* is that same *Word made flesh in us* because He wants to dwell in our midst and bring many sons and daughters unto Glory.

THE WORD MADE FLESH IS:
- The Power of the Word abiding in our earthen vessels.
- *The Knowing of the Spirit of God in us*. And like Moses, *at the Cleft of the Rock*, we also behold the fullness and form of the Word of Glory *burning in our hearts*.

This revelation is too magnificent for me; that every prophetic Word spoken to us is the *'Sent Word'* made a little lower than the angels, and becomes flesh in our beings, who carry the testimony of our Lord Jesus—The Spirit of Prophecy.

In other word, we are called to reveal His Presence.

We, who *carry the Word of Glory*, are the temple of the Most High, His dwelling place, and 'The Place Where He Speaks.'

We have become the Place of His choosing. And just like Christ, who was born and laid in a humble manger, so also must the Word be born in us.

We together have come into the light of that powerful revelation that *Christ in us, is the Hope of His Calling and the Hope of our Glory;* that one day, we shall no longer be lower than the angels of God, but be made again in the likeness of His Glory, by the Power of the Spirit at work in us (Ephesians 1:18-23 and Colossians 1:25-27).

And with gladness we establish the real meaning of what God meant by 'The Place Where He Speaks.'— *the Word sent to becomes REVIVAL in us.* It is also the Glory of the Word that comes to abide in our midst. That same Word of Power meets with those He has chosen at an appointed place of His choosing, to reveal His Glory and cause His Glory to rest upon them. He has come to mark His anointeds out and to send them forth with the Power and Authority of the Spirit of God. Their Commission is defined in that holy moment of encounter with the God of 'The Place Where He Speaks.'

> " The Place Where He Speaks
> is the Word of Revival made flesh in us

Everything I have written in this book is embodied in those holy Words from Heaven. It is the knowledge of God given to us to be caretakers and carriers of the 'Word made flesh.' That same Word that we behold, becomes the Word of Power that fills the atmosphere we soak in.

I can't give you a *God Encounter*, but I can tell you that there is a *Place before the Lord*, where the Lord calls you to ascend to. That Place is the *Cleft of the Rock*. I only speak in this manner because I know that Place.

The Place of *His Desire for us* becomes the place we shall *desire Him too; to be where He is and behold the fullness of His Presence, and to dwell under the weightiness of the Word resting upon our beings.*

I believe you know that place too. The Holy Spirit is also at work in you.

For those who have found that Holy Sanctuary and Humble Place, you have found it on your knees and with your faces bowed low to the earth. You have found it in brokenness before God and your hearts and minds have become closer to Christ.

This is the joy we have in Him, that as the world loses its lustre and fades gradually from us, the Glory of the Lord becomes thicker upon the Mantle that we are clothed with.

CHAPTER 19 — *The Place Where He Speaks*

This doesn't hinder us from living an abundant life here on earth; it only empowers us to walk with God. God is not stopping you from being an accountant, a lawyer, or a medical doctor (whatever your profession is). But God would rather reveal His Glory through you, even at your workplace. That's 'Heaven on Earth.' We are not just sent to preach His Gospel, but also to reveal His Presence. And the Gospel of Christ that we preach is the Gospel of *Peace and Power.*

When we live for God, it only expresses more of the God-nature through us. We are epistles of Christ written not with the ink of man but with the Power of the Holy Spirit that dwells in us. We are called as the wooden elements of God, covered in the gold of His Glory to carry the *Word made flesh.* For we are all called together, to *host His Presence* and also to *reveal His Presence.*

We, therefore, come away from that form of religious conformity and enter into *The Place of our ORIGINS*. We can trust that God knows everything about us and He delights to speak to us from His Holy Place. He knows that His Revival in us will stir the hearts of others. Some will receive the Move of the Spirit with willingness and gladness. Others will hesitate. Then some will completely reject the working of the Spirit.

But we must not be shaken by any of these. When we know the heart of our Father in Heaven, we are then led in a way, that our faith is steadfast, and our spirits are confident in the mighty flow of the Holy Spirit in us. Our greatest privilege is that God has chosen to speak to us and allow His Word to come in our midst.

CARRY - LEAD - SERVE THE MOVE
—WE ARE THE ARK OF GOD

Carry-Lead-Serve is the threefold discipline and principle of our ministry in God (I learned this only because of the Anointing dream I shared to you earlier in Chapter 10). 'Holiness unto the Lord' combined with being 'broken in unbroken fellowship' fits very well with this threefold statute of our Calling.

It has everything to do with how God wants to operate through us. This threefold principle is woven into the fabric of the Mandate of God's Call upon us. It carries the sovereign creed of our life hidden in Christ and the fullness of Christ revealed through us. Carry-lead-serve is the royal virtue of our true ministry in God. Let's observe together, the details of this threefold principle:

Carry the Move—

Is to become a vessel made ready by the Holy Spirit for the Glory to rest and reside. It means to be a Glory carrier or a carrier of the Word. It means we carry the revelation of the Kingdom and walk under the weight of that influence. When we carry the Move, we carry the burden of God's assignment, not by human-led efforts, but by God's Anointing. Carrying a Mandate from God requires obedience, willingness and discipline.

To carry the Move is to carry the cup of your calling, which is the cup of your Baptism. Like Jesus had to carry His to the Cross, then came resurrection day. And Jesus also instructed us to carry our cross. The word 'CROSS' in this context, means to carry the assignment of your calling given by God to you.

Lead the Move under the Leadership of the Spirit—

To Carry the Move also has everything to do with being led by the Spirit of the Move. The discipline of following the Holy Spirit is not a temporary task, but a part of who we are in God. It is our permanent role. And we *lead in the Move* by following the Holy Ghost who leads the Move; He is the Move of God. We lead by looking to the Glory of the Word. We do not go ahead of His timing. We wait till He Moves and we move when He Moves. This is the discipline I speak of.

Serve the Move—

This is the yielding and beholding part. We behold because we are being led and are blessed to carry the Glory. We are influenced and blessed by the Power that abides.

We want nothing but His Will to be done in us. When we serve, we know the desire of our God. Our hearts are overwhelmed with passion for God. We have become those who are broken before His Presence. We also serve through suffering, humility, patience and grace. We serve with joy and willingness. We serve with clean hands and a pure heart. We serve not begrudgingly or with emulation. We serve with a heart towards God first. Our service to God is not just with willingness but with obedience. We trust Him in all things. And when He says "Go," we go. And when He says, "Stay," we stay.

The threefold principle in essence—

'Carry-Lead-Serve'

When we faithfully and correctly fulfil all three requirements of our ministry in God, that should lead us to this amazing conclusion:

The Word of Power that you carry within you, is the *Kavod (weighty Glory) of God*—That same tangible Glory that rested upon the Mercy Seat of the Ark of God, where God met with Moses and spoke with Him. Jesus modelled it for us. He was the Ark of God—the Word made flesh. And in the likeness and similitude of God's Holy Ark, our very own lives, through Christ, (body, soul and spirit) have become the meeting place of God; we have also become the Holy Ark of God and 'The PLACE Where He Speaks.'

That's a big revelation to digest. Again, I only came into this knowledge by a vision that God showed to me and by revelation from the Spirit. When the Glory of God came upon my being in the vision, the same Glory also came upon the Ark of God, that was before me. That was so powerful to experience. I understood in that moment, that the same way in which the Lord God rested on the Holy Ark is exactly the same way He desires to rest upon us with His Glory. Diminishing nothing at all, but fulfilling all that God has purposed for us; to be 'one with Him in His Glory, and He with us, in our earthen vessels. That is truly magnificent.

You are comfortable with being called *the Temple of God—The Place of His Dwelling* (Exodus 25:8, 1 Corinthians 3:16), but are you comfortable with being called the *Ark of God—The Place Where He meets with us to Speak (Exodus 25:22)?*

When you read Ephesians 4:13, about reaching the fullness of Christ; that is this—the Glory of the Word coming into our spirit, soul and body. That is the same Glory that came upon the Ark of God. Two passages of scripture help us to understand this:

2 Corinthians 3:17-18

Now the Lord is that Spirit: and where the Spirit of the Lord is, there is liberty. But we all, with open face **beholding as in a glass the Glory of the Lord, are changed into the same image from Glory to Glory, even as by the Spirit of the Lord.**

CHAPTER 19 — *The Place Where He Speaks*

1 John 3:2 (KJV)

Beloved, now are we the sons of God, and it doth not yet appear what we shall be: but we know that, when He shall appear, **we shall be like Him; for we shall see Him as he is.**

The longer the Word of Glory abides in us, the more we are being transformed into the same Image of His Glory. We are being prepared as the Bride of Christ, made ready for Jesus our King, who will return in His Power and Glory.

If the Apostle Paul showed us by the Spirit that we are the Temple of the Holy Spirit and the Archangel Michael in that holy vision (in Chapter 6) confirmed it, then we who are *the Temple and Altar of God,* are also *the Ark of God, holy and sanctified for Him.*

The Holy Ark was made of wood, representing our earthen vessels, and it was overlaid with gold, representing the endowing of the Power of God. For God told Moses,

Exodus 25:22

And there I will meet with thee, and I will commune with thee from above the mercy seat...

The Lord also told Moses,

Exodus 29:42-46

...at the door of the tabernacle of the congregation before the LORD: where I will meet you, to speak there unto thee. And there I will meet with the children of Israel, and the tabernacle shall be sanctified by My Glory. And I will sanctify the tabernacle of the congregation and the Altar: I will sanctify also both Aaron and his sons, to minister to me in the priest's office. And I will dwell among the children of Israel and will be their God. And they shall know that I am the LORD their God...

Our very own lives as earthen vessels have become *The Place of His Communion; His meeting Place with us, and The Place Where He Speaks with us* (2 Corinthians 4:6-7).

You are clothed with the Power of God, to live and walk from that place of 'God-Influence' resting on you. That glorious Power from Above is Heavenly intent resting upon you to declare to the heavenliness and the earthly realm, what God desires for His people.

The Ark of God is a bold statement from God. And the Spirit of Lord Jesus Christ in us is that same bold statement from God.

Just as the Ark of God followed the Cloud to the Promise, the same is also with us who follow the *Presence;* For the Spirit will lead us *to the Promise of Glory*—Christ in us, the Hope of Glory (Colossians 1:27).

When you juxtapose the Ark of God, with our Hearts, you see in principle, that carrying *the Word of the Spirit*, is the same as carrying the *Ark of the Covenant*. The *Old* being the shadow of the *New*.

The Ark was dedicated by the blood of the Testament: anointed, consecrated and sanctified for the Lord. And we also have been dedicated by the Blood of the New Testament established by Christ, and are anointed by the Spirit upon us, consecrated and sanctified to serve the Will of our God.

For the saints of the Old Covenant, the law was carried in that Holy Ark and God desired continually to be in their midst.

For saints of the New Covenant, the same law is now written upon the hearts of man by the Spirit of God. The Presence that rested upon the Ark now abides upon the saints that carry the Glory of the Word in earthen vessels (2 Corinthians 4:6-7). We carry this Word by *revelation and grace*.

CHAPTER 19 — *The Place Where He Speaks*

For we are still being led by the mighty Cloud of Glory; that great pillar of Fire, not only manifested outwardly as it was in the days of old but now through *the Voice of the Word residing in us*.

Carry-Lead-Serve—We are called to be the people of 'The Place Where He Speaks.' We walk before the Lord as those who understand *The Meeting Place*. We are the Ark of God, chosen to carry, lead and serve the Will and desire of God upon our lives. We have by the Spirit of Christ, taken up our priestly calling in Him and have *become aware of the Word of the Spirit* that comes to us and is made flesh in us.

John 15:7-8

If ye abide in Me, and My Words abide in you, ye shall ask what ye will, and it shall be done unto you. Herein is My Father Glorified, that ye bear much fruit; so shall ye be My disciples.

A PEOPLE OF HIS PRESENCE

I marvel at this tremendous blessing to carry His Presence. What a wonderful and weighty revelation of *the Burning Bush, the Ark of God and of the Cleft of the Rock*. I am captivated by that *Place by the Rock*.

Exodus 33:21

And the LORD said, Behold, there is a place by Me, and thou shalt stand upon a Rock:

It is God's invitation for the Church to come up to that place of holy encounter and revelation. And while there before Him, we are given that holy opportunity to behold the Glory and Magnificence of the *Person and Presence of the Lord.*

He is raising a people of His Presence. It's not just about doing church, it's about *being* the Church of God. For the Spirit of Christ wants to raise a people of *the Cleft of the Rock.* He wants to raise a people that come to *Bethel; to the Place Where He Speaks.* This is our calling and our identity in Him. That is the place of our prestige and power with God.

Prayer: (Psalms 42:1-2,7-8)

As the hart panteth after the water brooks, so panteth my soul after Thee, O God. My soul thirsteth for God, for the Living God: when shall I come and appear before God?...Deep calleth unto deep at the noise of Thy waterspouts: all Thy waves and Thy billows are gone over me. Yet the LORD will command His lovingkindness in the daytime, and in the night His song shall be with me, and my prayer unto the God of my life.

CHAPTER 20

FINAL THOUGHTS

I have not been able to fit into this book all the other stories, visions and dreams, revival messages, revival lessons, miracles, healings, signs and wonders, testimonies and prophecies, I have received from the Lord over the years. If the Holy Spirit desires, maybe that will be included in book two, as a continuation of this wonderful Holy Spirit ordained Book.

With this, I want to thank you for reading right to the final Chapter of this book. I am confident that God has already begun a mighty work in you as a result of your obedience and alignment. It is my desire for Christ to be glorified in you. I remain fervent on my knees, and prostrated before the Lord of Glory, for you my friends.

I know the Father's heart, and I know He wants to make His Home with You. He desires your fellowship more than you realise.

I am confident that, it doesn't matter what the current status of your personal life is, your home, or your situation. God is looking down at you right now and He is asking you to have faith because I am confident that He is ready to do a mighty miracle in your life. God will, if you will only believe, and touch *the edge of His Garment*.

CHAPTER 20 — *Final Thoughts*

Now is the Time. Now is the Era for the Great Awakening and Outpouring of the Spirit of God. You are the chosen generation of God that will go up to the Holy Hill of our God (Psalms 24:3-4).

It will be my greatest joy when I see the Lord Holy Spirit descend upon your homes with an abundant wave of blessings that overtake you. The confidence of the Spirit has gripped my being on the matter. God is ready to descend upon the prepared vessel.

May your hearts soar to meet Him in such a way your feet never touch the earthly realm anymore but stand at the *Cleft of His Rock, made ready for you.* It is the place of His delight and His desire for You. May you find Him there, as I have and never stop resting in His Holy Presence. May the Glory of *Adonai Eloheinu,* find your heart acceptable and may the Lord make His Home with you.

You are called to be in His Presence, not just for a moment, but perpetually. You are called to carry His Glory and be Baptised in the Rivers of His Presence. You are called to walk in the Revival Fire of God. You are called as a Burning One, to carry the Glory of the Word. I desire that you be completely overtaken by His Presence, and remain soaked with Him continuously until the Spirit overflows.

My prayer is that you will go from Glory to Glory until you come to the fullness of Christ who abides in you. Unto you that fear the Name of the Lord, shall the Sun of righteousness arise with healing in His wings (Malachi 4:2). May the Lord God of the Great Revival Fire turn your hearts to Him and cause you to find His Heart also. For the Time of the Great Revival is at hand. The Break of Dawn has come. For you who have believed in Him and have been chosen by Christ, remember that you are the light of the world and the salt of the earth. This is your moment, *Burning Ones,* THIS IS YOUR MOMENT!

Final Thoughts   **CHAPTER 20**

OWN THIS MOMENT

Own this moment my brother and sister in the Lord. Make it one filled with your love for God. Pour out your heart upon God and let Him pour His Anointing upon you. Lay yourself down in the *River of His Presence*. For out of your believing, comes the overflow that grips the inside of you, it has one intent and that is for the Might of the Spirit to rise from your spirit. That *'overflow'* is the *abiding thoughts of God* that have settled as *the Dew of Heaven* upon your heart. For out from the soaking comes the overflow.

Heaven is orchestrating a new season of events appointed to *the anointed ones.* They are called Holy Ghost events because His markings are visible upon them. He has marked us for wonderful times of refreshing. He has appointed the Rivers of His Anointing to us by His abundant grace and mercy. Our loving Father has drawn us to the overflow of His Spirit. We have been called to live and express the new life we have in Christ. For us who have been born into a new life in Christ, and live now from that Holy Place of Divine Encounters, we have come to love the Identity of our new citizenship, which is the Kingdom of Heaven. This is our new story; hidden in Christ, so that we can manifest the fullness and Glory of our Lord. We are made anew continuously because of that abiding Presence. We are washed with abundant grace that we may walk in the liberty of the Spirit of God. Because we know that the Anointing given to us accomplishes what God establishes.

> " The Anointing given to us accomplishes what God establishes.

CHAPTER 20 *Final Thoughts*

GOD'S THOUGHTS BECOME OUR ATMOSPHERE

We have become those desiring the Atmosphere of our God. For we have chosen to come into the Light of His radiance and have rested in the sacred and Holy Words of the Holy Ghost. We have chosen God's Atmosphere. That verified air of Heaven has become ours because we have made room for the Most High God.

For we know in our hearts that the Thoughts of God become our Atmosphere when we have created a place for Him to work and for the Word of His Power to descend and abide. Our oneness with His Holy Spirit causes the *Dew of His Presence to fall upon us*. God wants to saturate us with the fullness of His Presence and Glory. That is where He has commanded a Great and Glorious Blessing upon us (Psalms 133).

Prayer:

Oh, Lord, Let the Dew of Heaven become our Atmosphere that we may breathe and live in the very Essence and Fullness of Your Presence. We lay ourselves down in the Rivers of Your Presence. We are here Lord, use us for Your Glory. Amen.

CONCLUSION

I conclude by saying, I want to give all Glory and honour to our Lord Jesus—He is worthy of it all.

As for me, I remain in pursuit of His Presence. I have continued to live in that humble and powerful place as a broken vessel before God. I believe I have not received these encounters

Final Thoughts **CHAPTER 20**

and experiences for myself. It's because God loves you and He wanted me to testify and reveal to you His revelation knowledge of how to walk in the Revival Fire and how to become a Glory Carrier. God has called and chosen you to walk in that magnificent place before Him. I want you to know that God loves you, and His thoughts for you overflow with great passion. He wants you to know His heart and to understand with powerful insight that in His Presence, you will experience the fullness of His Joy and at His Right Hand, there truly are pleasures evermore (Psalms 16:11).

I have enjoyed writing this book with the help of the Holy Spirit. I have spent many days and nights on my face before the Lord, because I have carried His burden for you, and I have felt the continuous waves of the Spirit come over me. The Fire of His Word burned in me, each time I sat to write. I have written for you oh precious Children of God. You are precious in His Eyes.

As I continue to walk in the Revival Fire of God, I have come to understand, what I call now, THE HOLY CREED OF GOD'S REVIVALIST. I will conclude on that note, with that proclamation.

THE REVIVALIST CREED:

"The platform assigned to me is not one out of ambition but of *Heavenly Commission*. It was born out of the *Fire of God*. It was the Holy One who called me, and I am glad I responded —now I burn with His Fire in my bones. The Glory is His, I am only His vessel. It is not of earthly conquest, but of His *Holy Anointing*. It has nothing to do with worldly pursuits but one completely filled with *the Glory and Passion of Yahweh; clothed with the Zeal of the Most High God.* (Galatians 1:11-12, Philippians 3:7-14). For this cause came I unto this hour: that the Glory of our Lord Jesus Christ may be revealed through my earthen vessel.

May God get all the glory, honour and praise. Amen"

"Not a man but You JESUS!

ABOUT THE AUTHOR

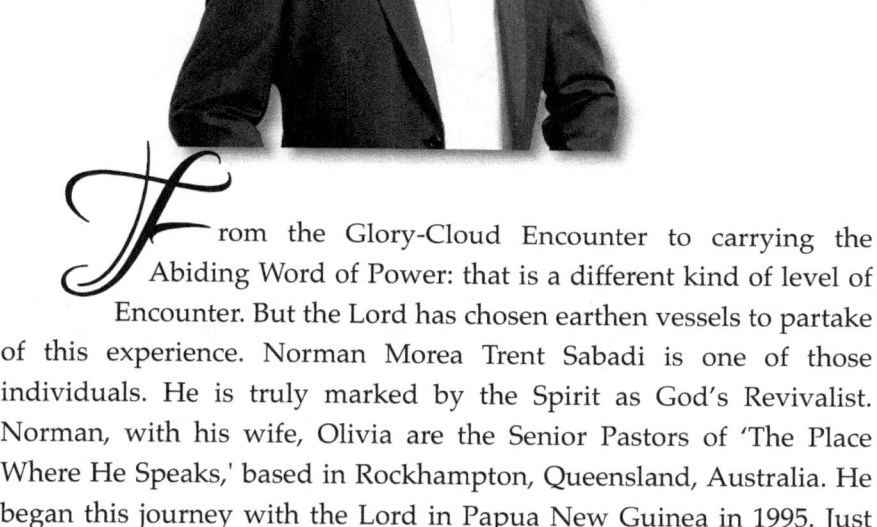

From the Glory-Cloud Encounter to carrying the Abiding Word of Power: that is a different kind of level of Encounter. But the Lord has chosen earthen vessels to partake of this experience. Norman Morea Trent Sabadi is one of those individuals. He is truly marked by the Spirit as God's Revivalist. Norman, with his wife, Olivia are the Senior Pastors of 'The Place Where He Speaks,' based in Rockhampton, Queensland, Australia. He began this journey with the Lord in Papua New Guinea in 1995. Just like the prophet Jeremiah told us about his call (Jeremiah 1:4-10), you have now also read about God's specific call upon Norman's life in this book.

> Then Jesus said, "Norman[1]...God Calls you and Anoints you to reach the nations with the Word of God. Preach His Gospel of Peace and Power."

> God has anointed Norman as the Carrier, Leader and Servant of *The Great Mandate of Revival* (the Great Awakening of God).

Through many years of nurturing and mentorship under the Holy Spirit, the appointed time has come for that Holy Mandate to be fulfilled, and to accomplish the call of mentoring God's people into the Great Revival Fire of God, the Knowledge of the Glory ready to be manifested to the world.

Endnote:
1 (Sabadi N.M.T. 2023. Chapter 10 - The Great Induction and Anointing Service, *Chosen to Carry the Glory - Carry the Fire of Jesus,* Norman Sabadi Publishing, Rockhampton, Queensland, Australia pp.165-207).

YOU CAN SUPPORT THE MINISTRY AND WORK OF PASTOR NORMAN BY:

* SHARING THIS BOOK AND SNIPPETS OF YOUR BOOKMARKS ON SOCIAL MEDIA
* BUY THIS BOOK AS A GIFT FOR SOMEONE.
* SHARING THE MESSAGE OF THIS BOOK WITH OTHERS.

DONATE TO

PAYPAL:
https://www.paypal.com/paypalme/normsabadi

Thank you so much for your support and May the Lord abundantly bless you

Other Books by Norman Sabadi

- Understanding the Laws of the Realms
- Wisdom Calls Out To You

Media

Connect with me through social media.

Facebook—The Place Where He Speaks Group:
> https://www.facebook.com/groups/652589851978873/

YouTube Channel—The Place Where He Speaks
> https://www.youtube.com/channel/UCqjypOfptKjmYNVB0_2I2wA

YOUTUBE HANDLE:
> @theplacewherehespeaks

YouTube Channel—Norman Sabadi
> https://www.youtube.com/channel/UC0OHqOX1OyciINWAhpLUJ9A

YOUTUBE HANDLE:
> @normansabadi

FOR MORE RESOURCE GO TO:
> https://www.normansabadi.com/

Contact Details

We would love to hear from you, about testimonies, praise reports, prayer requests and preaching requests also, or any other thing the Lord has impressed upon you to share. It would be our great honour to receive any communication from you about the *Work of the Great Revival and Awakening of God.*

ADMIN FOR THE PLACE WHERE HE SPEAKS

You can reach Pastor Norman through the following methods:

Email: theplacewherehespeaks@gmail.com

www.ingramcontent.com/pod-product-compliance
Lightning Source LLC
Chambersburg PA
CBHW070335240426
43665CB00045B/2026